"Clyde Toland can not only diss... ... ... and wax insightfully about silent film... ... Keaton, but he is also a meticulous historian who has researched and studied General Funston for decades.

Everyone knows that General Funston was a leading commander of the U.S. Army, a Medal of Honor recipient and – prior to World War I – developed future generals Eisenhower, Patton, Pershing, and MacArthur. However, Clyde has now expanded the Funston canon to include a comprehensive new trilogy.

Volume two of the trilogy, **Heat and Ice**, is a coming-of-age adventure that traverses Kansas, Death Valley, Alaska, and the British Northwest, and which brings to light Funston's life of exploration, science, hardship, and adventure. This is a new dimension in historical biographies.

As you are engrossed in the true story and the human achievement, you will be amazed about what you learn and how time flies as you read **Heat and Ice,** the chronicle of a great American being formed. This book is, quite simply, a towering achievement."

—**Richard W. Zahn** is a principal with HMJ Global Partners, a corporate strategy and governance group. He is the retired President of Schering Laboratories where he led change and grew the business to a $6 billion, 7,000 employee integrated pharmaceutical research development and manufacturing organization.

---

"Growing up on a farm a scant three miles from Frederick Funston's boyhood home and attending eight years of grade school in Carlyle, less than a mile from his home, I was always aware of the house and that somehow he was famous, but I wasn't sure of just what. It wasn't until I became involved in the Allen County Historical Society that I truly became aware of what an incredible set of life experiences he had lived. As president of the Allen County Historical Society for seven years, I was deeply involved with the establishment, design, and construction of the Funston Museum and Visitors' Center next door to the Funston Home Museum, both in honor of Major General Frederick Funston.

As a retired military officer, I have a keen appreciation of the military aspect of his life. As an avid traveler, I've been to Death Valley during the summer and experienced the extreme heat. I've been to Alaska and seen the jumping off place for the Chilkoot Pass and traveled into Canada to see places that he traveled to on the way to his wintering place. I can't imagine the physical challenges he faced and the determination he must have had. Having followed and crossed the Yukon River myself, it is beyond comprehension that he floated alone on the Yukon in a tiny wooden boat for more than 1,000 miles. Funston's adventures as a movie would make viewers think it was pure fiction. It was, however, all true. Clyde Toland's **Heat and Ice** is meticulously researched and sure to be the definitive work on this thrilling phase of Funston's life.

In 1992 I retired after 25 years as an officer in the U. S. Air Force and still have the farm that is three miles from where Frederick Funston grew up."

—**Robert G. Hawk**, Lt. Col. Ret., Iola, Kansas

---

*Additional endorsements appear on the back cover from:*

**Shirley Christian**, Pulitzer-Prize-winning journalist and author

**Bill Kurtis**, University of Kansas, BS in journalism (1962), honorary Doctor of Humane Letters (2021). Washburn University School of Law, JD (1966). In 1988 he founded Kurtis Productions to produce documentaries including *Investigative Reports* and *Cold Case Files* for A & E Network, 500 in all. Currently he produces *American Greed* for CNBC.

# Heat and Ice:
## Frederick Funston's Exploration of Death Valley, Alaska, and the British Northwest Territory, 1891-1894

### Volume Two
of
*Becoming Frederick Funston Trilogy:*
*A Tale of "cool courage, iron endurance, and gallant daring"*

### Clyde W. Toland

🌾Flint Hills Publishing

# Heat and Ice: Frederick Funston's Exploration of Death Valley, Alaska, and the British Northwest Territory, 1891-1894

Volume Two of *Becoming Frederick Funston Trilogy: A Tale of "cool courage, iron endurance, and gallant daring"*

Book Design by Carol Yoho

Cover Design by Amy Albright

Editorial Oversight, Thomas Fox Averill

This book was made possible by the Thomas Fox Averill Kansas Studies Collection, and through the generous support of the Washburn University Center for Kansas Studies.

Flint Hills Publishing
www.flinthillspublishing.com
Topeka, Kansas

Printed in the U.S.A.

ISBN: 978-1-953583-38-3
Library of Congress Control Number: 2022916242

Cover photo: Frederick Funston wore "a complete suit of furs consisting of a caribou skin coat or 'parkie,' with hood attachment..."

# Becoming Frederick Funston Trilogy
## A Tale of "cool courage, iron endurance, and gallant daring"

This trilogy tells the story of the coming of age of Frederick Funston, the future famous United States Army Major General and American hero at his death in 1917. At age thirty-two, he discovered who he was, and the course of the balance of his life was set. In the process of self-discovery, he lived a fascinating life of adventure, and that life, and certain of the times in which he lived it, are told in this trilogy.

Volume One: *American Hero, Kansas Heritage: Frederick Funston's Early Years, 1865-1890*

Volume Two: *Heat and Ice: Frederick Funston's Exploration of Death Valley, Alaska, and the British Northwest Territory, 1891-1894*

Volume Three: *"Yankee Hero": Frederick Funston, Expedicionario in the Cuban Liberation Army, 1896-1897*

The **Becoming Frederick Funston Trilogy** has forty chapters. The biblical number forty generally symbolizes a period of testing, and these chapters tell, in part, the testing of Frederick Funston in the formative years of his life.

The research and writing of this trilogy were done over a period of twenty-four years (1995-2019). The available time to research and write was the controlling factor. If there are any inconsistencies or errors in style throughout this trilogy, they have persisted despite my best efforts to eradicate them. My apologies for any such inconsistencies or errors.

# About the Author

Clyde W. Toland received a BA in history in 1969 from the University of Kansas, and in 1971 a MA in history from the University of Wisconsin-Madison. He received his JD from the University of Kansas in 1975. He is a member of Phi Beta Kappa and the Order of the Coif. Mr. Toland is a semi-retired lawyer in Iola, Kansas.

As a grade school student, he became fascinated by his local Allen County, Kansas, history and by Frederick Funston's early adventurous life in Death Valley, Alaska, the British Northwest Territory, and Cuba. For more than thirty-five years, he has been a student of Funston's life. As president of the Allen County Historical Society, Inc., in Iola, Kansas, he was the driving force in the successful move in 1994 of Frederick Funston's rural childhood home to the Iola town square and in its subsequent restoration and opening as a museum in 1995. He did the research and writing for most of the eleven exhibits in the Funston Museum and Visitors' Center, which opened in 1997 next door to the Funston Home Museum.

Mr. Toland founded the Buster Keaton Celebration, a nationally known humanities event held annually in Iola, Kansas, from 1993 through 2017. He served as co-chair of the Keaton Celebration Committee for the first five celebrations, and continued as a committee member through the 2005 celebration. He was a member of the committee which revived the Buster Keaton Celebration on September 24 and 25, 2021.

At age fifteen he became a Life Member of both the Allen County Historical Society, Inc., and the Kansas State Historical Society. Mr. Toland and United States Senator Nancy Kassebaum Baker in 1996 were the two first recipients of the Alumni Distinguished Achievement Award from the College of Liberal Arts and Sciences of the University of Kansas.

**For**
Nancy, my wife

**Our children and their spouses:**
David and Beth
Andrew and Anna
Elizabeth and Bart

**Our grandchildren:**
Caroline
William
Charlotte
Isaac

"History is the essence of innumerable biographies."
—**Thomas Carlyle**
(1795-1881)
\* \* \*

"But what a fortune in films Fred Funston's life would have been. That Death Valley experience, for instance, was movie stuff if there ever was any."
—**Martin Johnson**
"Motion Picture Explorer"
(1884-1937)
\* \* \*

"Fred Funston...in the University was known as 'Timmie.' His two years' trip alone to Alaska gained for him the title of 'Fearless Fred'..."
—*The Lawrence Daily Journal*
January 10, 1895
\* \* \*

"Some of the adventures of my early life, for instance, those in the arctic regions, have never been written."
—**Frederick Funston**
shortly before his death
\* \* \*

"Frederick Funston was a national hero and the object of great national affection."
—*The Miami Herald*
editorial on Funston's death

# Institutional, Article, and Book Credits for Illustrations:

## Institutions
Kansas State Historical Society, Topeka, Kansas
Pages 5, 125, 126, 127, 158 (bottom), 161, 199, 200

The Huntington Library, San Marino, California
Page 90

## Articles
Coville, Frederick Vernon, "Botany Of The Death Valley Expedition"
Page 42

Funston, Frederick, "Across the Great Divide in Midwinter"
Page 197

Funston, Frederick, "Along Alaska's Eastern Boundary"
Pages 158 (top), 172, 173

Funston, Frederick, "Baseball Among the Arctic Whalers"
Page 215

Funston, Frederick, "Over The Chilkoot Pass To The Yukon"
Page 162

Gleed, Charles S., "Romance And Reality In A Single Life. Gen. Frederick Funston"
Page 209

Spears, John R.,"Trees Of The American Desert"
Pages 40, 41, 43

## Books
*Stanford's Atlas of Universal Geography, London Atlas Series*, 1904 (Plate # 87)
Page 159

Wright, Marcus F., *The Official and Pictorial Record of the Story of American Expansion* (1904)
Page 160

# Table of Contents and
# Chronology of Funston's Years of Exploration

Page 1 **Introduction**

Part One
**Assistant Botanist
Death Valley, 1891**

8 **Chapter One** *The Death Valley Expedition, January 1, 1891– February 28, 1891*

49 **Chapter Two** *"A Winter Storm in Death Valley" by Frederick Vernon Coville*

57 **Chapter Three** *The Death Valley Expedition, March 1, 1891 – June 15, 1891*

75 **Chapter Four** *"A Wedding In The Mohave Desert" by Fred Funston*

79 **Chapter Five** *The Death Valley Expedition, June 15, 1891– September 3, 1891*

Part Two
**Botanist
Yakutat Bay, 1892
Alaska and the British Northwest Territory, 1893 – 1894**

98 **Chapter Six** *"A Summer on the Alaskan Coast": Yakutat Bay, Alaska, April 16, 1892 – October 15, 1892*

130 **Chapter Seven** *North to Alaska and the British Northwest Territory: The Next Adventure, 1893 – 1894*

135 **Chapter Eight** *"Over The Chilkoot Pass To The Yukon" by Frederick Funston, April 3, 1893 – May 23, 1893*

164 **Chapter Nine** *A Summer at McQuesten's Post (Forty Mile Creek), May 23, 1893 – August 25, 1893*

175 **Chapter Ten** *Ascending the Porcupine River and Lodging at Rampart House: Fred Funston's Account, August 25, 1893 – November 17, 1893*

184 **Chapter Eleven** *"Across the Great Divide in Midwinter" by Frederick Funston, November 17, 1893 – December 8, 1893*

202 **Chapter Twelve** *A Snowshoe Trip to the Arctic Ocean: Fred Funston's Account, March 10, 1894 – March 29, 1894*

211 **Chapter Thirteen** *"Baseball Among The Arctic Whalers" by Frederick Funston, March 29, 1894 – April 3, 1894*

216 **Chapter Fourteen** *The Return Trip and Rampart House Again: Fred Funston's Account, April 3, 1894 – June 18, 1894*

224 **Chapter Fifteen** *Homeward Bound: Descending the Porcupine and Yukon Rivers, June 18, 1894 – October 20, 1894*

232 **Afterword**

234 **Updated Acknowledgments**

237 **Bibliography**

**Notes** follow each chapter

# INTRODUCTION

"When the news of General Funston's death was flashed across the country, from the President to the humblest citizen we were shocked and stunned, and said surely a great man has fallen among us..." Thus spoke the minister officiating at Funston's funeral. President Woodrow Wilson wrote a personal letter of condolence to Funston's widow. *The Miami Herald* observed: "Frederick Funston was a national hero and the object of great national affection."

As a Major General of the United States Army, Frederick Funston, age fifty-one, held the highest filled rank at the time of his unexpected death from heart disease in February of 1917. A household name himself, Funston was the commanding officer of men whose names would later become household words—Lieut. Dwight D. Eisenhower, Lieut. George Marshall, Lieut. George Patton, Capt. Douglas MacArthur, and Major General John J. Pershing. To Pershing, not Funston, would go the command of the American Expeditionary Force when the United States entered World War I two months after Funston's death.

Prior to entering military service for the United States at age thirty-two in 1898, Funston's civilian careers had been many and variegated: farmer, business college student, country schoolteacher, high school and university student, rodman on a railroad survey crew, journalist, ticket collector on the Santa Fe Railway, Mexican coffee plantation promoter, lecturer, and magazine writer. As one of the young American men who volunteered to fight for *Cuba Libre* (Free Cuba), he fought in 1896-1897 on the bloody battlefields of Cuba for its independence from Spain before the Spanish-American War of 1898. Funston's Cuban experiences are the subject of the final volume of the *Becoming Frederick Funston Trilogy*.

Before his Cuban exploits, Funston in 1891 was a botanist and explorer in Death Valley as a member of the first scientific expedition to venture into the valley's hellish heat. For more than two years, botanist Funston, usually alone, next explored Alaska and the British Northwest Territory as far north as the Arctic Ocean, where whalers played baseball in 47° below zero weather. Funston's explorations and extraordinary adventures as a botanist are the subject of this second volume of the *Trilogy*.

The story of these explorations and adventures is primarily told through Funston's letters and articles. His letters are invaluable, since they are unfiltered by hindsight, and since even the best of

1

memories can fade over time, and facts and feelings can be incorrectly remembered or even forgotten. Funston's several published articles about his adventures have the concreteness of the recently-lived account. Funston was a skilled writer, utilizing vivid descriptions and crisp prose spiced with self-deprecating humor. Quoting extensively his letters and articles surpasses paraphrasing them, no matter how well that might be done. And, as will be seen, he was, at times, an amateur ethnographer.

Funston's letters and articles from and about Death Valley, Alaska, and the British Northwest Territory, and the quoted writings of other members of the 1891 Death Valley Expedition, are a rich contribution to the literature of the American West.

Major General Funston, idolized by his soldiers and the public as "the little General" and "the little guy," lacked typical heroic physical stature. Unlike Hollywood's hero Indiana Jones, as portrayed by six feet, one-inch tall Harrison Ford, Funston stood a mere five feet, four inches and generally weighed a scant 120 pounds. That Funston was able to lead such a physically demanding and rigorous life, particularly in Death Valley, Alaska, and the British Northwest Territory, is a testament to his courage, perseverance, intelligence, resourcefulness, physical strength, and sheer grit.

Frederick Funston was born on November 9, 1865, in an upstairs room of the Mitchell House, the hotel owned by his maternal grandmother in New Carlisle, Ohio. His parents, Edward Funston, known as Ed, and his mother, Ann Eliza Funston, who went by Lida, were physical opposites of each other. He was six feet, two inches in height, while she was either four feet, eleven inches or five feet, two inches (sources disagree). He weighed about 225 pounds; she weighed ninety pounds; had a nineteen-inch waist; and wore a size-one shoe. Ed had a booming voice, and in his political career was known as "Foghorn" Funston. He served as speaker of the Kansas House of Representatives and as president of the Kansas Senate before being elected to Congress in 1884.

Even though Ed had a large personality, that fact and the difference in physical size of father and son did not prevent their having a close relationship. Fred, as he was called and will frequently be called in this book, was the only one of his father's six children not overawed by him. Fred respected his father and confided in him. Fred's droll observations as a youth precipitated roaring laughter from him. Fred was devoted throughout his life to his mother; perhaps this was, in part, because they shared short physical stature.

In January of 1868, Civil War Union Army veteran Ed purchased a 162-acre upland prairie farm in Allen County located in southeast

Kansas. That spring, Lida, with their first born, Fred, and baby Burt, traveled from Ohio, first by train and then by stagecoach, to join Ed. As they traveled on the train, 2-year-old Fred picked out the ABCs on station signs. This farm was to be Ed and Lida's home for the balance of their lives, and Fred's until his marriage in 1898.

Fred had a typical upbringing as a farm boy. When he and Burt were small children, their father stationed them at opposite ends of his fields so that he could plow his furrows straight. As older boys, they helped with the plowing, harvest, and other farm chores. This hard work benefited Fred physically. An 1899 description: "Although small in stature, he has a magnificent physique. He can withstand hardships and exertions under which many a larger man would succumb."

When he was not working, Fred loved to fish and to swim in nearby Deer Creek, to hunt, and to read. Ed's library, stocked with the classics, was one of the finest in the county. Fred read all of these books as well as borrowing others from neighbors. Fred read history, adventure, and everything he could obtain of a military nature. From the age of sixteen, he subscribed to a humorous publication. He loved jokes, but seldom made one. He was constantly whistling.

Fred attended nearby Maple Grove School, a typical wooden, one-room rural schoolhouse. "Fred was recognized as a thorough student bubbling over with fun and full of all sorts of practical jokes. He always saw the funny side of any situation and was quick to analyze the situation." Fred also occasionally engaged in fist fights. Although he was small, he was wiry. He was also fearless. He worshipped with his family at the Presbyterian Church near the tiny community of Carlyle located northeast of the Funston farm.

Finishing his studies at Maple Grove School about 1882, Fred, at age eighteen, attended briefly in the spring of 1884 a business college in Lawrence, Kansas. Ed Funston had been a lieutenant in the Union artillery during the Civil War, and Fred was an avid listener to his father's stories. Not surprisingly, Fred competed that spring for an appointment to West Point. Although his five-feet, four-inch height exceeded the minimum height requirement, he came up short in the competitive examination, placing third. His score was impressive, however, since it was only slightly more than two points below that of the successful candidate. Military fame and glory on behalf of the United States would have to wait fifteen years.

Fred struck out on his own in the fall of 1884. Boarding at a nearby farmer's home, he taught at a rural stone schoolhouse about ten miles from the Funston home. The school was popularly known as "Stoney Lonesome" because of its composition and location. During his one term as a pedagogue, Fred's most notable experience was successfully disarming the school bully who had brought a gun to school. This was accomplished only after a violent fist fight and struggle between teacher and pupil. The rest of the class was so scared by this that they fled by jumping through the building's open windows.

In the fall of 1885, Fred entered the Iola High School, where he was classified as a senior. The town of Iola is located five miles south of the Funston farm, and Fred made the ten-mile round trip daily by riding a horse of a volcanic disposition which had the desire to throw his rider. Fred was not deterred. He so enjoyed such physical challenges that he would occasionally mount a wild calf while a friend held the calf in place, and then holding the calf's tail and after it was let loose, he would ride it as it tried to throw him.

Fred was of a restless and adventurous disposition and uncertain what he wanted to do with his life. After graduating from high school in May of 1886, he attended the State University of Kansas in Lawrence for one year before leaving to work. This was an important year for him, however. He pledged the social fraternity Phi Delta Theta, where he became close friends with several young men who, like himself, were to become nationally famous. One was William Allen White, the future Pulitzer Prize-winning editor of the *Emporia* (Kansas) *Gazette* newspaper. His nickname was Billy, and Fred's was Timmy. By those names, Billy and Timmy enjoyed a friendship severed only by Fred's death thirty years later.

After leaving the university, Fred first spent the summer working as the rodman for a railroad survey crew. Then, briefly, he was a newspaper reporter in Kansas City before fulfilling the same role in Fort Smith, Arkansas. There he became acquainted with the notorious hanging judge, Isaac Parker. Working for a Democratic newspaper did not suit Republican Fred. When the newspaper's owner was out of town one day, Fred wrote an editorial condemning the Democratic Party. Afterward, he resigned from the paper before leaving town. "I thought likely it might come out that way," Fred explained to his Kansas friends when he came back, "but I didn't like the town and I didn't like my boarding house, and I didn't like the job and I thought I might as well let them know I had been there before I quit." The newspaper never recovered from the uproar he had created. It failed.

Fred's next job had more permanence to it. For the year of 1888, he was a ticket collector for the Santa Fe Railway. He also bounced from the train cowboys who did not have the required fare. In response to Fred's request for his ticket, one cowboy pulled his revolver and responded, "I ride on this." Fred's response was laconic: "That's good, that's good." Later, he returned with a large-bore rifle and announced that he had come to "punch that ticket." Presumably, the cowboy complied. For the spring 1889 semester and the year 1889-1890, Fred returned to the university where he was "one of our most popular students..." It had become obvious to him that it was time to move on. The most important concept that he learned while at the university was that of independence. He chose to be in charge of his own life. Although he was uncertain what he wanted to do, he knew that the academic world was no longer for him.

Fred and his good friend, the future noted entomologist, evolutionary biologist, and science administrator Vernon Kellogg, spent the beginning of the summer of 1890 in Colorado collecting natural history specimens for the university. They had a nearly fatal experience when a blizzard developed while they were scaling a mountain. Fred turned this experience into his first published article, the thrilling "Storm Bound above the Clouds."

Fred returned home with the expressed intention of becoming a journalist. Yet, six weeks later he was on his way to North Dakota as a special agent for the United States Department of Agriculture. With his love of adventure and restlessness, Fred may have concluded that life as a newspaperman was more confining than he wanted. For two months, ending in October 1890, he collected for experimental purposes native grass seeds of North Dakota. A much more adventurous, physically challenging position soon appeared, and on New Year's Day of 1891, he was in California riding a horse toward the deadly, mysterious, fabled Death Valley.

Fred Funston on the morning in December 1890 when he left Lawrence, Kansas, to join the Death Valley Expedition.

# *Part One*
## Assistant Botanist
## Death Valley, 1891

CHAPTER ONE

# The Death Valley Expedition

January 1, 1891 – February 28, 1891

Uncle Sam scratched his head and concluded that if there was such a hell hole in his dominions he had a right to know something about it and so concluded to send out an expedition of scientists to thoroughly explore it.

—Fred Funston, Death Valley,
March 8, 1891, letter to a friend[1]

The top, center story on the first page of the second section of *The New York Times* of Sunday, March 27, 1892, was titled "Into The Valley Of Death." Written by 26-year-old Fred Funston, it was an account of the prior year's scientific exploration of Death Valley, California, and surrounding areas. Fred's Iola editor friend, Charlie Scott, had editorialized in January about Fred's making money by writing about his Death Valley experiences: "The Kansas City *Journal's* Kansas man has found out that Fred Funston is writing letters to a syndicate of newspapers about the horrors of Death Valley at $5 a horror. Fred had some hair lifting experiences in the Valley, and we are glad he is coining them into wealth."[2]

Fred's *The New York Times* feature began with the origin of the name Death Valley:

Away back in the days of the Argonauts, in the Summer of 1850, a large wagon train bound for the California gold fields passed through the Mormon colony at the great Salt Lake, the only settlement of importance between the Missouri River and the new-found El Dorado. This train was probably a fair type of the thousands that made the overland passage in the twenty years between the gold discovery and the completion of the Central Pacific Railway—a dozen unwieldy prairie schooners

8

each drawn by from four to six oxen, a few men on horseback, but more trudging along on foot, while in the wagons was an assortment of household goods and mining implements, and perched about on top of these a few worn-out, haggard women and tow-headed children. Accounts differ as to the number of persons in this particular train, but those who have the best means of knowing place it at seventy-two—men, women, and children.

Many trains had preceded this one in the course of the previous year, and there had come back gruesome tales of the hardships and privations endured by those who had crossed the 800 miles of sage brush desert and alkali plain that lay between the Mormon settlements and the foot hills of the Sierra Nevada, and of the prowling bands of hostile Indians who, with their Mormon allies, made a business of plundering every train too weak to offer effectual resistance. When the leaders of this caravan learned of the perils to be encountered if they followed the wagon road taken by their predecessors they held a council at which it was agreed to try an innovation; they would bear far to the south of the usually traveled route and cross the Sierra Nevada Mountains near their southern extremity. The Indians of whom they made inquiry assured them that there was "heap water" all through the country to the southwest. So it was determined to make the attempt. The new way could not be worse than the old one, and it might be vastly better.

Thus the caravan took its departure from the Mormon village. Of its subsequent history but little is known, save that it kept on its way for weeks over a burning, trackless desert and almost impassable mountains. Day after day the thermometer registered into the hundreds; they found the "heap water" that the lying Indians had told them of, but it was villainous alkaline stuff, worse than none at all. There was no forage for the oxen, and they were compelled to subsist on coarse weeds and sage brush. One by one the animals broke down and died, and several of the wagons had to be abandoned. A number of the members of the party succumbed to the hardships of the march and were buried on the desert.

More than a month after leaving Salt Lake City, the remnant of the train crossed the dry bed of the head of the Amargosa, and the next day, surmounting the rugged chain now known as the Funeral range, they saw, stretched before them, a tremendous depression in the earth. The shining white bottom, thousands of feet below them, had the appearance of water, and on the opposite side were to be seen the timbered slopes of the Panamint Mountains. The extent of the valley north and south could not be judged, and there was only one thing to do—cross it and reach the mountains on the other side, which they took to be a part of the main chain of the Sierra Nevada. So down they went, following the rugged, stony bed of Furnace Creek Cañon, where now there are several springs of warm but fresh water. They reached the bottom in the fierce heat of an August day, with the thermometer probably 130° in the shade, which means a great deal more out in the open glare of the sun. And here they found, not grass and springs of fresh water, but miles of treacherous alkali marshes, salt hummocks, and sand dunes.

The last of the oxen lay down and died, and all thought of further progress was abandoned, everything being given up to the hopeless search for water. The men scattered in all directions to scour the cañons of surrounding mountains, but in vain, and there the tragedy culminated. Many died where the wagons had been abandoned, and others, bereft of reason, wandered into the mountains and were never afterward heard from. Months afterward the two survivors, Bennett and Stockton, reached the settlements on the west side of the Sierra, and the civilized world heard for the first time of California's "Valley of Death."

In the circumstances, these two men can be pardoned for having given a somewhat highly-colored description of the natural phenomena of the region in which they had undergone such a bitter experience. The tale lost none of its sensational features by being told and retold in the hundreds of mining camps on the Pacific slope, until a region which has real terrors sufficient to entitle it to the distinction of being one of the most dangerous spots on the face of the globe was magnified into a sort of mundane hell, a veritable valley of horrors, from which no man could return alive.

The valley, surrounded on all sides by the vast expanse of arid, stony desert and precipitous mountain chains, remained practically unknown to the outside world for many years, although it was visited in the year 1867 by Lieut. Charles E. Bendire, and by Lieut. Wheeler in 1871.

In the early seventies silver and gold were discovered in the Panamint Mountains, and a mining camp established in

Surprise Cañon on the side of the range opposite Death Valley. It seems to be the lot of every unknown semi-mysterious region to have ascribed to it fabulous mineral wealth, and Death Valley was no exception to the rule. For several years after the discoveries in the Panamint Mountains prospectors set out, singly or in small parties, to search Death and Mesquit Valleys and the Funeral and Grapevine ranges of mountains, in the hope of other and richer finds. As a rule, these men were poorly equipped and were ignorant of the locations of the few springs of fresh water to be found in the country. The result was that many of them never returned, having perished from thirst or starvation. The fate of these prospectors did not improve the reputation of Death Valley and the surrounding country nor cause a general stampede to the locality. Those who did return, however, effectually disposed of many of the current ideas regarding the place, besides demonstrating that the valley and the mountains beyond it were devoid of precious metals.

The most important result of these spasmodic excursions was the discovery of large deposits of crude borax, both in Death Valley and on the Amargosa, near Resting Spring [spelled by some as Resting Springs]. At this time the world's supply of borax was far short of the demand, and the prevailing high price of the commodity induced a San Francisco company to make an attempt to utilize the deposit in Death Valley. Daggett, a station on the Atlantic and Pacific Railway, in the heart of this Mohave Desert, 150 miles south of Furnace Creek, was made the base of operations, and a considerable quantity of borax was freighted from Death Valley to that point for shipment. The heavy expense attendant on teaming across the long stretch of waterless desert and the fact that the work could be carried on only during the cooler season of the year caused the project to be abandoned, and the company's property is now lying idle, guarded by one of the old employees.

The accounts given by the prospectors and borax freighters did not add materially to the world's fund of accurate information about the famous valley. They only knew that it was a big sink in the earth, very deep and terribly hot. The flora they grouped under one general head as "greasewood," and the fauna under another as "varmints."[3]

Beginning annually in 1886, the United States Congress appropriated funds for a study of the geographic distribution of animals, the study to be conducted by the Division of Economic Ornithology and Mammalogy of the United States Department of Agriculture. In 1890, Congress enlarged the scope of the work to include the distribution of plants as well as of animals. The first of the biological surveys under the act of 1890 was of Death Valley and surrounding areas and was planned and conducted under the direction of Dr. C. Hart Merriam, Chief of the Division of Economic Ornithology and Mammalogy.[4]

Following the completion of the expedition, Merriam's Report at the end of 1891 about the expedition's goals succinctly explained the why and where of the expedition:

The most important work of the year has been a biological survey of a large area in southern California and southern Nevada. This region was selected because of the exceptional advantages it offered for studying the distribution of animals and plants in relation to the effects of temperature and humidity at different altitudes from the bottom of Death Valley, which is below the level of the sea, to the summit of the High Sierra, culminating in the lofty snow-capped peaks about Mount Whitney, at an elevation of nearly 15,000 feet.

The close proximity of precipitous mountains and deep desert valleys often brings near together associations of species which in a more level country are characteristic of widely remote regions. In one place on the east side of the Sierra all the life zones of the North American continent from the plateau of Mexico to the Polar Sea may be crossed in traversing a distance of only 10 miles.

The Death Valley expedition, for it soon came to be universally known by this name, was organized for the purpose of determining the actual boundaries of the several life zones of the region and studying the problems involved in the laws governing this distribution. The expedition outfitted at San Bernardino, in southern California, the last week in December, 1890, and set out through Cajon Pass, January 3, 1891, bound for the Mohave Desert and the region to the northward. In its personnel it comprised some of the ablest and most experienced field naturalists in the world. Vernon Bailey, E. W. Nelson, Theodore S. Palmer, Dr. A. K. Fisher, F. Stephens, and Basil Hicks Dutcher, belonged to the division force, and each was in charge of a branch party at some time during the season.

By cooperation with the Division of Entomology, experienced insect collector Albert Koebele was with the expedition for nearly six weeks. By cooperation with the Division of Botany, Frederick Vernon Coville, an Assistant Botanist, was appointed as Botanist of the Death Valley Expedition.[5] Coville, an honor student and star athlete from Oxford, New York, had graduated from Cornell.[6]

Using the available money, the plans for the expedition were well under way in the autumn of 1890 when Secretary of Agriculture J. M. Rusk "reported" that Frederick Funston, son of the chairman of the House of Representatives Committee on Agriculture, would be an expedition member. Merriam protested because he did not have enough money to cover Funston's salary and expenses. "This[,] however, the Sec. furnished and Funston was appointed as Assistant Botanist, though his knowledge of plant life was very meager," according to A. K. Fisher, fellow expedition member.[7] In a letter from Death Valley to his close friend, Edward "Buck" Franklin, the following March of 1891, Fred described his appointment as an expedition member: "By virtue of my 'Pap' being in Congress I managed to get on the thing as assistant botanist not that I know anything about botany, but then my work is to help collect plants and take care of the botanical specimens and do the cussing for the outfit for both of which tasks I am by nature amply qualified."[8] Ed Funston may not have actually requested the appointment of his son, since the Secretary of the Department of Agriculture may have, on his own initiative, added Fred to the expedition party in order to please Ed as the chairman of the House Agriculture Committee. This is particularly likely since, according to Fred's close friend, Charlie Scott, the prior expedition to North Dakota was the only time when Ed's influence had been used to have Fred appointed an expedition member. Now it was different. Fred had already worked for the department and had had some experience in the field. In his letter to Buck Franklin, self-deprecating Fred had, true to form, minimized his knowledge of botany, stating that he knew nothing about it, yet botany was a subject he had studied as a child and at the university.

In November of 1890, word of the proposed expedition appeared in newspapers, which noted that "[t]en celebrated scientists" would compose the expedition.[9] The details of the expedition had been arranged by the next month, and in late December members of the expedition not already in California traveled there from various locations, including Washington, D.C. One of those coming from the nation's capital was Dr. Albert Kenrick Fisher, known as A. K. and Doc to his friends. Fisher, like his classmate and friend, C. Hart Merriam, had received a medical degree from Columbia College, College of Physicians and Surgeons, which is now part of Columbia University in New York City. Thus, there were two non-practicing medical doctors on the expedition. Starting in 1885, Fisher served as Merriam's assistant in the U. S. Department of Agriculture Division of Economic Ornithology and Mammalogy, later renamed the Division of Biological Survey.[10] Fisher had reservations about how well the members of the Death Valley expedition would do: "Practically all the members especially for western work were tender feet, and I little knew at the time how much experience it would take to season them into veterans. Fortunately I knew the eastern out of doors very well, so that some of unpleasant experiences were not dealt out to me."[11]

Although Merriam was in charge of the expedition, he was not able to join it until April after Congress had adjourned and appropriations had been arranged for.[12] Then, he was to leave the expedition in mid-July on another assignment for the government. Surprisingly, the expedition members were generally quite young. At age thirty-five, Merriam was among the oldest members of the expedition. Two members who joined the expedition later in 1891 were older than Merriam: naturalist Frank Stephens, age forty-one, and entomologist Albert Koebele, age thirty-seven. In contrast, two expedition assistants who also joined the expedition later, Basil Hicks Dutcher and Fred W. Koch, were both quite young, Dutcher being nineteen and Koch was probably in his late teens. The topographers were only slightly older. J. M. Dikeman, one of the original seven expedition members, was likely in his early twenties and P. V. S. Bartlett was only twenty-one.

Like Merriam, original expedition member Edward W. Nelson was thirty-five, and original member A. K. Fisher was thirty-four. A fourth original member, Vernon Bailey, was twenty-six; Funston was twenty-five; and, at twenty-three, Coville was actually younger than his assistant, Funston. Of the seven initial members of the expedition, the youngest was 22-year-old Theodore S. Palmer. In Merriam's absence, leadership of the expedition was assigned to its youngest member, Palmer, a native Californian, who had graduated in 1888 from the University of California, and the following year had been appointed as a Field Agent by the U.S. Department of Agriculture.[13] Palmer left Washington for California on December 11.[14] Coville also traveled from Washington to San Bernardino, California, where he reported to Palmer, acting chief of the expedition, on December 26.[15]

Fred Funston would leave from Lawrence for San Bernardino in late December. Before his departure, he journeyed on December 1 from the Funston farm near Carlyle to Topeka, where he visited his sister, Ella, a student at Bethany College.[16] He likely traveled there to tell her goodbye before leaving for Death Valley. Then, on Thursday evening, December 18, he was one of the many guests who attended the evening reception given by the ladies of Pi Beta Phi in Lawrence. After a meal, the guests adjourned to Fraser Hall on the State University of Kansas campus "where they were soon gliding over the polished floor to the incomparable music of the Mandolin club."[17] Fred's imminent departure for California to join the government expedition had been noted the day before in a Lawrence newspaper.[18] When he left a few days later, *The Kansas City Star* observed that "Freddie is a mild mannered little fellow, who resembles his father about as a piccolo resembles a howitzer."[19]

One newspaper article noted in 1899 that "[o]ne trait of General Funston is to tell stories on himself that tend to belittle his real qualities; whereas if one seeks to learn of his heroic exploits he might as well interview a tombstone as to question Funston." One of Funston's characteristically modest stories that he told, at his own expense, involved an experience on his travel by train to California to join the expedition: "When I was on my way to join that Death Valley expedition, I stopped at Neevles [sic: Needles], Colo., to spend Christmas. A lot of cowboys were in town witnessing a dog-fight, and arrayed in holiday togs. I accidentally spit on the polished boots of one of these cattlemen. He fairly bellowed with rage, and was going to chew me up on the spot. I naturally apologized, which seemed to make him all the more furious. 'Wipe it off! wipe it off!' he roared: 'apologies don't go here.' I settled the matter by cleaning off his soiled boots."[20]

Fred reached San Bernardino near the end of December where he joined the other members of the expedition: Coville, Fisher, and acting chief Palmer. While the expedition was being outfitted, Fred wrote a letter to a friend back home in Iola. "The people here have a cheerful way of guying which is unique and exhilarating. One man gives us his lowest rates on metallic coffins. Others tell over and over to us the horrible tales of the hundreds who have gone into the valley never to return, and many of those who did return spending the remainder of their lives in the insane asylum. All of which is very bracing. But seriously, it is going to be a terrible experience without any doubt. Every man in the party except myself has insured his life, made his will and closed up all his earthly affairs, so you see it is regarded rather seriously." Charlie Scott published the foregoing excerpt in his *The Iola Register*, and observed: "It looks as if the boy were in for a pretty interesting trip, but we are guessing that he comes out on top. It is a way the Funston family has."[21]

On New Year's Day 1891, ready to start the journey to Death Valley, Fred and A. K. Fisher set out together on horseback. It was to be a most challenging eight months for all expedition members. In his

1892 *The New York Times* story, Fred detailed the first twenty days of this ordeal as supplemented here with additional material from other persons shown in brackets:

The expedition was sent into the field in two parties, and a rendezvous appointed at Lone Willow Spring, two days' journey southwest of Death Valley. Early in January Vernon O. Bailey, E. W. Nelson, and J. M. Dikeman left Keeler, the terminus of the Carson and Colorado Railway, 150 miles northwest of the rendezvous, and on New Year's Day T. S. Palmer, Dr. A. K. Fisher, F. V. Coville, and the writer left San Bernardino, 200 miles to the south. [Actually, only Fisher and Funston left on January 1; Coville and Palmer departed soon thereafter.] Besides the above mentioned, there were with each party several men employed as teamsters, packers, and cooks.

The expedition may be said to have been fairly well equipped and provisioned, though the necessity of economizing space and weight in the loads made it impossible to take with us many things that would have added materially to our comfort and well-being.

The party that started from San Bernardino left that place only partially equipped, it being the intention to purchase most of the supplies at Daggett, where the route crossed the Atlantic and Pacific Railway. The distance from San Bernardino to Daggett was covered in about a week. This part of the journey lay across the San Bernardino Mountains and the southern part of the Mohave Desert, and was without incident of note. Our progress was necessarily very slow, on account of the steep grades on the ascent to Cajon Pass and the deep, loose sand in the desert, which impeded the progress of the big freight wagon and almost exhausted the saddle horses.

## IN A WATERLESS LAND.

Reaching Daggett, three days were spent in purchasing supplies and pack animals and otherwise completing the outfit. The really serious work of the expedition was now at hand. North of Daggett the route lay over what was to the members of our party practically an unknown country. There was no forage to be had, and the first water hole was eighty [sic: about forty] miles distant. This scarcity of water was the greatest difficulty we had to contend with, and the possibility of not finding any at all added an element of danger that was fully appreciated. The necessity of a supply of water for the horses and for camp use was met by rigging up large barrels and casks on the outside of the wagon beds, and thus carrying several hundred gallons, which was made to suffice by putting the animals on limited allowance. [Author R. S. Dix wrote: Each person requires about three gallons of water per day there, as against three pints ordinarily, which adds much to the difficulty of travel, because it is all but impossible to carry enough water to last an exploring party from one drinkable stream to another....[T]he horses or oxen require the same increase in proportion ...[22]] Nobody, not even the cook, was allowed to wash his hands for three days after leaving Daggett, so important was it considered to save every drop of the water.

[Coville wrote: Bacon, flour, baking-powder, prunes, raisins, coffee, sugar, and rice were our chief supplies, things of which a sufficient amount could be packed on a mule to furnish a party of two with food for two months. We provided ourselves with a scant supply of fresh meat from the wild game we found. Potatoes, onions, and other vegetables we did not have.[23]]

The two freight wagons, one drawn by six and the other by four horses, were piled high with provisions and camp equipage and 3,000 pounds of grain and baled hay for the horses. [Usually grain and baled hay could be had only for the six-horse team that hauled our supplies from Daggett. The saddle horses and pack animals, and the general-utility horses, get what nourishment they could out of such grasses as grew about the desert water holes... However, notwithstanding our practice of camping as long as practicable where the feed was the best that could be found, the horses, in general, did not have sufficient feed.[24]]

The start from Daggett was made shortly after daybreak on the morning of the 10th, and the little caravan left behind the last remnant of civilization to be seen in many long and dreary months. To be sure, this remnant of civilization that we left at Daggett was rather ragged, and not up to the regulation standard; still there were, even here, some of the things that are supposed to go to make up the comforts of life.

The incidents of the first day after leaving here were not conducive to hilarity. The progress of the heavily laden wagons was painfully slow, and a cold wind was blowing from the north, making horseback riding about as disagreeable as can be imagined. The burros that had been brought along as pack animals seemed to have a premonition of the hard work and poor fare in store for them, and caused endless trouble by their attempts to take French leave of the expedition. One meek-faced, stubborn little brute had to be tied behind one of the wagons and literally dragged for several days. It was an object lesson in perseverance to see this animal a hundred times a day brace all fours and try to stop a four-horse wagon. The last I saw of this burro was when we were disbanded at Visalia eight months later. Though little more than an animated parcel of skin and bones, it was resisting the efforts of half a dozen men to force it into a stable.

## PHYSICAL ASPECTS OF A DESERT.

The popular idea of a desert is that it is a perfectly level stretch of sand, totally devoid of vegetation of any kind, but this would by no means be a description of the country through which we were now traveling, though it is as much a desert as the Sahara or Atacama. A succession of valleys from five to fifteen miles in width are separated by ranges of jagged and extremely broken hills or mountains, from a few hundred to several thousand feet in height. A person accustomed to the mountains of the Appalachian system, and those of the East generally, can have but little conception of what one of our party fitly termed the "upness and downess" of these desert chains, and of the difficulties to be surmounted in crossing them. Some of these, notably the Panamint, Timber, Inyo, and Grapevine Ranges, reach tremendous heights, and are impassable, except by pack train.

The characteristic feature of all the mountains of the region, however, is their brilliant and varied coloring. They may be steep, rugged, barren, and generally useless, but they are never monotonous. Within a few miles of each other can be seen mountains of half a dozen different shades of color. One peak will be composed of black volcanic rock, and the one next to it may be a gaudy yellow. The lower part of a cliff may be blood red and the upper part gray or brown, while in many cases the strata form large and well-defined bands of strikingly different colors. The most notable example of this display is to be seen in the northern part of the Funeral Range, and gives these otherwise respectable mountains a very cheap chrome appearance.

Everywhere and in the most unexpected places are the cañons, deep and gloomy defiles, with in most cases absolutely perpendicular sides. As the only way to cross one of these mountain ranges is to ascend a cañon to its head and go over the "backbone" to the head of a cañon on the other side, following it down to the valley, it can be seen that these gorges are one of the most important considerations for a person who would go from one valley to another without making a detour of, maybe, a hundred miles. And in this, I believe, is to be found one of the greatest obstacles to travel in this country, as it is certainly no exaggeration to say that nine out of every ten of these cañons are utterly impassable except by those on foot, and in many cases not even then.

As I have said before, the depressions separating these ranges vary in width from five to fifteen miles. On entering one of these valleys from the side, one crosses first a considerable stretch of tableland sloping gently toward the lowest part. This is composed of smooth, rounded rocks, packed tightly together as if cemented. Here and there are deep gullies torn out by the torrents of water that sweep down from the mountain cañons after the cloudbursts common to all desert regions. Leaving this rocky mesa, one crosses a comparatively narrow strip of loose deep sand mixed with gravel and small stones, and beyond this, forming a bed of the valley, a wide stretch of a soft, doughy mixture of salt, sand, and soil, or in some cases pure salt. These alkaline marshes forming the beds of the valleys are snow white, and in the bright glare of the sunlight have the appearance of water, making a most effective mirage.

### UNIQUE AND VARIED FAUNA. [sic: Flora]

No less interesting than the physical features of this region is its unique and varied flora. Wherever there is to be found any soil or sand, something of plant life has taken hold.

To be sure, this desert vegetation is totally different from that of the more favored sections of the country, and is composed almost entirely of plants that could not live in the conditions generally supposed to be necessary to plant life. The stony mesas and lower slopes of the mountains are tinged with the brilliant green of the creosote bush, (Larrea Mexicaus,) an evergreen shrub from two to six feet high, with bright yellow flowers and dark-green sticky leaves, having a most peculiar though not offensive odor. This shrub is characteristic of nearly all the Southwestern deserts and has no economic value, except that its dry twigs are the general fuel in those parts of the country out of reach of timber. The "giant yucca," (Yucca brevifolia,) often erroneously called a palm, is found in great numbers on the sandy slopes of all the valleys except those in the vicinity of Death Valley. It is a striking tree, with clusters of large sword-like leaves, and bunches of cream-colored flowers. Some of these yuccas are 20 feet in height and 18 inches in diameter, but are utterly useless as firewood, the trunk being soft, not unlike punk. In the lower parts of most of the valleys grow a number of bushes and shrubs generally called "greasewood" and "sage brush," though the later term is a misnomer. The most common of these are several species of the genus "Atriplex." The true sage brush is found only in the mountains at a considerable elevation.

Every where [sic] are the cacti in beautiful and varied forms, and in most cases with gorgeous blossoms of red or yellow. Only the most common plants are mentioned, and there are many others not so general. In some of the upper mountain cañons, removed from the heat of the desert, are many wild flowers, some of them very beautiful, which bloom in the early Spring months and die shortly afterward. The much to be desired grass family is almost totally lacking in this region. Several genera and species are found, but usually in small quantities, except in the most inaccessible mountains. As our party was not equipped with a balloon, we were unable to utilize these aërial pastures, and left our horses to eke out a scanty living on the coarse and wiry salt grass found along the edges of the salt fields.

### A PAINFUL JOURNEY.

But to return to the little caravan which we have left dragging itself through this wilderness of rocks and sand. On the morning of the 11th the summit of the Granite Range was crossed, and in the descent to the valley below the route lay for miles through a magnificent grove of yuccas. Valley after valley and many ranges of hills were left behind. The fact that we could carry only three days' supply of water made it absolutely necessary to reach a spring within that time, so that several hours of each night were consumed in travel. When the darkness became so thick that further progress was impossible, the panting horses were unhitched and doled out their pitiful allowance of water, grain, and baled hay, while the men, hungry enough to eat anything, regaled themselves on bacon, hardtack, and coffee, and, rolling up in their blankets, lay down on the sand to sleep until daybreak. In the morning, even before it was light enough to see, everything was astir. Horses were fed and hitched to the wagons, and the cook again distributed his collection of indigestible bric-à-brac.

Each day was like its predecessor, except that as we progressed the grades became steeper and the horses were more easily fatigued. On the evening of the 12th we reached Granite Spring, the first water seen in three days, and it was well that we did, as all the barrels and casks were by this time empty, and another day of work without water would have proved a most severe trial for the horses.

This spring was found to contain about two barrels of excellent water in a hole ten feet deep, which had been dug by the borax freighters years before. Here the horses drank their fill, and the men were allowed to wash their hands and faces.

One long day's march now lay between us and the rendezvous at Lone Willow Spring, and this was accomplished on the 13th. Here we found in camp Messrs. Bailey, Nelson, and Dikeman, who had come down from Keeler with a wagon and buckboard and several pack animals. They had also brought with them a packer and Ti Sing, the irrepressible Chinaman who was to be our chief cook and general camp boss during the remainder of our stay in the field. This man had been with the geological survey for several years, and was a model camp employe—cleanly [sic], intelligent, and obedient. It was in no small degree due to his efficiency that the members of the party endured so well the unavoidable hardships and privations of camp life on the desert and experienced so little sickness. [As Funston's party had approached the camp at Lone Willow Spring, the first man they heard was Ti Sing, who was nonchalantly whistling one of the popular tunes of the day, "Sweet Violets."[25]]

Last and least of our number was "Hat," [full name was Hattie Lewis [26]] the Chinaman's black shepherd dog, that followed us in all our wanderings…

Our party now numbered eleven men and about thirty horses, mules, and burros. In the four days since leaving Daggett the animals had subsisted on a scanty allowance from the supply of feed brought along in the wagons. I did not see a single spear of grass in that four days' march; but in the range of low mountains back of our present camp was a scattering growth of bunch grass, not much, but enough for a few days' forage; and as the animals were sorely in need of rest it was determined to remain here two days before resuming the march to Death Valley.

During the stay at this place Messrs. Bailey, Coville, and Dikeman, and the writer made the ascent of a considerable mountain, marked on the chart of the Wheeler survey as Brown's Peak. This peak rose about 6,000 feet above our camp, and, though very steep, can be climbed without serious difficulty. The view from its summit is one long to be remembered. More than a hundred miles to the west, rising above all the desert mountains, is the snow-white main chain of the Sierra Nevada—Whitney, Tyndall, and other famous peaks. To the north rises the huge broken mass of the Panamint Range, surmounted by Telescope Peak, lifting its great square cap more than two miles above the surrounding valleys. Between the Panamint and Argus Ranges is to be seen the entire length of Panamint Valley, a strip of snow-white salt, sixty miles long and fifteen broad.

But the sight that interested us most was far to the northeast. Lying lower than any of the other valleys, nestling down between precipitous red and brown mountains, half hidden in dim gray haze, was the shining white of the alkali marshes and the yellow sand dunes of the bottom of the Valley of Death.[27]

Although Fred provided in *The New York Times* article the overview of the twenty-day journey, his personal experiences during this period starting in San Bernardino and ending on the edge of Death Valley are not only interesting, but also provide insight into his personality. When A.K. Fisher arrived from Washington, D.C. at the hotel in San Bernardino, he found Fred there. A.K. later described Fred as "rather a chubby rounded out fellow about 5 ft. 2 in. in height. At the time he was quite retiring and altho pleasant had very little to say."[28] After departing from San Bernardino on January 1, Fisher and Funston headed across the plain to Cajon Pass, a pass with an altitude of 4,195 feet located in the Sierra Madre mountains, which form the southern boundary of the Mohave Desert.[29] Many years later, Fisher typed rough drafts of his memories related to the Death Valley Expedition and to some of its members: Bailey, Merriam, Nelson, and Funston, whose surname he frequently misspelled. In quoting from Fisher's memories, I have, without notation, corrected spelling, punctuation, and grammar, as appropriate.

On that first day of travel for Funston and Fisher, Fisher later recollected that "[f]or sometime we rode with orange and other citrus orchards on either side of the road. As we approached higher ground, Funston thought he saw a no. of oranges lying on our side of the fence. He said as he was thirsty, he was glad of this opportunity to find such nice looking fruit. He galloped ahead and when I arrived he had a disgusted look upon his countenance, for what he mistook for oranges were merely wild squashes which resembled oranges in color and size."

About halfway up Cajon Pass, the two men decided to stay the night at a small hotel, and the following day collected specimens before going to the town of Hesperia.[30] This was located just north of Cajon Pass and thirty-six miles from San Bernardino.[31] Fisher later described this adventure in collecting:

> The next morning we went out into the country bright and early and visited the open ground as well as the brushy chaparral. I collected quite a no. of birds which were moderately common but new to me in life. Funston had collected quite a no. of plants and finally when lunch time came and we were in an open space he placed the drying papers in a row and carefully allotted to each one plants for his botanical box. There was quite a no. of specimens and he looked upon them with some pride. A few min. later there was, however, an ominous sound and before we were aware a gust of wind came which upset all the plants off the dryers and sent the light sheets of paper floating into the air. Up to this time, Funston was quite mild mannered, but the profanity which he let forth on this occasion made me give him the appropriate name which was "The Parson." All this, however, was charged up to experience and really was worth the happening.[32]

Fisher described Funston's swearing on this occasion: "the way that cuss-words were rattled out by the score indicated that he had had some previous experience along this same line."[33] Billy White succinctly explained Fred's swearing: He had "a wide eclectic Spanish-Texan-Kansan-and-Old English collection of oaths which he loved to juggle with in emotional moments. For he was an emotional creature."[34] Fred apparently never renounced swearing, a positive trait in the eyes of a fellow U. S. Army officer: "The dignity of the eagles [Fred's rank as general] did not take from him the prerogative of his fine, old-fashioned anger-purging profanity. He believes, I think, in the virtue of that vice, as many another man has. This human quality was, in the first days, seen the most often in his frank boyishness."[35]

To collect and preserve the plants they collected, botanist Coville and assistant botanist Funston used a knife, a pick, a portfolio, and two board presses. The knife was of the kind used by cotton inspectors in opening covers of cotton bales. The pick was modeled after one commonly used by plant collectors in the southwest of the United States. Its head was made of steel, with a slightly curved blade about five inches long, and, at the extremity, an inch wide, and the head, about two inches long, narrowed to a point. The handle, made of strong tough wood, was slender and about three feet in length.[36] Coville heartily approved of this style of pick: "For digging plants in hard clay soil, in gravel, or among broken stones, or for uprooting cactuses and other spring shrubs, this instrument is by far the best that I have ever used. In loam, mud or sand the knife is best."[37] The portfolio consisted of binders' boards covered with canvas and was usually carried tied to the saddle. The presses, to press the specimens, "were ordinary ones made of boards, and straps were used for applying pressure."[38]

By experimenting in the early part of the expedition, Coville established a three-part system for keeping field notes. First, there was a catalogue of specimens collected. For each new specimen, with its duplicates, the collector assigned a number, the date, locality, station, altitude, and any "desirable short remark." "A specimen with these data accurately recorded is, for the uses of geographic botany, inestimably more valuable than many specimens whose history is but vaguely known." Second, he used a journal. In this the collectors recorded under each date "the location of the night's camp, the course of the day's journey, and a few notes indicative of the general and vegetative features of the new country seen." Whenever the camp was stationary for several days, collecting excursions were noted. Third, there were slip notes. On these were recorded all kinds of facts which related to the botany of the region, but which were not shown by the specimens themselves or in the catalogs. These slip notes were kept in large envelopes filed by subject.[39]

Coville's clothing reflected the weather conditions at the start of the expedition. His clothing was ordinary, but heavy "for the weather was often cold." Over his coat he wore a canvas hunting coat, and often also an overcoat. He began the expedition wearing commonly worn shoes, but later in the season when he had to climb mountains, he wore heavy, thick-bottomed miners shoes, the soles and heels of which were "thickly set with hobnails." In the winter, a wide-brimmed felt hat or sombrero was best, while in the summer a cork helmet or its equivalent "which will shade the eyes is cooler and pleasanter." Coville carried a .44 Colt magazine carbine, but for general camp use, a breech-loading shotgun was better. An aneroid was used to measure the differences in altitude.[40]

Returning to the experiences of "Doc" Fisher and Fred Funston during the twenty-day journey, on the day following the incident of Fred's collected specimens blowing away, the two men traveled on to the town of Hesperia just north of the Cajon Pass, where they were to remain until Coville and Palmer arrived. While waiting, A.K. and Fred hunted for specimens, including mammals for Fisher's collection. "At one locality where we found a no. of wood-rats' nests, we drove out some of the animals by means of smoke. We were interested to find that these animals had a regular place to deposit their droppings. As these droppings were of uniform size and shape, Funston jokingly suggested that we leave the party, sugar coat these droppings and sell them for pills which were strictly vegetable."[41]

"Doc" found Fred to be an agreeable companion. "Funston was an amusing fellow, told some good stories and gave peculiar names to all our horses, or to various people we subsequently met. A little mare which he rode he called Venus de Medici. This white cow pony of mine was christened Appollo Belvedere, and a bigger raw-boned horse which Coville owned Katharine Brandegee [American botanist] because it had a brand mark of K.B. on its right shoulder. As Coville was a tall fellow, several inches over 6 ft., when I saw him and Funston riding through a street in Victor it reminded me of Don Quixote and Sancho Panza."[42]

Funston not only named the horses ridden by the expedition members, he also named the burros who carried the vital water casks for the expedition:

> Speaking of the burros, the Mexican donkey is an interesting though not very intellectual beast. We were afflicted with an especially depraved and unregenerate lot. The task of naming them was the cause of much discussion, but they were in the course of time all fitted out. There were Sarah Bernhardt [French stage actress], Fay Templeton [American stage actress], George Francis Train [American entrepreneur], Herr Most [anarchist politician and newspaper editor] and others. There was one pair that the other burros would not associate with. These two seemed to be the sole proprietors of an immensely vacant and meaningless bray. A bright thought worked its way into my head, and with tears in my eyes I beseeched the chief of the expedition to allow me to christen these darlings. The hard-hearted man was moved by my artless manner and gave his assent and thereafter when anything went wrong with the pack train Jerry Simpson and Mrs. Lease were sure to be the targets of a shower of maledictions from everybody within reach.[43]

Republican Funston's obvious pleasure in naming, and then verbally assaulting, the recalcitrant burros, Jerry Simpson and Mrs.

Lease, stemmed from Kansas politics. Simpson and Lease belonged to the People's Party, the members of which were commonly known as Populists. In the election in the preceding November of 1890, "Sockless" Jerry Simpson had been elected to the United States House of Representatives from Kansas. Mary Elizabeth Lease was a Populist orator who supposedly advised Kansas farmers to "raise less corn and more hell," the result of the growing revolt by many Kansas farmers against high mortgage interest rates and high railroad rates.[44]

On January 5, Palmer and Coville arrived at Hesperia where they joined Funston and Fisher. The four men rode on to the town of Victor where they camped for the night. Coville wrote in his journal: "It was our first night in the [Mohave] desert, and the frost that formed upon our bed-canvasses and the coyotes (kī-yō' tez) that howled about the camp gave us a hint of our coming experiences."[45] The next morning, January 6, they left Victor for Stoddard's Wells, fording the shallow Mohave River, and followed the road northeast through the desert, with their ultimate goal being the town of Daggett.[46] Coville recorded that they made their "first close acquaintance with the mountains of the desert, in this region perhaps better called hills for they were only a few hundred feet in height, rocky, treeless, with only scattered creosote-bushes visible from the plain below, and even these wanting on steep slopes. The whole view was that of a rugged mass of bare rock, and an impression constantly forced itself upon a stranger to these regions that the mountains had never been moistened with rain."[47]

The little group arrived at Stoddard's Wells at nightfall. "We found this a dreary camping spot," wrote Palmer.[48] Coville described what occurred next. "The water of a sluggish spring in the barren mountain-slope had been conducted to the roadside in an iron pipe, and there accumulated in an immense iron-bound wooden tub or tank. It could be let out through a hole near the bottom into a drinking trough for horses and other stock."[49] This was the only source of water on the approximate forty-mile trip between Victor and Daggett. Only a "broken-down stone wall" was left of a house which had stood there, "and in the lee of its chimney we threw down our table-canvas, set the lantern in the chimney-hole and shivering ate our cold supper. The wind was cold and piercing, the sky clear—a typical winter night in the desert. We spread our beds on the dry fine gravel among the creosote-bushes and, chilled and without a fire crawled into our blankets."[50]

That next morning, January 7, the little group left the wells "without regret," Palmer noted.[51] They traveled through a country similar to that of the day before. Jack rabbits were abundant, and several were shot. Crossing a low range of hills, they reached Daggett about 3 p.m.[52] "This is a settlement of perhaps thirty buildings, which serves as a railroad connection for silver and borax mines in the adjacent mountains."[53] Here the little expedition was to stay for two days while supplies were purchased and water barrels were put on the wagon. A team was hired to assist in hauling the freight to Granite Springs.[54] Palmer dismissed the driver, Samuel Smith, who had brought their wagon from San Bernardino, and hired George W. Porter as driver and Michael Barnes as packer and cook.[55] While at Daggett, Coville and Fisher made a side trip to obtain various specimens.[56]

Provisioned for the next stage of their journey, the small group of Palmer, Fisher, Funston, and Coville on horseback, and a four-horse team and a temporary two-horse team with their drivers and a cook, set out about 9 o'clock on the morning of January 10.[57] While they were packing to leave, a burro broke loose, and Coville and Funston rode to the Calico mining camp six miles away in search of it.[58] Whether they were successful is not recorded, but there is another story about Fred Funston purchasing burros at Calico, which must have occurred at the time of the provisioning at Daggett. Palmer stated, in a later interview, that one day he asked Funston to go to the Calico mining camp to purchase a couple of burros. "'We heard nothing from him until about nine o'clock at night,' said the doctor [Palmer], 'when we heard a crashing noise in the distance. 'Clear the road! Get out of the way! I'm coming!' were the shouts heard in the darkness, and Funston dashed into camp with two galloping jackasses tied together with a 25-foot rope. He rode one, while the other wildly circled about, twisting the rope around bushes and trees, frequently landing both Fred and the burros in a promiscuous heap."[59] Fisher provided this additional detail: At one point, the burros, each at the end of the rope, started to run, each "staying on the edge of the road so that the intervening rope would have upset 2 pedestrians if they had not heard Funston yell, 'Get out of the way.' Just what they said to Funston when he joined them is merely problematical, but Funston did not seem anxious to furnish the information."[60]

The little group stopped at Evans Wells, four miles from Daggett, to water the horses, since the next water was nearly forty miles distant at Copper City Spring. They camped that evening about a mile or two below the summit of the ridge north of Daggett. By hitching six horses on the big wagon the next morning, January 11, the summit was successfully crossed. They traveled through Paradise Valley, and camped without finding water, making thus a second dry camp. That fact plus a cold wind "made things rather unpleasant," Palmer recorded.[61] On January 12, Palmer and Coville walked about one and a half miles and located Copper City Spring, about thirty-nine miles from Daggett. There they found the water was a little sulphury, and they baled the spring out about half. The team and horses were watered, and then, after traveling five or six miles to the northwest, they arrived at Granite Springs, just southwest of Granite Mountain (or Pilot Knob). Although Granite Springs, sometimes called Granite Spring, had good water, it was too far from the road, so after packing ten gallons of water on a burro, the party moved to a better spring on the north side of Granite Mountain, where they unloaded the wagons and dismissed the extra team.[62]

When the party pulled out the next morning, Fisher and Funston were left in camp "to watch load of stuff" while the rest of the men and the wagon went on with the "bulk of feed provisions + baggage" to Lone Willow Spring, located at the south end of Panamint Valley. This was the long-awaited rendezvous point for the members of the two parts of the expedition. Arriving at the nearby Lone Willow Tanks after covering about twenty-five miles from Granite Springs, Palmer and Coville and their helpers found in camp Edward Nelson, Vernon Bailey, and J. M. Dikeman with their cook and packer, they having arrived the day before.[63] The cook was Ti Sing (also spelled Tie Sing), whom Funston had so complimentarily described in his *The New York Times* article. Fred was not alone in his high regard for Ti Sing. Vernon Bailey, many years later, described Ti Sing as "efficient, always cheerful, honest and intelligent. His favorite song was 'Clementine' and his quaint rendering of it did as much for our good cheer as his good cooking did for our hungry bodies."[64] According to A. K. Fisher, Ti became "very fond of me..." As a result, Ti would hurry to finish his own work, and then would help A.K. skin mammals that A. K. had trapped. On one occasion, Ti set traps to catch a gopher. A. K. later described what he did when he passed Ti's traps early the next morning. He "found a gopher and taking it out I placed my finger tips together and made an imitation of a cat track in the soft dirt. While I was skinning some mammals later in the A.M. Ti came up laughing and said, 'You make cat tracks with fingers, I could see nail thence,' which showed how that minute details were not lost by chinamen." A.K. had used his saddle for a pillow on one occasion, and two or three days later Ti brought him a flour bag filled with duck feathers, and remarked that this was "a softer pillow than a saddle."[65] Ti had A. K. keep his money from his wages throughout the expedition, and when A. K. gave him the whole amount at the end of the journey, A. K. warned Ti not to gamble with his fellow Chinese "because all would be taken from him."[66]

Coville also complimented Ti Sing. He "was the most original and resourceful Chinese I have ever seen in a camp." If a cottontail rabbit hopped into the camp, he wound up in Ti's stewpot. "Funston told a story on himself of shooting at one mountain sheep and killing another, but Ti Sing never missed a pot shot." If fuel was short in camp, Ti "would catch a horse, saddle it, ride off into the desert, and come back dragging a load of dead creosote bush stems at the end of a lariat. Whistling popular tunes, using a shotgun with efficiency, and catching and riding western saddle horses were not ordinary accomplishments of a Chinese cook."[67]

While at the Granite Mountain camp, Fisher secured a fine coyote specimen when the coyote died after eating one of the poisoned dates Fisher had set out. Fred asked what the animal was, and Fisher said "Canis latrans." Fred responded "Oh, Chinese Lanterns." Thereafter, coyotes were known as Chinese lanterns.[68] The next day, January 14, Fisher and Funston arrived at Lone Willow Spring about 2 p.m., and later Porter came into camp with the remainder of the "stuff" which had been left the day before at the Granite Mountain camp. There were now eleven men in the party, including the seven scientists, a driver, two packers, and the cook.[69]

Lone Willow Spring continued as the expedition's camp until January 19. In the meantime, on the 16th, Fred, Coville, Bailey, and Dikeman ascended Brown's Peak as described previously by Fred in his *The New York Times* article. The next day, Coville and Fred set out on horseback for Lone Willow Peak, a high point about eight miles southwest of Lone Willow Spring in the Slate Range. They followed an old wagon road up the steep mesa and entered the mouth of a cañon about a mile above. As far up into the mountains as the horses could be ridden, the two men followed the cañon. After staking the horses to feed on bunch grass, the two men continued up the cañon on foot nearly to its source, and upon ascending a steep ridge to the right, they found themselves upon the shoulder of the mountain. Coville went about three miles farther up the "broken but ascending slope"; he does not say in his record what Fred did.[70]

On the afternoon of January 18, Coville returned to Lone Willow Peak by nearly the same route that he and Fred had used the previous day, going about halfway to the summit, but climbing the mountain proper along the hog-back west of the cañon.[71] Meanwhile, Fred, with the expedition's mail, left for the post office at the mining camp of Panamint, about forty-eight miles away. He would thus miss the expedition's entry into Death Valley.[72]

Fred's *The New York Times* article continued:

## IN THE VALLEY ITSELF

On the 19th the horses and mules were driven in, the wagons reloaded, and the barrels refilled with water for the last long pull before reaching the valley. The first two days were spent in surmounting the low divide above the "Wash of the Amargosa," [Coville wrote: "During the [first] day, we had been reminded of the country that lay before us by passing a roadside grave with the inscription on the headboard, in pencil, 'James Coleman. Buried by Gomer Jones June 16, 1879,' and another board at the fork of an old mining road, bearing the legend 'Taylors Mine 16 miles to Hell,'"[73]] and then began the steep descent into Death Valley, down a long and tortuous stretch of sand and loose rocks and then over the level of treacherous, doughy "salt-rising ground," past the brine pit called Mesquit Well, and the graves of the borax freighters who perished here from thirst, until the evening of the 21st, when we went into camp at Bennett's Well [spelled by some as Bennett Wells], in the bottom of Death Valley, below the level of the sea. It was a weird, uncanny sort of place, in thorough keeping with the stories of the ill-fated wagon train and the lost prospectors. Immediately west of our camp was the Panamint Range, forming the western wall of the valley, and extending its entire length north and south.

Telescope Peak, as seen from this point, is one of the world's finest mountain views, rising more than 11,000 feet above the beholder, a tremendous mass of black, red and brown, unobstructed by intervening foot hills or mountains. Looking east across the valley, the view lies over the field of salt and alkali, level as a floor along the edges, but broken into hummocks in the middle. On the further [sic] side, rising almost perpendicular, is the rugged mass of the Funeral Range.

Death Valley proper, that part of the depression extending from Mesquit Valley on the north to the "Wash of the Amargosa" on the south, is about forty-five miles long and fifteen broad. Mesquit Valley is nothing more than an extension of Death Valley, and has all the characteristics of the latter place, from which it is separated by only a low range of sand hills. It is oval in form, about thirty by fifteen miles in extent, and has a slightly higher altitude than Death Valley.

In both valleys there are considerable clumps of mesquit (Prosopia juilflora) several kinds of greasewood, and, as a matter of course, the inevitable creosote bush; but, besides these, there is little vegetation. Animal life is not abundant. Mice, moles, horned toads, lizards, a few insects, and fewer birds constitute about all the living creatures.

There is little or no wind, and over the whole region hangs an awful and most impressive silence. Day after day and month after month a fierce sun beats down from a cloudless sky, making these valleys veritable furnaces of dry heat. The atmosphere is apparently totally devoid of moisture, and this, in addition to the intense heat of the Summer season, is the cause of a constant longing for water which cannot be satisfied by drinking a reasonable amount. Every member of our party carried a gallon canteen on the horn of his saddle, and no one ventured any distance from camp without taking with him this supply of water.

In such conditions of heat and dryness there is, of course, rapid evaporation. The body of a horse or man will not decompose, but becomes dried up or desiccated, and finally crumbles to dust. It is the above fact that has been the foundation for a lot of arrant nonsense about the mummified remains of human beings being scattered all over the bed of the valley. A corpse does become, in a certain sense, mummified, but not for all time. Several years ago, in the month of June, an employe of the borax company perished from thirst in the southern part of the valley, and his body, which was not discovered until the following September, was at that time in a good state of preservation. This man's grave is the first one south of Bennett's Well.

[Charlie Scott later reminisced about "a joke on Fred Funston." While Fred was on the Death Valley Expedition, "two of his University girl friends were talking about him. 'Where and what is Death Valley?' queried one. 'Why, it is away out west in the mountains and is a horrid hot place where people just wither up into mummies,' was the reply. 'How perfectly awful!' responded her friend. And then with a tone of enthusiasm in her voice she added, 'But what a dear, sweet little mummy Fred would make!'" [74]]

[Although "in midsummer the bottom of the valley is so hot that language can hardly provide exaggeration...," in the winter the temperature at a given spot could be cold at night and hot during the day. The day after the expedition reached Bennett's Well, the temperature was 31° just before sunrise, but, by afternoon, in the shade it was 73°, a range of 42° for the day.[75]]

In such a region as this Bennett's Well is an anomaly hard

to understand, but very thoroughly appreciated by travelers. Situated on the west side of the valley, about fifteen miles from its southern extremity and not more than 300 yards from the edge of the salt field, is this shallow hole, filled with good fresh water. The spring was named in honor of Bennett, one of the survivors of the wagon train of 1850, who is supposed to have here found the water that enabled him to reach the Panamint Mountains.[76]

After a successful trip over the Panamint Mountains to Panamint to deliver and pick up mail, Fred rejoined the expedition on the night of January 20 at the camp at Bennett's Well, where Bailey and Nelson had arrived ahead of the main party, which reached there the next day.[77] Like Funston, Bailey wrote positively about the benefits of the "anomaly," Bennett's Well: "Instead of being a 'terrible region of death' this is the pleasantist camping place we have had this winter. Here at Bennetts Wells we get plenty of good water. Splendid grass for the horses, + good wood. The weather, for the past 5 days, has been as near to my liking as it could be. The coldest has been 30° + the hottest only 75°. Clear + pleasant all the time. That is all right for January but I dont [sic] want any of it in August. It must be terrible then. Men do stay here + work all summer but the graves scattered over the valley are an evidence of what it is in summer. The stories of deadly gasses [sic] + poison water are all bosh. It is pure heat + dense air that kills people. The dense air becomes heated + conducts heat rapidly."[78]

Two days after Fred's arrival at Bennett's Well, Fred, Fisher, and Palmer left there on the morning of January 22 and headed north across the valley to Greenland Ranch, located at Furnace Creek.[79] Furnace Creek was a small stream which entered Death Valley on its east side and which came from a cañon of the same name in the northern part of the Funeral Mountains. The Greenland Ranch, also known simply as Furnace Creek, was owned by the Pacific Coast Borax Company and was supplied by water from Furnace Creek.[80] It was nearly 8 p.m. when the little party reached Greenland Ranch, where they found James "Jimmy" Dayton of the borax company in charge. They camped for the night outside the gate of the ranch yard.[81] Many years later Coville paid tribute to Jimmy: "Rough on the surface, Jimmy was in spirit courteous and helpful to every member of the expedition and they all came to hold him in the respect and affection he had earned."[82] Although Dayton offered them the use of the buildings at the unused borax works a mile north of the ranch, Palmer concluded that the ranch offered a better place for their collecting work. Thus, they put up their tent just outside the ranch gate. Palmer sent the driver Porter to Daggett with the team to obtain a load of provisions and instructed him to meet them at Resting Spring on February 3.[83]

Greenland Ranch, located about a mile north of the mouth of Furnace Creek Cañon, had about forty acres of alfalfa surrounded by a row of young cottonwood trees on the east and south sides. Near the house was a vegetable garden and a few fig trees. Dayton told his visitors that the prior summer on July 3 the temperature had reached 136° in the shade.[84] That was the summertime, but this was wintertime when "the months of December, January and February are painfully cold..."[85] Fred had been told while still in Kansas that Death Valley was very warm, and he brought with him only very light blankets. Early in his travels with Fisher, there was one place where they stopped for the night that Fred would have suffered greatly from the cold if Fisher had not invited him to share with him the heavy, double-mission blankets and canvas covering that Fisher had. The temperature that night was only about ten degrees. At Greenland Ranch, Fred was still sleeping with Fisher under his blankets, and twice he was disturbed by noises. One moonlit night a killdeer plover called excessively, as far as Fred was concerned, and he grumbled that he wished they could shoot it in the morning.[86] "One evening there was a mosquito with rather a bass voice humming around our bed." This again irritated Fred, who "remarked that there was a damn mosquito trying to bite him that was as large as a bumble-bee. He assumed that the tone of its voice indicated a very large insect."[87]

"Doc" Fisher recorded that Fred's "sense of direction was very poor and it caused us some little worry lest he would wander and be difficult to find. Once he went outside with mules to bring in some grain and did not return that night, all of which worried us a great deal and taking the trail the next morning, we found him sitting on a bag of barley which had become dislodged from one of the pack mules."[88]

On January 25, 26-year-old Vernon Bailey wrote from Death Valley a descriptive letter describing other members in the expedition: "The men are all first rate fellows, but I like Palmer + Coville the best. They are quiet, thoughtful men, well educated + know a great deal that I don't. Another thing is, they are not always swearing. The amount of profanity in camp is fearful. The men seem to get worse the longer they are out here." "[Coville] is a splendid walker, is 6 feet, 2 ½ inches in stockings & weighs 175 is splendidly built + very strong.... He is 23 years old, graduated from Cornell College when 20. He is reckoned among the few best botanists of the country."

"Palmer is a quiet, pleasant fellow, has a very good classical education, is clear headed and has a talent for managing men—is better at that than at managing horses. He is a good worker but does hate to get up in the morning. He is a little younger than I am. I dont [sic] know just how old, is just beginning to raise a moustache + has a boyish look." "Dr. Fisher is about 35. He is always joking till his face has settled down to a funny, dry smile, except when he rides horse back. Then it wears an expression of painful endurance. He is about my size, light complexioned + is, all round, a jolly fellow to be with."

As for Fred, Bailey noted that he was assistant botanist "[n]ot because Coville needed an assistant nor because he is a botanist but because he is a 'Senators son.' He has very little to do + draws good pay. That makes one senator solid with the division + helps in getting appropriation. Fortunately Funston is not a disagreeable fellow but takes what comes in a philosophical manner. He is obliging + good natured has a shammy[spurious imitation] kind of education (I think) but has seen a good deal of the country + is fairly well posted. Writes some for papers Saint Nicholas for one." Bailey described Fred as "a short, thickset fellow, + is especially noted for funny, dry remarks, + for adapting his profanity to the occasion, for which they call him the 'parson.'"

As for the four "teamsters, cooks, packers + etc." Bailey noted that "[t]he man that drives the big ticm [sic: team] gets $60.00 a month but it is a mean job. I wouldnt [sic] do it for twice that. All of the men have more work than they can do in 16 hours a day + are hustled about by one + then another. Tie [Sing] does first rate since he has nothing to do but cook. The big wagon ran over his toe + took a nail off the other day." Bailey noted that one man "is going to leave soon, can't stand the work. I dont [sic] blame him." [89]

Nearly a month later, farm boy Bailey was clearly disillusioned by his experiences on the expedition.

> We are all getting along all right + are likely to for the rest of the trip. I am tired of writing about country + places + people. It all doesnt [sic] amount to shucks. I am tired of being bossed around + having to boss others around, tired of being alone + tired of company that I dont [sic] like. The more I think of quiet farm life with a few people around that I care for + a few common comforts the more I feel disgusted with this sort of life. If I come out with a few dollars ahead next fall, I believe I will come home to stay, settle down to work on the farm along side of the rest of you. I think we can make a living + all enjoy ourselves better that way.... To be sure I earn more

money than I can on a farm, still I go ragged + dirty + live on coarse grub—bacon + boiled beans + camp bread + black coffee + dried apples. How I would like some good fresh milk –not skimmed– + a couple of fried eggs + a piece of Ma's bread with butter on it. [90]

Bailey, however, was to pursue a career as a field naturalist. [91]

On January 26, Coville arrived at Greenland Ranch from Bennett's Well, but two days later he returned to Bennett's Well. The expedition divided into two parties the following day when Coville, Bailey, Nelson, and Dikeman with a packer headed south to Saratoga Springs at the south end of Death Valley.[92]

On February 1, while still at Greenland Ranch, Fred wrote to his mother from "Death Valley":

Dear Ma:

I received your letter at Panamint a few days ago. Am getting along splendidly and like my work more every day.

We are all together now, eleven of us. We left Dagget [sic], where I wrote you my last letter on the 10th and reached here on the 20th.

We were ten days going 152 miles and had some rather vivid experiences Death Valley is a great sink 40 miles long, 2 [?] wide and 10,000 feet deep and is surrounded on all sides by tremendous mountains. The bottom is lower than sea level and is a crust of salt and soda as white as snow.

The people who have died here nearly came in during the summer, and I don't think there is any danger now. It is about as warm now as Kansas is in June, but in the summer time gets awfully hot up to 140 degrees in the shade. We have a good camp and plenty of water, and have been in here now ten days. We leave tomorrow for a months [sic] trip in western Nevada. I don't think there will be any chance for me to mail a letter from there, so you must not be alarmed if you don't hear from me for some time.

We are 50 miles from Panamint postoffice and 152 from the nearest town. After we get back from this trip, we will be in here for a short time again and then go into the mountains. I have no idea when we should be through. Maybe not until next fall. You must not be alarmed about me. There is no great danger and I am able to take care of myself, no difference what happens. We are not going to be in here in the warm weather.

I had two letters from Pa and wrote him one today. We have a Chinaman for a cook and he is a good one. You must not be uneasy. If you don't hear from me for a month, as it will be that long before I can send a letter out, probably. I send this one to Daggett by one of our teamsters. Write, as before, to Panamint, Inyo Co., Calif.

Your son, Frederick Funston[93]

Fred's *The New York Times* story told what occurred next and, as supplemented in brackets with an excerpt from his letter published in *The Iola Register*, follows:

We spent ten days at Furnace Creek, and while here several trips were made to the higher peaks of the Funeral Range. On Feb. 4 we left for Resting Spring on the Amargosa sixty miles southeast where we were to meet those of our party who had gone by way of Saratoga Spring [also spelled Saratoga Springs] around the southern end of the range. After two and half days of travel over a most exasperating country we were again united.

This so called river, the Amargosa, is one of the freaks of nature so common in this region. In some unknown spot in the southwestern portion of Nevada a number of mineral hot springs unite to form a little stream, which sneaks off toward the south, winding and twisting about among salt marshes and sand dunes, crossing the line between California and Nevada in half a dozen places, here and there disappearing from sight only to reappear a little larger a few miles further [sic] on, until more than eighty miles from its source it makes a bold sweep around the southern end of the Funeral Range, and is lost for the last time among the salt marshes of Death Valley. Such is that strangest and most unaccountable of rivers, the Amargosa. Its waters are inconceivably vile, holding in solution large quantities of salt and suds, and are worse than useless, being rank, deadly poison. The water has the appearance of very dirty soap suds. [94] [We are told that nothing was made in vain, but I am thinking that when the final round-up comes the Amargosa will be classed with the dude and the mosquito as one of the things pretty hard to explain away.[95]]

Resting Spring was one of the few places in the region where fresh water was found. At Resting Spring lived two white men, brothers "Cub" and Phi Lee. They had settled there many years ago; both "married Piute squaws and seem well contented with their lonely life." One day Cub Lee was giving me [Fred Funston] some reminiscences of the early days in Nevada when Virginia City and Gold Hill were great mining camps and incidentally mentioned a 'young feller name of Sam Clemens what I hearn [sic] tell wrote a book about the country what was mostly a pack of lies.' I was not long in guessing that the 'young feller' was Mark Twain and the 'pack of lies,' 'Roughing It.' The only description he could give of the immortal Mark was that he was a 'hatchet-faced young smart Aleck.'"[96] Interesting comments in view of the future acrimony that marked the Fred Funston–Mark Twain relationship.

Fred had an arrangement with his friend, Charlie Scott, to write letters specifically intended for publication in *The Iola Register*. Fred wrote two, one published July 17 and the other September 11. Knowing that the good people of Iola—and perhaps also of Iola's rival, Humboldt, eight miles south of Iola—would be reading this prose, Fred wrote the following: "At Resting Spring the expedition was joined by Mr. W. C. Burnett, of the San Francisco *Examiner*, who was sent out by his paper to write up the desert region, and who reached us by driving overland from Daggett. Mr. Burnett is a native Kansan, having been born at Humboldt. Very naturally he induired [sic: inquired] of me the present standing of his birthplace. I broke it to him gently and he took it like a man, only saying that he had expected as much."[97] Ah, the Iola-Humboldt rivalry!

The expedition attracted much interest nationwide through newspaper stories. Vernon Bailey described this journalistic interest:

> [Mr. Burnett of the *Examiner*] has a team + outfit of his own + is going to keep with us to report what we do + see. The San Francisco Chronicle employs our base-barometer-reader at Keeler as a special correspondent on the expedition, Dikeman furnishes him notes as often as he can get mail out. You see we are of some importance in the world when the two leading western papers have to keep so close an eye on our work. Our reporter is a pleasant + obliging fellow—he has to be + we have no objection to his going along. We tell him all the yarns we can think of but have to place him under bonds not to tell the whole truth. These intrepid + daring sons of science would not show up well in dirty, ragged clothes + mounted on old bony plugs.[98]

In a letter he wrote in December on his way to join the other members of the Death Valley Expedition, Bailey discussed the interest in the expedition he personally experienced:

> It is going to be a trip of uncommon interest. I have had several letters from people wanting to go with us. Did you

see a piece in the papers about the expedition? I did not, but everyone out here has + they were all expecting us. We cant [sic] go through a town without having a crowd around us wherever we stop. We get acquainted with some very pleasant people, but I dont [sic] care for such acquaintances.[99]

While the party was at Resting Spring, several members, including Fred, took a ten-day trip to Charleston Peak in the Timber Mountains of Lincoln County, Nevada, sixty miles northeast of Resting Spring and more than a hundred miles from Death Valley. A part of their route lay through Pahrump Valley where there was a "remarkable oasis":

> The soil here is much better than that in any of the other valleys, there being very little salt and gravel. At one point there bursts from the ground a powerful stream of warm, fresh water with sufficient force to turn a small mill wheel. A man by the name of Winters has taken upon [sic] his abode here with several other white men, and has utilized this spring to great advantage by irrigating a tract of ground on which he raises alfalfa, barley, and garden vegetables, and has a fine orchard and vineyard in bearing. As the nearest town is Daggett, 150 miles distant, those men have no market, but subsist on their own produce.
>
> Returning to Resting Spring, we found that our party had received an addition in [naturalist] Mr. Frank Stephens, who had driven up from Daggett.
>
> During all this moving from place to place the work of the expedition was being actively carried on. Large numbers of all the small mammals found in the country were taken in traps, birds were shot, and reptiles were captured is [sic: in] almost any way that seemed practicable. The skins of the birds and mammals were cured and packed in boxes to be sent to Washington, and the reptiles were pickled in alcohol. The botanists collected and pressed a number of specimens of all the plants found. A record was kept of the altitude of the locality where every specimen of whatever nature was procured.[100]

A.K. recollected years later that "Funston, who seemed to have the faculty of falling into water whenever it was found, made no exception at Resting Spring when he slipped and went into his waist. On another occasion, when he stood astride an irrigating ditch washing his face, he possibly got dizzy and fell in. I happened to be close by and grabbed him by the collar and pulled him out."[101] A.K. did not recollect the foregoing details identically in another document, stating there that Fred stepped on a board which broke and threw him waist deep into a spring. As to Fred's pitching into the irrigating ditch while washing his face, A.K. wrote that he "grabbed him by the seat of his breeches so that he could struggle onto the shore. These things came to mind in later years when we heard of him swimming across a large river in the Philippines with his sword in his mouth."[102] The sword in Fred's mouth is an exaggeration, but the swimming of the Filipino river is true. Like Fred's contemporaries, I am surprised, based on Fred's early awkwardness and mishaps, that he was such an accomplished soldier in the Philippines. But, we have yet to see his development in Alaska and Cuba.

A.K. noted that Fred "often caused considerable amusement" during times "when he was in difficulty because his remarks were often droll or contained a lot of dry humor. From this time on, he and I seldom were together as he would go with Nelson or some other party to work up new localities. While together, he often recited past experiences which at the time may have been unpleasant but at that time far enough in the back ground to make the incidents amusing to him. He was telling about having breakfast one morning at some eating-house where the girl asked him if he would have an egg or if he had had one."[103]

Pranksters A.K. and Fred joined forces at Resting Spring to teach the topographer Dikeman a well-deserved lesson. Dikeman, according to A.K., "had a voracious appetite for prunes, and he also had long fingers, which he would poke thru a hole in the box, and thereby manage to stuff himself with sweetmeats, leaving the rest of us to eat bacon." Fred "growled" about this, and at his suggestion, A.K. "fixed a heavy mouse-trap in the prune-box opposite the crack..."[104] Fred sat on a horizontal pole and watched Dikeman, when he arrived, run his fingers into the box of prunes. The mouse trap snapped, catching one of Dikeman's fingers. He quickly pulled his hand out, in the process dropping several of the prunes on the ground.[105] Watching this, and in his excitement while roaring with laughter, Fred fell backward off the pole into the mud.[106]

After an additional stay of a few days at Resting Spring, the party again divided. By doing so, they could cover more ground in their search for specimens. One group followed the Amargosa to Ash Meadows, while Coville, Bailey, Dikeman, and Fred, with one packer and a pack train of five animals, left for the west to work in the extreme southern part of the Funeral range.[107] Frederick Funston and Frederick Coville were soon to have a demanding, and nearly fatal, adventure.

THE YUCCA-PALM OF THE MOJAVE DESERT.
This Trunk was one foot in Diameter.

A YOUNG YUCCA.
Four feet tall.

Cactus at entrance to Death Valley.

A MESQUITE GROVE IN DEATH VALLEY, CALIFORNIA.
Diameter of largest Trunk shown five inches.

# Chapter One Notes—*The Death Valley Expedition*

1. Fred Funston to Edward C. Franklin, March 8, 1891 (Frederick Funston Papers, hereafter FFP) (Archives Division, Kansas State Historical Society).

2. "Editorial Notes," *The Iola Register*, January 22, 1892.

3. F.F. [Frederick Funston], "Into The Valley Of Death," *The New York Times*, March 27, 1892. Interestingly, the Lieut. Charles E. Bendire (1836-1897) who visited Death Valley in 1867 was also an ornithologist, oologist, and curator of birds' eggs. He began serious collecting of eggs and nests about 1868. According to C. Hart Merriam, "No other American naturalist in modern times has spent half so much time in the field as Bendire." He retired from the U.S. Army in 1886 due to disability (Keir B. Sterling, Richard P. Hammond et al., ed., *Biographical Dictionary Of American And Canadian Naturalists And Environmentalists* (Westport, Connecticut: Greenwood Press, 1997)), 75.

4. Frederick Vernon Coville, *Botany Of The Death Valley Expedition* (U.S. Department of Agriculture, Division of Botany, Contributions From The U.S. National Herbarium, Vol. IV. Issued November 29, 1893, Washington: Government Printing Office, 1893), 1. The use of the word "Economic" before Ornithology and Mammalogy was significant. It referred "to the study of the economic implications—both beneficial and harmful—of organisms on farming, ranching, and other economic endeavors. It was an important aspect of late nineteenth century natural history, especially with regard to receiving winning funding from state and national governments, because it demonstrated the 'use' or 'utility' of natural history" (Matthew Laubacher, "Cultures of Collection in Late Nineteenth Century American Natural History") (dissertation, Arizona State University, May 2011), 1.

5. C. Hart Merriam, "Report Of The Ornithologist And Mammalogist" (contained within *Report Of The Secretary Of Agriculture 1891*, 52D Congress, 1st Session, House of Representatives, Ex. Doc. 1, Part 6, Washington: Government Printing Office 1892), 267.

6. F. C. Brown and Arthur W. Palmer, "Frederick Vernon Coville (1867-1937)" (*Cosmos Club Bulletin*, Vol. 20, No. 1 (January 1967)) (Frederick V. Coville Collection, American Heritage Center, University of Wyoming), 2.

7. Albert Kenrick Fisher, *C.H. Merriam a narrative of Death Valley Exp* (manuscript, container #40, A. K. Fisher Papers, Manuscript Division, Library of Congress, Washington, D.C.), 27.

8. Fred Funston to Edward C. Franklin, March 8, 1891 (FPP).

9. "Death Valley," *Sacramento Daily Record-Union*, November 9, 1890. This brief article is datelined November 7 from Washington.

10. A. K. Fisher Papers Finding Aid, Manuscript Division, Library of Congress, Washington, D. C.

11. Albert Kenrick Fisher, *C.H. Merriam a narrative of Death Valley Exp*, 27.

12. F. F. [Frederick Funston], "Into The Valley Of Death," *The New York Times*, March 27, 1892.

13. W. L. McAtee, "In Memoriam: Theodore Sherman Palmer, "*Auk* (Vol. 73, July 1956), 367. In 1895, Palmer received a medical degree but did not intend to practice, merely desiring the same title that his boss, Hart Merriam, and his co-worker, A. K. Fisher, held (Keir B. Sterling, *Last of the Naturalists: The Career of C. Hart Merriam* (New York: Arno Press, 1974)), 162.

14. Theodore Sherman Palmer, *Diary, Death Valley expedition 1891, Dec. 11, 1890*

- *May 25, 1891* (manuscript, Call No. HM50827, The Huntington Library, San Marino, California), December 11, 1890, entry.

15. Frederick V. Coville, *[Death Valley Expedition] Itinerary* (Smithsonian Institution Archives, Accession 11-253, Frederick Vernon Coville Field Books, 1890–1924, folder Death Valley Expedition, Itinerary, 1890-1891), 1. This is the manuscript of Coville's itinerary published in *Botany Of The Death Valley Expedition* (U.S. Department of Agriculture, Division of Botany, Contributions from the U.S. National Herbarium, Vol. IV, Issued November 29, 1893). The manuscript was much reduced when published, and thus provides detail not included in the published work.

16. "Personal Mention," *The Topeka State Journal*, December 1, 1890.

17. "Pi Beta Phi Reception," *The Lawrence Daily Journal*, December 20, 1890.

18. "University Items," *The Lawrence Daily Journal*, December 17, 1890.

19. "The State Press," *Hutchinson News*, December 27, 1890 (reprint from *The Kansas City Star*).

20. William E. Johnson, "The Making of Brigadier Funston," *The New Voice,* May 13, 1899 (FPP).

21. "Local Matters," *The Iola Register,* January 9, 1891.

22. R. S. Dix, "Death Valley," *Chautauqua*, August 1891, 629.

23. Frederick V. Coville, *Botanizing In Death Valley In 1891 And Forty Years Afterward* (manuscript, folder #B-C878-fv, Frederick V. Coville Collection, American Heritage Center, University of Wyoming), 13.

24. Frederick V. Coville, *Botanizing In Death Valley In 1891 And Forty Years Afterward*, 14-15.

25. Frederick V. Coville, *Botanizing In Death Valley In 1891 And Forty Years Afterward*, 12.

26. Albert Kenrick Fisher, *C.H. Merriam a narrative of Death Valley Exp*, 29.

27. F.F. [Frederick Funston], "Into The Valley Of Death."

28. Albert Kenrick Fisher, *C.H. Merriam a narrative of Death Valley Exp*, 28.

29. U.S. Department of Agriculture, Division of Ornithology and Mammalogy, *North American Fauna No. 7. The Death Valley Expedition. A Biological Survey Of Parts Of California, Nevada, Arizona, and Utah, Part II* (Washington: Government Printing Office, 1893), 364.

30. Albert Kenrick Fisher, *C.H. Merriam a narrative of Death Valley Exp*, 28.

31. U.S. Department of Agriculture, Division of Ornithology and Mammalogy, *North American Fauna No. 7. The Death Valley Expedition. A Biological Survey Of Parts Of California, Nevada, Arizona, and Utah, Part II* (Washington: Government Printing Office, 1893), 370. Distances, unless otherwise stated, indicate the number of miles measured in a straight line between two points, and not the distance by road, except for railroad stations, where the distance between stations is that given by the railroads (301).

32. Albert Kenrick Fisher, *C.H. Merriam a narrative of Death Valley Exp,* 28.

33. Albert Kenrick Fisher, *Frederick Funstun* [sic] (manuscript, container #40, A. K. Fisher Papers, Manuscript Division, Library of Congress, Washington, D.C.), 3.

34. William Allen White, *The Autobiography of William Allen White* (New York: The Macmillan Company, 1946), 143.

45

35. Louis Stanley Young and Henry Davenport Northrop, *Life and Heroic Deeds of Admiral Dewey* (Philadelphia: Globe Bible Publishing Co., 1899), 348. Quoted is William A. DeFord, the first commissioned officer appointed in Kansas at the outbreak of the Spanish-American War. As adjutant, he recruited the entire Twentieth Kansas Regiment.

36. Frederick V. Coville, *[Death Valley Expedition] Itinerary*, 11-12.

37. Frederick V. Coville, *[Death Valley Expedition] Itinerary*, 12-13.

38. Frederick V. Coville, *[Death Valley Expedition] Itinerary*, 13.

39. Frederick V. Coville, *[Death Valley Expedition] Itinerary*, 13-14.

40. Frederick V. Coville, *[Death Valley Expedition] Itinerary*, 10-11.

41. Albert Kenrick Fisher, *C.H. Merriam a narrative of Death Valley Exp*, 29.

42. Albert Kenrick Fisher, *C.H. Merriam a narrative of Death Valley Exp*, 29.

43. Fred Funston, "Death Valley," *The Iola Register*, July 17, 1891.

44. Kansas State Historical Society Website www.kshs.org. Go to Kansapedia.

45. Frederick V. Coville, *[Death Valley Expedition] Itinerary*, 4-5.

46. Frederick V. Coville, *[Death Valley Expedition] Itinerary*, 5, and Theodore Sherman Palmer, *Diary, Death Valley expedition 1891, Dec. 11, 1890 – May 25, 1891*, January 6, 1891, entry.

47. Frederick V. Coville, *[Death Valley Expedition] Itinerary*, 6-7.

48. Theodore Sherman Palmer, *Diary, Death Valley expedition 1891, Dec. 11, 1890 – May 25, 1891*, January 6, 1891, entry.

49. Frederick V. Coville, *[Death Valley Expedition] Itinerary*, 5-6.

50. Frederick V. Coville, *[Death Valley Expedition] Itinerary*, 6.

51. Theodore Sherman Palmer, *Diary, Death Valley expedition 1891, Dec. 11, 1890 – May 25, 1891*, January 7, 1891, entry.

52. Theodore Sherman Palmer, *Diary, Death Valley expedition 1891, Dec. 11, 1890 – May 25, 1891*, January 7, 1891, entry, and Frederick V. Coville, *[Death Valley Expedition] Itinerary*, 7.

53. Frederick V. Coville, *[Death Valley Expedition] Itinerary*, 7.

54. Theodore Sherman Palmer, *Diary, Death Valley expedition 1891, Dec. 11, 1890 – May 25, 1891*, January 7, 1891, entry, and January 9, 1891, entry.

55. Theodore Sherman Palmer, *Diary, Death Valley expedition 1891, Dec. 11, 1890 – May 25, 1891*, January 8, 1891, entry.

56. Frederick V. Coville, *[Death Valley Expedition] Itinerary*, 8-9.

57. Frederick V. Coville, *[Death Valley Expedition] Itinerary*, 10.

58. Theodore Sherman Palmer, *Diary, Death Valley expedition 1891, Dec. 11, 1890 – May 25, 1891*, January 10, 1891, entry.

59. William E. Johnson, "The Making of Brigadier Funston."

60. Albert Kenrick Fisher, *C.H. Merriam a narrative of Death Valley Exp*, 30.

61. Theodore Sherman Palmer, *Diary, Death Valley expedition 1891, Dec. 11, 1890 – May 25, 1891*, January 10, 1891, entry, and January 11, 1891, entry.

62. Theodore Sherman Palmer, *Diary, Death Valley expedition 1891, Dec. 11, 1890 – May 25, 1891*, January 12, 1891, entry.

63. Theodore Sherman Palmer, *Diary, Death Valley expedition 1891, Dec. 11, 1890 – May 25, 1891,* January 13, 1891, entry, and Frederick V. Coville, *[Death Valley Expedition] Itinerary,* 20-22.

64. Vernon Bailey, "Into Death Valley 50 years Ago," *Westways,* December 1940, 8

65. Albert Kenrick Fisher, *C.H. Merriam a narrative of Death Valley Exp,* 35.

66. Albert Kenrick Fisher, *C.H. Merriam a narrative of Death Valley Exp,* 56.

67. Frederick V. Coville, *Botanizing In Death Valley In 1891 And Forty Years Afterward,* 12-13.

68. Albert Kenrick Fisher, *C.H. Merriam a narrative of Death Valley Exp,* 30.

69. Theodore Sherman Palmer, *Diary, Death Valley expedition 1891, Dec. 11, 1890 – May 25, 1891,* January 14, 1891, entry.

70. Frederick V. Coville, *[Death Valley Expedition] Itinerary,* 25-27.

71. Frederick V. Coville, *[Death Valley Expedition] Itinerary,* 28.

72. Theodore Sherman Palmer, *Diary, Death Valley expedition 1891, Dec. 11, 1890 – May 25, 1891,* January 18, 1891, entry.

73. Frederick V. Coville, *[Death Valley Expedition] Itinerary,* 29.

74. *The Iola Register,* June 23, 1893. Editorial.

75. Frederick V. Coville, *Botanizing In Death Valley In 1891 And Forty Years Afterward,* 16.

76. F.F. [Frederick Funston], "Into The Valley Of Death."

77. Frederick V. Coville, *[Death Valley Expedition] Itinerary,* 33.

78. Vernon Bailey to "My Dear Friends," January 25, 1891, "Death Valley, Cal. (Bennetts Wells)" (Vernon Bailey Papers, Box 9, Folder 3, American Heritage Center, University of Wyoming).

79. Theodore Sherman Palmer, *Diary, Death Valley expedition 1891, Dec. 11, 1890 – May 25, 1891,* January 22, 1891, entry.

80. U.S. Department of Agriculture, Division of Ornithology and Mammalogy, *North American Fauna No. 7. The Death Valley Expedition. A Biological Survey Of Parts Of California, Nevada, Arizona, and Utah, Part II,* 368.

81. Theodore Sherman Palmer, *Diary, Death Valley expedition 1891, Dec. 11, 1890 – May 25, 1891,* January 22, 1891, entry.

82. Frederick V. Coville, *Botanizing In Death Valley In 1891 And Forty Years Afterward,* 7.

83. Theodore Sherman Palmer, *Diary, Death Valley expedition 1891, Dec. 11, 1890 – May 25, 1891,* January 23, 1891, entry.

84. Theodore Sherman Palmer, *Diary, Death Valley expedition 1891, Dec. 11, 1890 – May 25, 1891,* January 24, 1891, entry.

85. R. S. Dix, "Death Valley," 629.

86. Albert Kenrick Fisher, *C.H. Merriam a narrative of Death Valley Exp,* 30-31.

87. Albert Kenrick Fisher, *Frederick Funstun* [sic], 5.

88. Albert Kenrick Fisher, *Frederick Funstun* [sic], 5.

89. Vernon Bailey to "My Dear Friends," January 25, 1891, "Death Valley, Cal. (Bennetts Wells)" (Vernon Bailey Papers, Box 9, Folder 3, American Heritage Center, University of Wyoming).

90. Vernon Bailey to "My Dear Friends," February 20, 1891, "Funeral Mts., Cal. (Mesquit Spring)" (Vernon Bailey Papers, Box 9, Folder 3, American Heritage Center, University of Wyoming).

91. See David J. Schmidly, *Vernon Bailey: Writings of a Field Naturalist on the Frontier* (College Station: Texas A&M University Press, 2018).

92. Frederick V. Coville, *[Death Valley Expedition] Itinerary*, 37-39.

93. Frederick Funston to Ann E. Funston, February 1, 1891 (typescript, Eckdall collection of letters, Allen County Historical Society, Inc.).

94. F. F. [Frederick Funston], "Into The Valley Of Death."

95. Fred Funston, "Death Valley," *The Iola Register,* September 11, 1891.

96. Fred Funston, "Death Valley," *The Iola Register*, September 11, 1891.

97. Fred Funston, "Death Valley," *The Iola Register*, September 11, 1891.

98. Vernon Bailey to "My Dear Friends," February 8, 1891, "Resting Spring, California" (Vernon Bailey Papers, Box 9, Folder 3, American Heritage Center, University of Wyoming).

99. Vernon Bailey to "My Dear Friends," December 14, 1890, "Lone Pine, California" (Vernon Bailey Papers, Box 9, Folder 3, American Heritage Center, University of Wyoming).

100. F.F. [Frederick Funston], "Into The Valley Of Death."

101. Albert Kenrick Fisher, *C.H. Merriam a narrative of Death Valley Exp*, 32.

102. Albert Kenrick Fisher, *Frederick Funstun* [sic], 6.

103. Albert Kenrick Fisher, *Frederick Funstun* [sic], 6.

104. William E. Johnson, "The Making of Brigadier Funston."

105. Albert Kenrick Fisher, *C.H. Merriam a narrative of Death Valley Exp*, 32-33.

106. Albert Kenrick Fisher, *C.H. Merriam a narrative of Death Valley Exp*, 33, and William E. Johnson, "The Making of Brigadier Funston."

107. F.F. [Frederick Funston], "Into The Valley Of Death."

# CHAPTER TWO

# *"A Winter Storm in Death Valley"*

—By Frederick Vernon Coville

Frederick Coville's account of his and Fred Funston's arduous trip to obtain the expedition's mail at Panamint was published in 1897 in *The Youth's Companion* under the title "A Winter Storm in Death Valley."[1] It is reprinted verbatim below and includes in brackets additional detail taken principally from another account written by Coville many years later.

\* \* \*

Walled in on the west by the Sierra Nevada and its continuations, on the north by the plains and mountains of the Great Basin, and on the east by the southern Rockies and the high plateau of eastern Arizona and New Mexico, the Mohave Desert derives its scant supply of rain from the Gulf of California. A few times each year the southwest winter winds bring up, along the broad valley of the lower Colorado River, sufficient moisture to cause a mild rainfall for several days. A storm of this type, but of unusual violence, occurred in this region in February, 1891.

An expedition had been sent out by the government to ascertain the conditions of plant and animal life in Death Valley, the most desolate portion of the Californian desert. We were camped at Resting Springs in the valley of the Amargosa River. For a month we had received neither official nor private mail, and a trip to Panamint, the nearest post-office, became a matter of necessity. [Mail arrived at Panamint each Sunday and then outgoing mail was sent the next day.[2]]. A party of five crossed the Amargosa Valley, and ascending the eastern slope of the Funeral Mountains, camped at a small spring in an obscure cañon [Mesquite Spring, about a mile east of the summit of the Funeral Mountains, at a point west of the old abandoned Amargosa Borax Works and about fifteen miles north of Saratoga Spring[3]].

On the second day afterward, February 21st, Mr. Frederick Funston and myself, each with a saddle-horse, bed-blankets, and a small

49

quantity of provisions, climbed to the summit of the mountains, and there viewed the country before us. We had to descend the long western slope of the Funeral Mountains, cross Death Valley, travel northward along its western side, and then ascend the snow-capped Panamints, on the western slope of which lay our objective point.

The pass on which we stood was about five thousand feet above the bottom of Death Valley, and the larger peaks of the range rose nearly two thousand feet higher. In all the Funeral Mountains, stretching many miles to the north and south, not a tree was visible—only brown and gray rocks, naked and desolate.

We mounted and set off down a wash [for ten or twelve miles[4]], our horses travelling at a swinging walk. About eight miles southeast of Salt Wells we reached Death Valley, and after stopping for lunch, went on again past the wells, then along the western edge of the great white saltmarsh, past Mesquit Well. Finally we struck out westward across the mesa that lies at the foot of the Panamint Mountains.

It was nearly dark, and from the clouds, which for two days had been gradually thickening, the rain began to fall. The mesa was traversed by arroyos, and in the bottom of one of them, when darkness prevented our going farther, we camped. Our troubles now began.

The horses, after travelling about forty miles, had no food nor water, for the arid desert could furnish neither. The sprinkling rain, the darkness, and the lack of anything with which to make a good fire spoiled our supper, so hurriedly we spread our blankets and crawled into them.

All night it rained, and early in the morning, after a breakfast no more satisfactory than our supper, we were about to set out again. Then my sorrel mare, always a nervous animal, began to tremble and snort, looking steadfastly up the arroyo.

I felt sure that she saw or smelled a wildcat; so taking up my carbine, a Colt's forty-four repeater, I carefully examined the surrounding cliffs. Nothing was seen nor heard except the rain. I walked cautiously up the arroyo a few rods, until a sight met my eyes that made me shiver.

It was only a little white band of foam just sinking into the sand and gravel, but it meant that the mountain above us had sent down its first warning of a torrent. If the night's rain had been more severe, we should have been carried down the arroyo, horses, beds, and all.

Mile after mile we ascended in the pouring rain until we reached the mouth of Johnson Cañon. Once, between the showers, the low, overhanging clouds that drove over us broke away for a few minutes. Then, looking backward across the valley, we saw a high peak of the Funeral Mountains white-capped with snow—a condition which must have been very rare for them.

Our journey up the cañon was a continuation of the morning's experiences, the monotony somewhat relieved by an occasional climb up the wet and slippery sides of the cañon to avoid some impassable barrier at the bottom. For much of the distance we were obliged to walk, both because our horses were worn out and because at the increasing altitude the air grew colder and our wet clothes chilled us.

Late in the afternoon we reached some deserted Indian wickiups, or brush-houses, situated at the lower edge of timber; for the Panamint Mountains rise so high—nearly eleven thousand feet—that an evergreen forest is borne for several miles along their crest. [The Indians were away from [Indian Gardens] for the winter.[5]]

Leaving our horses near the wickiups, we set out on foot up the trail. Above us rose the steep, main ridge of the mountains, whitened with deep snow, and lost amid dark, whirling clouds. At first we tramped through slush, but after walking a mile or more, we found the snow gradually deepening, but still moist.

The zigzag trail finally became so obscured that we could no longer follow it. So, selecting the most promising gulley, —for the mountain-top and the pass enveloped in clouds gave us no guidance, —we attempted to climb the slope to the indefinite heights above.

Night was falling. We were wet to the skin; the mountain winds were cold, the snow was already three feet deep, and there was nothing but the direction of the slope to guide us in ascending. Furthermore, we had not eaten a full meal since breakfast of the preceding day, and we were fatigued from the vicissitudes of our day's climbing.

We saw it was useless under such conditions to attempt to reach the pass, and turned back disappointed and disheartened to the point at which we had left our horses. The knowledge that only six miles away, on the other side of the mountain-crest, were well-roofed houses, comfortable fires, hot beefsteak and sympathetic human beings, did not make our immediate situation more pleasant.

A small field of alfalfa had been cultivated by the Indians near the wickiups, and in this we staked our horses. We found an axe but no firewood, so we sacrificed a cedar fence-post. Our saddle-blankets and provisions were carried through the low door of a roofed wickiup. The fire-wood followed, and finally we ourselves.

That night was the most wretched I had ever experienced. The structure covered a circular space nine feet in diameter, and so low that we could not stand up in it. The poles of which it was constructed curved and converged to a central point, where there was a small chimney-hole. This aperture we had been obliged to cover to keep out the direct fall of rain, while the door was barricaded in an attempt to prevent the wind from blowing in.

The moist wood did not burn well, and several times the rain, dripping through the roof, extinguished our fire. Finally, amid smoke, water and dirt we made a successful blaze and cooked our few slices of bacon.

For a frying-pan we used a tin plate, into which we had inserted a handle made of baling wire, while a tin tomato-can answered the purpose of coffee-pot. I recollect with great distinctness that the frying-pan had a persistent tendency to slide off the fire, the coffee-pot to upset into it.

Our bread, coffee and sugar were water-soaked, and so mixed together that they required considerable sorting before they could be used. I can still see Funston squatting beside the fire, holding in one hand a fork with which to turn the frying bacon, the other hand wiping the tears from his smoke-filled eyes [cussing the weather, the construction of the wickiup, the Indians, and all other contributory agencies[6]].

"I have been in mean situations before, but for out-and-out, low-down, useless misery, this takes the cake!" said Funston, with energy.

The only pleasurable prospect was the dryness and warmth of our beds. The bed-canvasses in which our blankets were rolled had thus far kept them comparatively dry. For an hour or more after going to bed we were supremely happy, except for the dripping of the rain on our heads.

Our most careful precautions, however, did not keep the water from running into the blankets, so that from midnight on we were about as comfortable as if sleeping in a cold bog.

The storm outside was terrific. [Lying in our bed in the wickiup that night, I listened to the most terrific storm of my experience.[7]] There was a constant downpour of rain, accompanied by a high wind, while at frequent intervals louder and wilder blasts whirled down the cañon. The broken topography of the Panamints, and the fact that the wind came from the west, eddying over the mountain-crest, seemed to give peculiar opportunity for the formation of miniature hurricanes.

We could hear a blast howling far up the cañon one instant, and the next it would go rushing past us with fury indescribable [a living super-siren[8]]. It seemed as if the very rocks must be torn away. The immensity of the storm gave one an impression of grandeur combined with malignancy. Some conception of the fury of the wind is furnished by the fact that we did not notice during the night the sound produced by a torrent of water rushing down the cañon, not thirty yards from our beds.

In the morning we took account of stock. There was left, after a breakfast of short rations, bacon and bread enough for one full meal. It was ninety miles to the rendezvous of the expedition in Nevada. Forty miles of that distance were over a portion of the desert that we had never traversed. The cañon up which we had come was filled with a rushing torrent, and would be impassable for at least a day. If we returned, we must do so without the mail. The alternative was to reach Panamint before night, and that we determined to do. [I had left a bride of two months three thousand miles away, and I wanted to hear from her.[9]]

The forenoon wore away slowly, showers and hurrying clouds alternating with short intervals of sunlight and blue sky. At noon we made a hearty dinner of the last of our food.

It had now ceased to rain, but the mountain-crest was still girdled with clouds, and the summit of the pass was obscured. Our horses were staked in fresh parts of the alfalfa-field, our saddles snugly stowed away in the wickiup, and our wet blankets hung on the bushes outside. Then, feeling more invigorated by a sufficiency of food and the brighter outlook, we set off up the trail down which we had returned so disconsolately the night before.

The first part of the ascent was a repetition of the preceding day's experiences, for, after a mile or more of climbing, we lost the trail in the deepening snow, and began the struggle up the slope; but with renewed determination we waded upward through the snow, climbing over boulders and nearly buried bushes whenever an opportunity offered.

After an hour or two of this vigorous exercise, steadily rising to a higher altitude, we reached a point where the snow was more than three feet deep. Our progress became slow and very difficult. In addition, a new obstacle presented itself in the form of an icy crust.

In snow only a few inches deep a thin crust is of little consequence. Under the conditions in which we were placed, it caused us no little annoyance. It scraped our shins and bruised our thighs, or required to be constantly broken in front of us by our elbows. After three hours' climbing at high altitudes, to which we were unused, we were nearly exhausted.

The clouds had lifted, and the outlines of the mountain-crest showed that we were approaching it at a point that necessitated our climbing about five hundred feet higher than the real pass. The sunshine was streaming through the piñon-trees above us, while we were still in the cold shade of the mountain. Before us lay fully half a mile of deep, smooth snow, inclined at an angle of thirty to thirty-five degrees.

We knew that in our state of exhaustion, and at the rate at which we were progressing, the summit never would be reached; but more in desperation than from any feeling of confidence in the result, we pushed on. Soon we were rewarded by the discovery that the crust had now become sufficiently thick to support us when lying down or crawling on our hands and knees, but not when standing erect upon it.

For some time we used the new method of climbing, and found that more rapid progress was made than before, yet the effort was terribly exhausting. At each step, if that term may be used for our movements, we were compelled to strike the toes of our shoes through the crust to prevent shooting backward down the slope against the scattered tree-trunks or rocks below.

One went ahead making these holes, the other followed. We tried to alternate, but Funston, who was lighter and less strong than I, at last became too much exhausted to take the lead.

My shoes, from several weeks of desert wear and mountain-climbing, had become so broken and worn that the rough crust tore a hole two inches long in one of them. The stocking soon followed; and then, each time I struck my shoe into the crust it cut and bruised the bare flesh.

The physical exhaustion and the nervous strain were terrible. I could not crawl ten feet without throwing myself down to rest, but for nearly an hour we kept it up. It was the most fearful physical experience of my life.

Lying with my face against the crust, panting like a dog, my teeth gritted in the determination not to give up the fight, the whole problem of success or failure lay clearly before me. To hesitate would bring sure privation and possible starvation; to keep on meant success and relief. It required the last ounce of strength, with bulldog determination, and those we gave.

[At early noon we began our crawl, and[10]] [j]ust as the sun was setting clear and yellow in the west, we dragged ourselves across the huge drift that overhung the roof-like crest of the Panamints. Nine thousand feet above the bottom of the Death Valley we stood upon the frozen snow, the icy wind that followed the storm blowing through our clothing and chilling us to the very bone.

The first part of the descent, although not exhausting, was dangerous, for the slope was steep, and the crust so thick that one could hardly make an impression upon it with his heel. Farther down, upon a gentler slope, the breaking crust would trip us, and throw us down. Stumbling and sliding along in the darkness, Funston fell heavily again and again; but he was so worn out that he seemed hardly to care what happened to him.

The sight of the Black Sea was not more welcome to the soldiers of Cyrus the Younger than the lights of Panamint to us.

[In its early days Panamint had been a thriving mining town. In 1891 its population had dwindled to three, the postmaster, the caretaker of a mining property, and the scion of an eastern family who were financing his activities in that particular part of the world under the delusion that since the saloons were gone, liquor could not be had at Panamint. The last time I saw this jovial person he was on his way back from the town of Darwin and was lying under the shade of his buckboard at Brewery Spring in Surprise Canyon, with a gallon demijohn of whiskey beside him.[11]]

[When a desert mining town begins to play out, its abandoned wooden buildings disappear like snow, for they furnish the remaining population with a commodity highly in demand in the treeless desert, fuel. Among the outlines of streets and buildings that marked the ground of Panamint in 1891 after the buildings themselves had been used for fuel, stood a billiard table abandoned and exposed to sun and weather but still respected by the axman because of the beauty of its inlaid wood.[12]]

[On our way back, two days later, by the proper pass on the trail, which was hundreds of feet lower than the ridge up which we had crawled, we threw the four sacks of mail down the mountain-side, and slid on our backs, with our heels as brakes, just as I had learned to do as a boy on the snow-clad hills of Oxford, New York.[13]]

We found our horses where we had staked them. They had eaten all the alfalfa within reach, and were very glad to see us. The very arroyos on which we camped had been washed and torn away by the violence of the storm, the worst, it was said, in southern California in twenty years.

Railroad and highway bridges had been swept away, towns inundated, and cañon passes gutted during that very night when Funston and I lay shivering in the Indian wickiup and the wind went howling down the cañon.

[When we joined the expedition again at Ash Meadows, Nevada, four days later, we found that one of the camp hands had seen the snowy cap of the Panamints from the top of the Funeral Mountains, and had bet the topographer five dollars that we wouldn't get through to Panamint. It was well worth nine days work to help the topographer win a bet off that desert reprobate, for he was old, wise, and wicked.[14]]

# Chapter Two Notes—"A Winter Storm in Death Valley"

1. Fred Funston to Edward C. Franklin, March 8, 1891 (Frederick Funston Papers, hereafter FFP) (Archives Division, Kansas State Historical Society).

2. Vernon Bailey to Dear Friends, January 11, 1891, "Panamint Valley, Cal" (Vernon Bailey Papers, Box 9, Folders 3-5, American Heritage Center, University of Wyoming).

    I was initially surprised that the expedition members had connection by mail with persons elsewhere while in Death Valley. That there was even a post office at Panamint, with its negligible population of three persons, was also a surprise. For an impressive study on the spread of post offices throughout the West as whites settled it, see Cameron Blevins, *Paper Trails: The US Post and the Making of the American West* (New York: Oxford University Press, 2021).

3. Frederick V. Coville, *Botanizing In Death Valley In 1891 And Forty Years Afterward* (manuscript, Frederick V. Coville Collection, American Heritage Center, University of Wyoming), 16.

4. Coville, *Botanizing*, 17.

5. Coville, *Botanizing*, 17.

6. Coville, *Botanizing*, 17.

7. Coville, *Botanizing*, 18.

8. Coville, *Botanizing*, 18.

9. Coville, *Botanizing*, 18. Mrs. Coville later joined her husband on the expedition. See Chapter Five.

10. Coville, *Botanizing*, 18.

11. Coville, *Botanizing*, 20

12. Coville, *Botanizing*, 20

13. Coville, *Botanizing*, 18.

14. Coville, *Botanizing*, 19.

# CHAPTER THREE

# *The Death Valley Expedition*

### March 1, 1891 – June 15, 1891

**I have seen men fall on the field of battle like stalks of corn under the mower's scythe, and I have seen a part of these men in Cuban jungle hospitals in the malarial districts, with rotting limbs and putrid flesh, but never have I suffered or seen suffering such as that I underwent in two days when I rode alone in Death Valley.**

**—Fred Funston**

Before Fred and Coville left Panamint with the mail, Fred wrote a letter to Charlie Scott, who published an extract of it in *The Iola Register*. He introduced the piece by noting that "Fred Funston is evidently too tough for even Death Valley to make way with..." The published extract adds nothing new to our story, except a postscript in which Fred wrote that his "favorite yearn" is for beef steak and pumpkin pie.[1]

Ash Meadows, where Fred and Coville arrived with the mail, was unimpressive. In Fred's words to readers of *The Iola Register*, "There may have been some reasons for naming the spot Ash Meadows, the main one being, I think, because there was not an ash tree nor a blade of grass within a day's ride."[2] He was a little more informative in his *The New York Times* article: "At Ash Meadows are a number of powerful fresh-water hot springs, but the soil is so impregnated with alkali that its cultivation is out of the question. The only inhabitants at this place are one lone white man and a few harmless Indians."[3] One Indian, named Indian Mary, gave several expedition members haircuts, an experience which A. K. Fisher later described as an "ordeal." A steer was butchered by the Indians, and Fisher found it "interesting to see the squaws take the intestines, squeeze out the contents and begin to chew the cut end." Fisher further noted, "I shall refrain from putting down the remarks that Funston made on this occasion for the very sight of this performance seemed to have a bad effect on his stomach."[4]

From Ash Meadows on March 8, Fred wrote a lengthy letter to Buck Franklin. Various details, though overlapping our story to date, are included here, particularly because some of them provide Fred's perspective on the journey, which he candidly shared with one of his closest friends:

> My dear Buck
> I have just received your letter of December 25th forwarded to me from Carlyle Kas I wrote you about the same time from San Bernardino Cal. so you doubtless know by this time what sort of a fool expedition I am on. And I am going give you some of my experience in my poor weak way. You may have known before that in the extreme eastern part of California near the Nevada line and some distance south of the middle is the most unknown and desolate region of the United States and in the middle of this is the famous Death Valley of which so many gruesome tales have been told... Uncle Sam scratched his head and concluded that if there was such a hell hole in his dominions he had a right to know something about it and so concluded to send out an expedition of scientists to thoroughly explore it. By virtue of my "Pap" being in Congress I managed to get on the thing as assistant botanist not that I know anything about botany, but then my work is to help collect plants and take care of the botanical specimens and do the cussing for the outfit for both of which tasks I am by nature amply qualified. The members of the party were... bird and animal collectors; J. M. Dikeman, topographer, F. V. Coville and myself, botanists, beside teamsters, packers, cook ect [sic]. The expedition was divided into two parties... I was with the San Bernardino outfit. We left San Bernardino Jan 1st and on the 18th joined the northern party and on the 20th whole party entered Death Valley via the dry bed of the Amargosa. It would be too big a job to write up in detail that awful twenty days trip across the [Mohave] desert. It was <u>hell</u>. The country is absolutely uninhabited a great wilderness of sand and rocks cut up by ranges of red, bronze and yellow mountains from 500 to 10,000 feet high. Here and there were great flats of salt and soda. The mirages made by these are said to be finer than those of the Sahara. There was no vegetation but sage brush, grease wood and many kinds of cactus besides

the grim yuccas, some of them thirty feet high. Not a spear of grass in the whole country. Sometimes we would be three or four days between water holes and then the supply for the men and the seventeen horses and burros had to be carried in barrels rigged up on the outside of the wagon beds or in casks on the backs of the burros. In such cases everything was put on a limited allowance and we were not even allowed to wash our hands. The feed for the animals had to be carried with us and a team, or rather a six horse freight wagon, was sent a head and cached 3000 lbs. of barley and baled hay 150 [sic] north of San Bernardino.

We rode horse back. My charger is a little roan broncho as tough as wire. But we finally entered Hell, and spent several weeks exploring that and the country for a hundred miles south and east. Our next work will be north of here and as warm weather comes on we go into the Sierra Nevadas. If the whole program is carried out, we shall be out until Sept. though we may be called in any time after April. I know all about Death Valley now I think. It is forty miles long and about ten wide. The bottom which is a treacherous crust of soda and salt over a sort of hell broth of alkala is 150 [sic] <u>below</u> the level of the sea. The eastern boundary is formed by the Funeral range 6000 feet high and the western by the Panamint 10,000 feet. These mountains rise sheer up from the valley for two miles and are covered with snow. There is nothing to compare with them in Colo. The only camera in the outfit is a d____d Kodak. This is too bad. While we were in Death Valley in January the mercury hit 88° in the shade. Capt. Bendire of the regular army who was in here in August 1875 found the thermom. to reach 140 day after day. The body of a man or animal will not decay here. It simply dries up and mummifies. It would be a great place for you to jerk sheep. We found the place where the emigrants perished in 1850. It was a sad sight. An acre of ground strewn with wagon tires ox bones and cooking utensils where they abandoned them 41 years ago. As I said before, the bodies of the seventy men, women and children were buried in 1860. We found some other graves all marked "Unknown" where prospectors had found bodies and buried them. Most of the people who came in here and were never heard of afterward mired in soda marshes and their bodies were never recovered. I have mired myself and horse many a time but always managed to get out. We keep a six horse wagon running between here

and Daggett on the Atlantic and Pacific R.R. 152 miles hauling supplies. Our postoffice is Panamint a little mining camp
with half a dozen inhabitants where the mail comes in once a
week. It is distant 100 miles southwest and we have a hell of
a time getting our mail and have only got it three times since
entering the country. Coville and I started after it Feb. 20th
and made a hell of a mess of the job. We left a point 10 miles
southeast on horseback with our bedding and four days provisions. We found no trails and the country was unknown to
us. All went merry until the morning of the second day when
a terrible storm came up and raged for four days. We were in
a terrible pickle but had to keep going and on the 23rd had to
abandon bedding and and [sic] horses and make Panamint
or starve. The snow for miles up the cañon [illegible] to the
summit of the range was ten feet deep and awfully steep. At
one time we crawled on our hands and knees for 500 yards on
the crust. But we got over and got our mail two sacks full and
reached our horses on the 25th and found them O.K. We joined
the party at Ash Meadows Nye Co. Nevada having been out
eight days and ridden 178 miles across mountains without
any trails. How is that for a trip to the post office.

On account of this expedition I have given up my trip to
Estes Park next summer. I dont [sic] know what the others
are going to do. I have got my belly full of roughing it for a
number of years to come. If we are out here until October I
may go from San Francisco to New York via Panama. The fare
cabin is only $75, and the trip six weeks. It would be a fine ex-
cursion. "Storm bound above the Clouds" will be out sometime
during the spring or summer. Dont [sic] try to get it as I shall
not neglect to send you a copy. I wish the d____d fools would
hurry up and bring it out. Would like to see what it looks like.
When do you expect to come back to God's country? I feel that
I am as far away as you are [Buck was in Europe], but am not
a dam [sic] bit homesick [illegible] any of the girls now and
so dont [sic] care whether school keeps or not. Are you going
to send E. June Scotte [sic] a rose bud when [illegible] she
graduates. Chas. F. Scott is going to Europe next summer and
wants me to run the Register for him but fear that I will not
be able to accommodate him.

By the last mail I had two long letters from the only Goat.
Write me as before at Carlyle. Give my best to Tar Baby, Cap.
[Will] and Mrs. Franklin, and say that I love them all just as
much as I used to.

Yours lovingly,

Tim

It may be a long time before I can get this letter to a post office.[5]

Although Fred had been an expedition member for only just over two months, he was clearly disillusioned by the physical challenges he was experiencing. As he wrote: "I have got my belly full of roughing it for a number of years to come." Famous last words.

When Fred and Coville arrived at Ash Meadows on February 28, they found that one of the two parties of the expedition had already arrived.[6] Once the two parties had reunited, a party consisting of Coville, Bailey, and Nelson left on March 4 for a two-week trip to the Grand Cañon of the Colorado.[7] Another challenge was soon in store for those, including Fred, who remained at Ash Meadows. He told the readers of *The Iola Register* about it in one of his letters, as supplemented here in brackets with material from Fred's *The New York Times* story:

> It was here that we experienced what is now referred to as "the starving time." [We had been at Ash Meadows only a few days when the teamster who had gone to Daggett for supplies came in on horseback [on March 6] with the startling information that he had abandoned the six horse freight wagon, mired to the axles in a salt marsh, 120 miles south, at Coyote Holes.]...[O]ur provisions were exhausted and we lived for about two weeks on climate, helped out by such delicacies as gophers, blackbirds[,] badgers, chuck-wallies, etc. The chuckwally is a big, [black and yellow] clumsy lizard, about a foot long. Its flesh is white and tender, somewhat suggestive of spring chicken. However I do not predict that the chuckwally is destined to become a popular dish with the best people. There is something funny about this "starving time" as I look back on it now, though at the time it was a very serious affair.[8]

During this challenging time, Fred set out on March 13 for Panamint to take and pick up mail. The horrible details of this nearly fatal trip Fred recounted in a breezy letter to an unidentified friend in Lawrence, Kansas. In brackets below are additional details from a biographical sketch of Fred's life that appeared in 1899, a sketch which may have relied upon the reporter's prior communication with Fred about this trek:

Dear _____: I've made the trip. I am "trooly grate." Listen to my narrative of how a Brave Man suffered.

Left Ash Meadows (name for a small spot somewhere in the desert) Friday, March 13, and that night reached the edge of Death Valley, forty-eight miles. The next day I played the trombone. Against all common sense and reason, I tried to reach Panamint by going around the north end of the Panamint Range, a mountainous desert without water or trails, this was on Saturday. I rode hard all day, passing around the north end of Death Valley and around the end of the range. When night came I found that I was in a country of which I could make neither head nor tail and I couldn't tell where in the desert I was, except that I had half a gallon of water left and was forty miles from the nearest water at Furnace creek. Lay down and went to sleep. Coyotes sat around me and howled all night. Got up at six the next morning and saw if I did not take a back track, was a goner. Horse was so weak from hunger and thirst that it could not carry me, had not had a drop nor a mouthful since the morning before. I started back over that stony mesa leading the horse. The sun was awfully hot, water gave out, and I suffered tortures that day and the following night. It would take too long to write it, but to make a long story short my thinker got all bejiggered. Before I knew it I was loony, but I tried to keep my mind off of it, and kept pounding the mesa. The horse could barely walk.

[His head seemed to split open with the dry, awful heat. His ears tingled and roared. Suddenly he stopped, for he heard two distinct shots, like those a rifle would make. There was no smoke anywhere on the desert that Funston could see, and no sign of anything human. He thought it must be hunters or miners in distress and as the shots seemed to come from the left, in spite of his own distress, he went in that direction to do what he could for the desperate men. Again he heard the shots, but in another direction, and he ran to answer them; but after running a short distance he was forced to stop from exhaustion and to lie down. He got up again, but his pony, not so strong as the man, fell on the alkali crust and refused to go farther. For the third time then Funston heard the shots, but this time he knew they did not come from the desert nor from the mountains, but from his own faculties, which were deceiving him. It was the fever brought on by the terrible heat that caused the snapping of the nerves in his head to sound like rifle shots. The pony arose after Funston had emptied a part of his canteen of water into its throat and trudged on patiently with the indomitable man. "I must keep going on," said the man to himself. "I must not stop, I must not, I must not! Whatever happens, I must keep going on, or I am lost."

[He kept going on. That evening when his water was all gone he fell to the ground fainting and saw a mirage of grass and trees and water, a beautiful, delicious, cool pool of water. He leaped to his feet—and he went on. He saw maddening images of beauty; he saw lakes and pools and springs and clusters of trees and great fields of long green grass—but he went on.[9] ]

From 6 a.m. Sunday to to [sic] 3:30 a.m. Monday I did not stop ten minutes all told, then lost my way and waited for daylight two hours and at 7 a.m. reached Furnace creek.

I had not eaten a bite from Saturday night till Monday morning and was nearly as long without water. I had grub but was so thirsty that I could not eat. The pony had not had a drop of water or a mouthful of food from Saturday morning until Monday morning. Old hermit at Furnace creek, Jim Dayton took me in, filled me full of Chili sauce and some other hot stuff. I rested and ate and drank all day very assiduously, and the next Tuesday borrowed another horse from Dayton and today reached Panamint by leaving my horse in charge of some Shoshones and coming over snow on foot.

Start back from [sic: for] Ash Meadows tomorrow. By the time I get back shall have been out eight days.[10]

In publishing this letter, Charlie Scott noted that "he is having a tough time,—and getting a barrel of fun out of it."[11]

Theodore Palmer in his diary noted that when the expedition reached Greenland Ranch at Furnace Creek on March 22, it found Fred there with the mail. Fred had apparently stopped there on his return trip to Ash Meadows. Palmer recorded that Fred had traveled about 230 miles, having walked "a good part of the way."[12] Reminiscing a few years later about Fred's nearly fatal trek, Palmer added:

We thought that was the last of Funston, and it came near to being so. He was nearly finished when he reached camp, but really seemed to enjoy the adventure. He always made the best of everything no matter what it was. When our water got so bad with borax that it would make lather in our mouths, Funston saw only the funny side of the situation. He used to have a favorite song about a mythical bird, which he would sing over and over again by the campfire—

"She was a hen that laid eggs;
Sometimes two and sometimes ten."
"The next best thing to eating a good fresh egg is to sing
that hen song," Fred would say, after going eggless for six
months at a time.[13]

Eight years after Fred's escape from death, Jimmy Dayton, the
caretaker at Greenland Ranch, was not so fortunate. Through prior
arrangement, he set out in the heat of midsummer, 1899, for supplies
at Daggett, 150 miles away. When he failed to arrive, two men went
in search of him. About a mile north of the abandoned borax works,
they found Jimmy's outfit: four horses harnessed to a heavy wagon,
a light spring wagon in tow, and two led horses. All the horses were
dead, having been unable to free themselves to get to the feed in the
big wagon and to water within a mile. Jimmy himself was also dead,
having died as he had lived in Death Valley—alone. Apparently ill, he
had stopped to rest under a mesquite bush, where his body was found.
Jimmy's little black dog had survived and would not let the two men
touch Jimmy. "Protection of his master's body was not necessary, however, for in the burning heat of August neither coyote nor buzzard had
ventured into the bottom of Death Valley."[14] Jimmy was buried where
he had died, and one of the men spoke these words: "Well, Jimmie, you
lived in the heat and you died in the heat, and after what you been
through I guess you ought to be comfortable in hell."[15]

On March 19, Vernon Bailey also ventured forth from Ash Meadows, even though his horse had had only salt grass and no grain to eat.
The destination was the town of Keeler, 150 miles away over the Funeral, Panamint, and Argus mountain ranges and across Death Valley and Panamint Valley. He was sent by Palmer to get three horses
and a buckboard sent from Reno, Nevada, for Dikeman's use. After a
horrendous trip, which included no water for his horse for more than
thirty hours and almost as long for Bailey, and with Bailey leading his
horse when it was too weak to carry him, they reached Keeler.[16]

Our story of the expedition continues with Fred's account for the
readers of *The Iola Register* (without identifying it, I have divided one
paragraph into two paragraphs):

But everything has its end—and so had the "starving time."
The supply wagon came in from Daggett [Palmer and the
teamster brought it in], the expedition got on its feet again
and, leaving Ash Meadows and the Amargosa, turned westward once more and winding down across the stony wash of
Furnace Canon, crossed Death Valley to the mouth of Johnston's Canon [spelled by some as Johnson Cañon] in the Pan-

amint Mountains [which they reached about 5 p.m. on March 25[17]]. The ascent of Johnston's Canon to the Shoshone camps was one of the incidents that will not soon be forgotten. I do not think it possible for one who has not had some experience in mountain work to conceive the terrible ruggedness of this great gorge. Imagine a great canon [sic: cañon hereafter] fifteen miles long, the sides from one to three thousand feet high, and the bottom a mass of smooth bowlders from the size of a bushel basket to that of a country school house, all piled and jumbled as if dropped from the sky, and you have some idea of the task before us. Of course the wagons were left behind at Bennett's Hole in Death Valley and the entire camp outfit packed on the backs of the *burros*.

The start was made at day-break. All led their horses, it being too dangerous to ride. It was a terrible place for men to travel, and worse for the horses. They would fall down repeatedly and became so terror stricken that we could hardly urge them along. The burros did pretty well until, as we were moving along on the top of a smooth egg-shaped bowlder about twenty feet high, Jerry Simpson's feet flew out from under him and, with a terrified squeal, the namesake of the Medicine Lodge statesman bolted into Fay Templeton and the two went end over end off from the big rock. You can't hurt a burro by throwing him off from anything, and ours were no exception to the rule. Jerry's pack consisted of bedding and was not injured, but Fay was laden with an assortment of table delicacies, so that for the next week or two our Chinese cook spent all his resting time sifting broken glass out of the coffee and separating the syrup from the potatoes. It only needed this one disaster to start the trouble, and in ten minutes more half a dozen men were pulling and prying George Francis Train out of a big crevice. And so the fun went on through all that long day and when darkness settled down we had gone about half the distance,—eight miles in twelve hours. It was impossible to camp in such a place without wood, water or grass, so the procession moved along. I have been out a few dark nights in my time, but never saw one to equal this for muddy, inky blackness.

During the forenoon we had joked over our predicament and taken it all rather good naturedly, but human patience has its limit, and very little was said toward the close of the day other than the continual yelling at the animals of the pack train. But after dark our troubles were multiplied and the worn-out, hungry and exasperated men began to snarl at each other and to make some rather interesting remarks about the plan of things in general and this canon in particular. We had in our party one meek-faced, squeaky-voiced little fellow whom none of us thoroughly understood. He never talked about himself and all that we knew of his past history was that he came from some place in New England; but we agreed among ourselves that he was a theological student taking a year off and roughing it for his health, and it was further agreed that none of us would ever say anything in his presence that might tend to hurt his feelings. Those of the boys who were in the habit of swearing a little when angered, did so under their breath when in the vicinity of "Brer Calvin," as we called the New England youth, for fear that individual would burst into tears and have to be assisted to his bed.

Well, it happened that "Brer Calvin" was in it at the ascent of Johnston's Canon. He had been quiet as usual during all the day and well into the night, but about midnight, while picking his way over the slippery rocks he fell into a crevice about the size of the one that George Francis Train had graced the morning before. The clumsy big horse that he was leading fell in on top of him. All that the rest of us heard was a little girl-voiced shriek and a few pitiful groans. Rushing to the spot a torch was hastily improvised from a magazine that one of the party had in his pocket. Not a sound came from the bottom of the crevice and we agreed that the Massachusetts brother had gone to his reward. By main force we lifted off the horse and then began hunting for the lad, whom we found about ten feet down, pretty tightly wedged in. Two of us went down and, having got him loose, tied a rope about his waist and the others hauled him up. We thought he was dying and some of the boys began to clear their throats to sing something appropriate like "Rock of Ages." But soon he began to recover his breath, and was hastily asked the address of his parents. He did not say a word until he had got all the wind he wanted, and then we found that we had been fooled in "Brer Calvin." Lying there on a rock that youth unburdened his mind in a way that was simply horrifying to a mild, everyday criminal to listen to. All the swearing that he had not done in the twenty years of his life came then between gasps and groans in five minutes of time. It was wonderful and artistic and as well put up as if he had written it out beforehand with a typewriter and committed it to memory. He recovered. We changed his name from

"Brer Calvin" to "Mephistopheles." It is only fair to state that we found out afterward that he was not a theological student.

But to return to the pack train. It kept moving along, and at three o'clock in the morning, after twenty hours of hard work we unpacked the burros, rolled up in our blankets and went to sleep. Nobody got up until noon, but at day-break the Indians whose village was a short distance away came down in troops, men, women and children, to inspect their visitors. We were too tired to get up, and entertained our morning callers while lying on the ground in our blankets. It was what would be called a strictly informal affair, but they seemed well pleased and we did not care. These Indians are not Piutes, like those surrounding them, but are called Panamints, and are a branch of the great Shoshone nation, from which they separated many years ago, but whose language and customs they still retain. They are industrious and well-behaved Indians, supporting themselves by gardening, and hunting, helped out by pine-nuts and the beans of the mesquite tree. Their gardens are well up in the mountains away from the heat of the desert and the water is conducted to them by ditches which the Indians have dug to connect them with the mountain streams. They plow with a forked stick drawn by a burro, and all of their work is done in a primitive and clumsy way. The products of their gardens are corn, black beans, cabbage, turnips and squashes, besides which they have a few grape vines and fruit trees. Their houses are mere "wicky-ups," built of brush, but that does not matter much in a mild climate. Take it all in all, I doubt very much if there is anywhere in the United States such a well-disposed lot of Indians as this little band of Pana-mints, the Pueblos of New Mexico, alone, excepted. They know nothing of Government aid, missionaries, whiskey, or any of the other things which generally come from contact with the whites. If they were a band of lazy, thieving butchers like the Apaches they wouldn't have to work; this Government would feed them. But as it is no Kansas farmer works harder than do these Indians, and a white man would be as safe among them as on the streets of Iola.

We remained at the Indian camp two weeks, and then re-packing the burros we mounted our horses and rode over to the other side of the range and camped at the all but "desert-ed" mining town of Panamint. This old mining camp is a study for one who enjoys wrecks. Fifteen years ago it was a turbu-lent, busy place of four thousand inhabitants, and the "Hemlock" "Nellie Grant" and other rich mines made their owner, the present Senator Stewart, of Nevada, a many times millionaire. To-day the wide canon is filled with acres and acres of tumble-down houses and demolished cabins. The mines became exhausted and were closed down, and the four thousand people, miners, saloon-keepers, gamblers and the denizens of the dance hall, drifted down Surprise Canon, and scattered themselves among the camps. Panamint's boom was "busted," and to-day its only inhabitants are half a dozen old fellows who would not or could not leave the place where they had risked their all and lost the stakes. The mail comes in to them once a week from Keeler, seventy miles away, and gives them their only communication with the busy world of which Panamint was once a part.

I forgot to say that there were thirty-one others who could not leave. The postmaster took me up into a little side gulch and showed me where they had been "planted," as he expressed it. *Twenty-eight of them died with their boots on.* I did not inquire the manner of the taking off of the other three, but infer that they were shot in bed. These were the "good old times" that the old fellow sighed for, when he could get five dollars for a day's work, and it was considered an off night if there was not a "shootin" down at Nagle's saloon. He showed me the wreck of this popular *abattoir*. The man who conducted it in the boom period was the same Nagle who afterward became known to fame as the slayer of the notorious Judge Terry.[18]

Palmer had remained at Ash Meadows after his return from Daggett with supplies on March 18. On March 21, the party moved to Greenland Ranch, where Fred was, and on March 27 arrived at Bennett's Well. The next day, Palmer, with a driver, Mike Barnes, and a four-horse wagon, left for Daggett, where they were to meet the expedition chief, C. Hart Merriam, who had finished his work in Washington, D. C., and was ready to take from Palmer the reins of control of the expedition. The trip proved to be harrowing for Palmer and Barnes. During the following night of March 29-30, their horses broke away, and headed for Granite Springs. Taking "a little food + a canteen," the two men started on foot about 10 a.m. looking for the runaways. They walked until 9 p.m., when they stopped for a cold night "without even a fire." The next day, March 31, Palmer and Barnes set out walking shortly after 5 a.m. They tracked the horses up to the spring where they lost their tracks among the tracks of numerous cattle. Palmer recorded: "Food being scanty we could not wait to look for them so reluctantly continued on our way to Daggett on foot." They walked until 8 p.m. when they stopped for the night, making a "good fire" out of a dead tree. "Cold wind blowing made sound sleep impossible." The next morning, April 1, they started at 5:15 and "[f]inally arrived at Evan's Wells where we found team going into Daggett. We were pretty well exhausted having made over 20 miles during forenoon." At Daggett, Merriam was not there, having gone with a new packer to Los Angeles to get a team of mules. Dr. Merriam returned by train the next evening, and the mules arrived the following morning of April 3.[19]

Additions to the expedition at that time were Fred W. Koch, a young man, likely a teenager, Merriam had brought on as a general utility man, and Albert Koebele, entomologist. While Merriam had been at Escondido, California, Koch and his mother had called upon him, attempting to secure a place on the expedition for young Koch. Merriam recorded in his journal that "[h]e seems to be an intelligent + very enthusiastic young man who wants to get started right in Natural History work."[20] Fred Funston had a dim view of young Koch, whom, after meeting him, he described as "a 'bloomin' ass."[21] The little party, under Merriam's leadership, left Daggett on the morning of April 4. Palmer felt sick all morning and could not sit up in the wagon in the afternoon. He was so sick in the night that the next day Merriam permitted him to return to Daggett and from there to go to his home in Claremont, California, where he was hospitalized part of the time while he recuperated. Palmer was absent on sick leave from April 6 to April 30 before returning to the expedition.[22] How Mike Barnes fared during their joint ordeal was not recorded by Palmer.

Although it is difficult to compare Fred's hardships during his 230-mile solo trek against the hardships experienced by Palmer, the fact that Fred apparently rebounded from his ordeal without significant difficulty, and "really seemed to enjoy the adventure," is to his credit and another sign that under that genial, joking, somewhat chubby exterior was a man of tremendous physical and mental strength and endurance. Fred Funston possessed grit.

On April 19, Fred and Coville met Merriam and his party at Hot Springs in Panamint Valley and delivered to them mail from Panamint.[23] Merriam divided the men into groups that went in different directions so that work could be done over a wider field, scattering them to "the 4 winds." Merriam and Bailey with a camp wagon, a fresh team of mules, their two saddle horses, and a camp man covered on horseback in a month and a half 960 miles, which was measured by the odometer on the wagon wheel. They collected 240 mammals, a considerable number of birds, reptiles, and even plants. "[M]ost important, [they] noted every change of life zone limits on every slope traversed." Not only were traps for mammals set each evening when they camped, the two men also collected during the day mammals, birds and reptiles "as we both carried shotguns on our saddles and our horses were well trained to our shooting from the saddle." [24]

Fred remained at Hot Springs until April 24 when he and eight others left heading west. In a May 3 letter from Darwin, California, to his mother, Fred told about the extreme physical challenge endured by this group and about the upcoming ordeal that he would prefer not to face:

> Dear Ma:
> I had a letter from you a few days ago and am glad to hear that everybody is alive at home. I also received the handkerchiefs that you and Ella sent me and am much obliged for them. Our party which now numbers 17 men is scattered everywhere from the Colorado river to the Sierra Nevadas. A party of nine of us with wagons and horses left Panamint going west on April 24th.
> The only way was to cross a tremendous range of mountains through an almost impassable canon. The whole force of us went to work with picks and shovels, cutting down trunks, filling up holes, and clearing out brush until after seven days of hard work we got the wagon through empty and then had to pack the loads over on the backs of mules. We were one week going five miles. This will give you some idea of the difficulties of travel in this country. We are now camped in what is called Coso Valley fifty miles west of Death Valley and about the same distance east of Mount Whitney the highest mountain in the United States. The view of the Sierra Nevada range from our camp is the finest mountain view I ever saw. Tomorrow Nelson and I go with the Chinese cook on a trip that I would rather not take but there is no help for it. We are to go horseback and carry our provisions on pack mules on a trip into the unexplored country lying north of Death Valley. We are to be gone six weeks and may not get to a post office in that time so if you dont [sic] hear from me before June 15th dont [sic] be alarmed. I will try to make at least one trip for the mail in that time but may be able to get it oftener. When we three come back from this trip we will join the expedition at Keeler and from there go into the Sierra Nevadas. Until you hear from me again my address will be Keeler, Inyo Co. Calif. but if you have sent any mail to me at Panamint I will get it all right.
>
> > Your son
> > Fred Funston.[25]

The almost impassable "canon" that Fred and the others ascended using picks and shovels was Sheppard Canyon. Rattlesnakes were very common in this cañon, and the party killed a dozen before reaching the summit to Coso Valley. On occasion, Fred, tiring of the physical work of clearing a way upward, and mindful of his job as assistant botanist, went off collecting "weeds and brush." One time he had gone only a short distance before he called out that a rattlesnake had bitten him. "Doc" Fisher quickly got a flask of whiskey and hurried toward Fred. "He had shirt sleeve rolled up on one arm and was looking at a little blood on the skin midway between the elbow and the shoulder. No snake was visible, and I [Fisher] asked him where the accident occurred. From his description I made up my mind that the snake, to inflict the wound, would have to strike at least 6 ft. After making rather facetious remarks that the snake might have been 10 ft. off, without opening the flask I returned to camp. I expect this was a disappointment to Funston because I imagine that he would like to have had the medicine even though the snake had not bitten him."[26]

As to the trip that Fred "would rather not take," Edward Nelson described, many years later, this branch expedition undertaken by Fred and himself. Nelson collected and studied the birds, mammals, and other animal life, and Fred collected the plants. Their guide and camp man was a Shoshone Indian, "Indian Mike," and their cook was Ti Sing, who left the main party. All four men rode horses, and they had three pack mules and one pack horse. Nelson, as the one in charge, had a "roving commission" for them to visit those surrounding areas that the expedition had not yet explored.[27]

The Nelson expedition left on May 4 and by May 17 had been to Maturango Spring, the town of Darwin, and Willow Creek Cañon.[28] On May 17, Fred went from the Nelson camp at Willow Creek Cañon to obtain provisions at Keeler. There, he met Coville, and the following day the two men traveled to the camp, and then the next day collected specimens.[29] From May 23 to June 15 the expedition traveled through Cottonwood Cañon, across Mesquite Valley to Grapevine Peak, and then to Keeler by the same route.[30] It likely was during this time period that Fred, Nelson, and Ti Sing had the experiences that Fred so colorfully described in the article reprinted in the next chapter.

Before enjoying Fred's writing, it should be noted that traveling horseback on mountain trails could be dangerous. On one occasion, Fred's horse slipped and rolled over a cliff to its death a thousand feet below. Although Fred was dragged to the cliff's edge, he grabbed a nearby shrub and pulled himself back to safety.[31] Once again, it was lucky Fred.

# Chapter Three Notes—*The Death Valley Expedition*

Epigraph: "Funston, Brig. Gen., U. S. V.," *The Kansas City Star*, May 7, 1899 (Frederick Funston Papers, hereafter FFP) (Archives Division, Kansas State Historical Society).

1. "Local Matters," *The Iola Register*, March 6, 1891.

2. Fred Funston, "Death Valley," *The Iola Register*, September 11, 1891.

3. F.F. [Frederick Funston], "Into The Valley Of Death," *The New York Times*, March 27, 1892.

4. Albert Kenrick Fisher, *C.H. Merriam a narrative of Death Valley Exp* (manuscript, container #40, A. K. Fisher Papers, Manuscript Division, Library of Congress, Washington, D.C.), 35.

5. Fred Funston to Edward C. Franklin, March 8, 1891 (FFP). In this letter, Fred wrote: "Here and there were great flats of salt and soda. The mirages made by these are said to be finer than those of the Sahara." David Haward Bain in *Sitting in Darkness: Americans in the Philippines* (Boston: Houghton Miftlin Company, 1984), 31, claimed that Funston "thrived on comparisons" in his letters and articles. As an example, Bain both noted and criticized Funston: "Mirages in the California desert were 'finer than those of the Sahara,' quite a pronouncement for a young man who had never been to Africa."

   Although this quotation by Bain of Funston's writing matches the quotation above from the March 8, 1891, letter, it lacks the modifier of "these are said to be finer than those of the Sahara." Bain cited as his source a letter from Fred Funston to A.E. Funston, May 3, 1891 (FFP). Review of this letter shows that this quotation is not included so I do not know where Bain found this quotation without the modifier "these are said to be finer." As for Fred's making comparisons with familiar subjects in his letters and writings, I regard that as a benefit to his readers in their understanding what he was describing.

6. Frederick V. Coville, *[Death Valley Expedition] Itinerary* (Smithsonian Institution Archives, Accession 11-253, Frederick Vernon Coville Field Books, 1890–1924, folder Death Valley Expedition, Itinerary, 1890-1891), 6.

7. F.F. [Frederick Funston], "Into The Valley Of Death," and Frederick V. Coville, *[Death Valley Expedition] Itinerary*, 63 for date of departure.

8. Fred Funston, "Death Valley," *The Iola Register*, September 11, 1891, and F.F. [Frederick Funston], "Into The Valley Of Death." The date of March 6, 1891, is from Theodore Sherman Palmer, *Diary, Death Valley expedition 1891, Dec. 11, 1890 – May 25, 1891* (manuscript, Call No. HM50827, The Huntington Library, San Marino, California), March 6, 1891, entry. Black and yellow color from Vernon Bailey to My Dear Friends, May 13, 1891, St. George Utah (Vernon Bailey Papers, Box 9, Folder 3, American Heritage Center, University of Wyoming).

9. "Funston, Brig. Gen., U. S. V."

10. "Local Matters," *The Iola Register*, May 1, 1891.

11. "Local Matters," *The Iola Register*, May 1, 1891.

12. Theodore Sherman Palmer, *Diary, Death Valley expedition 1891, Dec. 11, 1890 – May 25, 1891*, March 22, 1891, entry.

13. William E. Johnson, "The Making of Brigadier Funston," *The New Voice*, May 13, 1899 (FFP).

14. Frederick V. Coville, *Botanizing In Death Valley In 1891 And Forty Years Afterward* (manuscript, folder #B-C838-fv, Frederick V. Coville Collection, American Heritage Center, University of Wyoming), 7-8.

15.  Richard E. Lingenfelter, *Death Valley & The Amargosa: A Land of Illusion* (Berkeley: University of California Press, 1986), 14.

16.  Vernon Bailey, "Into Death Valley 50 Years Ago," *Westways*, December 1940. Theodore Sherman Palmer, *Diary, Death Valley expedition 1891, Dec. 11, 1890 – May 25, 1891,* March 19, 1891, entry for date and purpose of Bailey's trip.

17.  Theodore Sherman Palmer, *Diary, Death Valley expedition 1891, Dec. 11, 1890 – May 25, 1891,* March 25, 1891, entry.

18.  Fred Funston, "Death Valley," *The Iola Register*, September 11, 1891.

19.  Theodore Sherman Palmer, *Diary, Death Valley expedition 1891, Dec. 11, 1890 – May 25, 1891,* March 18, 1891, entry; March 21 – April 3, 1891, entries.
     Vernon Bailey did not like Palmer's management style: "Palmers [sic] management doesnt [sic] suit me very well but I hope M[erriam] will make some changes when he comes. Palmer would make a good school teacher, but he dont [sic] know much about horses + does some foolish things for the sake of economy.... He is a first rate fellow but is absurdly ignorant about some things + is to [sic] muleish [sic] to hear to reason. I can manage M[erriam] better because he knows what is needed" (Vernon Bailey to My Dear Friends, Bennetts Wells, Death Valley, April 15, 1891, Vernon Bailey Papers, Box 9, Folder 3, American Heritage Center, University of Wyoming).
     After Merriam arrived and the ill Palmer did not return for some weeks, Bailey wrote: "I think [Merriam] will run things on a better system than they have been going" (Vernon Bailey to Dear Friends, Bennetts Wells, California. April 8, 1891). Bailey soon was able to write: "Things go on now in a more satisfactory manner since M[erriam] has taken the wheel..." (Vernon Bailey to My Dear Friends, Panamint Valley, California, April 22, 1891). One wonders if Palmer's young age of twenty-two with its attendant lack of experience was at the root of his management problems.

20.  C. Hart Merriam, M.D. *Death Valley Expedition I – Journal of a trip across Southern California + Nevada including NW Arizona + SW Utah 1891,* Vol. I (March – July) (manuscript, container #4, C. Hart Merriam Papers, Manuscript Division, Library of Congress, D.C.), March 20, March 28, and April 4 entries.

21.  Frederick V. Coville placed with his *[Death Valley Expedition] Itinerary* manuscript six small pages of penciled notes, which he identified as written by Fred. These pages are about plants collected, except one page which told very briefly of Funston's movements on April 16 and 17, 1891. On the latter date, he wrote that he and Coville "have our hands full of work."

22.  Theodore Sherman Palmer, *Diary, Death Valley expedition 1891, Dec. 11, 1890 – May 25, 1891,* April 4, 1891, through April 30, 1891, entries, and, for hospitalization, Vernon Bailey, "Into Death Valley 50 Years Ago," *Westways*, December 1940, 8.

23.  C. Hart Merriam, M.D. *Death Valley Expedition I – Journal of a trip across Southern California + Nevada including Northwest Arizona and Southwest Utah 1891* Vol. I (March – July), April 19, 1891, entry.

24.  Vernon Bailey, "Into Death Valley 50 Years Ago," *Westways*, December 1940. Bailey wrote of the arrangements "to scatter to the 4 winds" (Vernon Bailey to My Dear Friends, April 22, 1891, Panamint Valley, California, Vernon Bailey Papers, Box 9, Folder 3, American Heritage Center, University of Wyoming).

25.  Fred Funston to Ann E. Funston, May 3, 1891 (FFP).

26.  Albert Kenrick Fisher, *C.H. Merriam a narrative of Death Valley Exp*, 40-41.

27. E. W. Nelson to Mrs. Frederick Funston, February 9, 1931 (Frederick Funston Papers on microfilm) (Archives Division, Kansas State Historical Society).

28. Frederick Vernon Coville, *Botany Of The Death Valley Expedition* (U. S. Department of Agriculture, Division of Botany, Contributions From The U.S. National Herbarium, Vol. IV. Issued November 29, 1893, Washington: Government Printing Office, 1893), 7. This work contains a Catalogue of Specimens, and from that one can obtain a detailed record of where and when Fred collected specimens. In the text, I have used only Coville's brief summary of where Fred was.

29. Frederick V. Coville, *[Death Valley Expedition] Itinerary*, 86-87.

30. Frederick Vernon Coville, *Botany Of The Death Valley Expedition* (U. S. Department of Agriculture, Division of Botany, Contributions From The U.S. National Herbarium, Vol. IV. Issued November 29, 1893, Washington: Government Printing Office, 1893), 7. This work contains a Catalogue of Specimens, and from that one can obtain a detailed record of where and when Fred collected specimens. In the text, I have used only Coville's brief summary of where Fred was.

31. Charles S. Gleed, "Romance and Reality In A Single Life. Gen. Frederick Funston," *The Cosmopolitan Illustrated Monthly Magazine,* July 1899, 326.

# CHAPTER FOUR

# "A Wedding In The Mohave Desert"

## —By Fred Funston

Fred Funston wrote the following account the year after the Death Valley Expedition. It was published in the State University of Kansas *University Review*, Vol. 13, no. 3, November 1891, 66-68. A student newspaper noted that "'Fearless' Fred Funston in his inimitable style describes a wedding in the Mohave Desert" (*The University Courier*, December 14, 1891).

* * *

During the early part of last summer a small detatchment [sic] from the United States Death Valley expedition, consisting of Mr. E. W. Nelson and myself, with our irrepressible Chinese cook, Ti Sing, and a train of five pack animals, was engaged in collecting specimens of the plant and animal life, and making an exploration of the vast mountainous desert region lying east of the Sierra Nevadas and north of Death Valley.

We had already been separated from the main party nearly a month, and in all that time had not seen a human being, other than a few vagabond Indians, when one day while descending a rugged canyon in one of the numerous mountain ranges scattered over the desert, we came suddenly upon a camp of about forty Panamint Indians.

These Panamints are probably more totally cut off from intercourse with the whites than any other Indians in the United States. They do not live on a reservation, and have no connection whatever with the government, roaming at will over a country which the white man has never wanted to take from them.

Probably all of the adult members of the tribe have, at some time in their lives, visited the settlements in the Owens river valley, eighty miles to the west; but most of the children had never seen a white man, nor for that matter, a Chinaman, and as we came suddenly upon the camp around a sharp turn in the canyon, there was a chorus of shrieks from behind a clump of mesquit trees, where a dozen copper-colored little chaps were busily engaged in digging a lizard out of his hole. They didn't stand still to shriek, however, but lined out for the brush wickyups in a way that would have been a pointer to some people who fondly believe themselves sprinters.

One round-faced little four-year old evidently had not heard the story of Lot's wife, for he looked behind him as he ran, and stumbling over a bush, fell headlong into the sand. Our Chinaman, who was, strangely enough, a splendid rider, spurred his horse into a gallop, and reaching down, caught the little redskin by the arm and lifted him on to the pommel of his saddle.

This was something new to the Chinaman's horse, and the animal began to buck and plunge savagely. In this predicament the only thing Ti could do was to drop the little savage on the softest place he could find; but as one place was about as soft as another, and something had to be done quickly, he simply let loose of young Mr. Lo, and that much abused individual fell into some sage brush, and picking himself up, scampered for the paternal wickyup with commendable energy. By this time the Indian camp was in an uproar; squaws were running hither and thither, taking a hurried census of their progeny; but the most alarming result of the Chinaman's foolish playfulness was that several men emerged from the camp carrying rifles, and started toward us.

My companion, Nelson, understood the Indian character well, and as the men approached, dismounted from his horse, and holding his hands above his head, walked out to meet them. At this one of their number, laying his rifle on the ground, came forward in like manner. After a short parley in broken English, Nelson convinced the Indians that the Chinaman meant no wrong, and we were invited into the camp.

As soon as we came inside the brush inclosure [sic: enclosure] which surrounded the dozen wickyups, it was evident that something unusual was on the program for that night; the wickyups, horses, dogs, guns, in fact every thing that a string could be tied to, were decorated with bits of gaily colored cloth; the faces of men, women and children were made hideous by great daubs of red and yellow paint; three old squaws were busily engaged in roasting about two bushels of chuck-wallies (big fat lizards) in a rude stone oven, while two others, younger and more comely, were preparing great bowls of pine-nut soup.

As yet we did not know the meaning of all this preparation, but I suggested to Nelson that we remain and participate in the orgies whatever they were to be. My companion replied that he was not in the habit of running away from a social gathering, and that the prospect of a square meal was more than his weak, worldly nature could withstand. So in a few moments the tired and hungry animals of the pack train were relieved of their burdens and turned loose to nibble on the bunch grass, if they could find any. We three, Nelson, Ti and myself, at once proceeded to make ourselves at home,— to do in Rome as Romans do.

Of course none of us could speak a word of the Panamint language, but two of the men knew a little English, and explained to us the cause of the approaching festivities, which was nothing less than a wedding between a son of the chief of this band and the daughter of the chief of the Hot Springs band, forty miles to the south. A wedding was something right in our line, so we agreed to see it through to the finish.

The prospective groom was pointed out to us, but the young lady in the case was not on exhibition, but we were comforted with the assurance that we could see her after awhile.

By this time the sun was just setting, and the medicine man of the tribe, a tough looking old reprobate of eighty summers, emerged from the largest of the brush houses carrying a small drum of home manufacture. As the old fellow passed out of the inclosure he looked neither to the right nor the left, but hastened with his popular musical instrument to a commanding knoll about three hundred yards from the village, where he proceeded to execute a solo, as one of the Indians explained to us, in order to drive away the evil spirits, who were supposed to take an especial delight in hovering about weddings. I do not know how badly the spirits were alarmed, but I did notice that at the first rub-a-dub-dub of that old heathen's drum, every one of our horses and burros started off up the canyon, head and tail in air.

For nearly an hour we could see the tall form of the old medicine man outlined against the evening sky, and hear the monotonous roll of his rawhide drum; but just as the twilight began to fade away he returned to the village, evidently satisfied that the evil spirits were hunting their holes.

No sooner had the medicine man reentered the inclosure than the members of the tribe seated themselves on the ground in two circles, the men in one and the women [in] the other; all eyes were bent on the ground, and the chief, the father of the groom, began a monotonous chant, which was soon taken up by the other men.

While the chant was in progress the groom arose from his place in the ring, and walking to the center, stood upright; two old women of the tribe went to one of the wickyups, and removing the screen from the entrance, led forth the bride.

Suddenly the chanting ceased, and the bride, walking into the circle of men, stood before the groom, who did not deign to notice her; she fell down on her face before him, and he without looking at her, placed his moccasined foot on her head and held it there an uncomfortably long time. We supposed that this was done in order to remind her that she was to be forever subject to his will. Finally the young brute thought he had pressed the poor girl's face into the dirt long enough, and removed his foot. She rose at once and stood before him, and for the first time during the ceremony he looked at her – a cold, sullen, brutal stare.

There was some more chanting and the medicine man got out his drum again and began to pound it vigorously, while the men and women rose, and forming a circle about the fire, the newly married couple with the others, began a wild, fantastic dance; this was kept up at intervals for more than two hours, the intervals being spent in taking a foretaste of the feast which was to complete the ceremony.

At nine o'clock at a signal from the medicine man the dancers left the circle and gathered about the piles of roast chuckwallies and bowls of pine-nut soup. Up to this time we three had taken no part in the proceedings, but now it was our turn, and at a signal from the father of the groom we came forward, the Chinaman in the lead, his eyes fairly sparkling in anticipation of the feast. Roast chuckwally was by no means a new dish to us; we had been compelled to eat them when we could get nothing else. Most people I dare say, will feel creepy at the thought of eating lizards, but I wish to remark right here that I have eaten worse stuff in Lawrence at the Phi Delt club, when I was steward, however. Pine-nut soup, as one would surmise from its name, is a broth made from the fruit of the nut pine converted into coarse flour by grinding between stones. Zest is given to this dish by the seasoning, rabbits, gophers, and dogs whose usefulness has been impaired by age. If one is able to overcome any prejudice against the seasoning, the dish is quite palatable. Nelson remarked, I thought rather unkindly that these were put in, in order to give the soup "body."

The delicacies were handed around by the squaws, and the feast began in earnest. I might say in justice to ourselves, that we partook sparingly. The Indians gorged themselves until midnight, and that began another dance, making the hills echo and re-echo with their yells and whoops. A great bonfire was built of sage-brush, and lighted up the steep canyon walls and added to the weirdness of the wild scene. We rolled up in our blankets and lay on the ground watching them; I could not keep my mind off from the story of the dance of the witches in "Tam O'Shanter."

Finally the fire burned out and the yelling ceased. I spoke to Nelson, but he was already asleep. The wedding was over, and I drew my blanket tighter about me, and was soon dreaming of chuckwallies, witches, painted faces and the old heathen with his kettle drum.

# CHAPTER FIVE

# *The Death Valley Expedition*

### June 15, 1891 – September 3, 1891

**This side Expedition on which Funston accompanied was the most adventurous and interesting of the entire Expedition...**

> —Edward Nelson to Mrs. Frederick Funston,
> February 9, 1931

We left Nelson's expedition on its arrival, with "a good lot of specimens," at Keeler on June 15.[1] The town of Keeler is located on the eastern shore of Owens Lake, at the east base of the Sierra Nevada Mountains, southeast of Mount Whitney.[2] The next day, Fred and Nelson journeyed to Lone Pine to join the general camp.[3] Lone Pine, a town on the west side of Owens Valley, was located four miles north of Owens Lake.[4]

The Nelson party, consisting of Fred, Nelson, Ti Sing, and the guide, "Indian Mike," soon set out on their next expedition.[5] By June 24, the little party was on the west slope of the Inyo Mountains; the next day on the crest of the mountains; and on the 26th and 27th on the east slope.[6] The Inyo Mountains, known for their height and steepness, form the eastern wall of the Owens Valley.[7] By June 30, Nelson's party was in Saline Valley, where tragedy struck.[8] Hat, Ti Sing's black shepherd dog, "perished from thirst after his master had divided with him the last drink in his canteen."[9] The temperature was 114° in the shade, and the men suffered greatly from heat.[10] The topographers, Dikeman and Bartlett, nearly suffered the same fate as Ti Sing's dog. At the beginning of July, while crossing the desert during the night from Owl Holes to Calico, they "broke down." Their water was so hot it was unfit to drink. "[T]hey were nearly insane." The temperature the next day was 123° to 124° in the shade. The two men had "to walk in order to get out before death from thirst overtook

79

them. They finally reached Daggett and rested up, but suffered much from their experience."

Fifty years later, Vernon Bailey recollected about the heat of Death Valley:

[A. K. Fisher and I in June] found the temperature at mid-day 116 degrees in the shade at Furnace Creek, but there was only one little spot of shade in the whole valley, the cottonwoods around the ranch. Out in the sun my thermometer, which was limited to 135 degrees, soon went to the top and blew off the bulb at the bottom. But during the summer our weather observer obtained temperatures of 136 degrees, in the shade and protection of the regular Weather Bureau box [the U.S. Weather Bureau detailed to the valley a field observer]....

In the summer the heat was bad, but not unbearable. It did not bother us if we could get enough water for ourselves and for our horses. Two gallons of water a day to a man would keep us comfortable. [Much of the water we drank was strongly impregnated with soda and in Ash Meadows and Amargosa desert it was very strong of borax. It was not pleasant to drink but it did not do any harm. In that country when you are thirsty any kind of water will do.] We had to wear gloves and wide hats in the summer, for otherwise our noses would burn hard and crisp, and our hands would swell up from the heat in the open.

I had to go to my traps before sunrise. If the sun struck the specimens caught in the traps for a few minutes they would be cooked. Many a time I would break a mouse open and it would smell like well-done meat. Throughout the summer the temperature usually ran from 117 to 120 degrees, perhaps 125. The highest was 136, I think.[11]

At a now unknown time and place in that awful valley, Fred had another thirst and extreme heat experience. "The air did not contain one particle of moisture and in the midst of all this, one day when the thermometer was 147 degrees above zero, the water supply ran out. When we came to a spring, two days later, I plunged my head into the water and held it there until I could drink no more. But the water would not stay on my stomach. I tried it again and this time my thirst was slacked [sic: slaked]. It was several days before I came to myself, and one member of the party, the driver, has never recovered. He is now in an insane asylum."[12]

A happier experience for Fred occurred with the publication in the

July issue of *St. Nicholas Magazine* of his story, "Storm Bound above the Clouds." In the *El Dorado Republican* managed by Billy White, he complimented this article as "very well-written" and "graphically illustrated from photographs and is very interesting both in narration and description." Billy then described his friend glowingly: "Fred Funston is probably the luckiest, clumsiest, wittiest, bravest, most tender-hearted boy in Kansas. He is now in Death Valley, Colorado [sic], on a Government exploring expedition." [13]

On July 1 and 2, Nelson's party was in Waucoba Cañon in the Inyo Mountains, and by July 7 had reached Black Cañon in the White Mountains. On July 12, they were at Cottonwood Creek in the White Mountains, and by July 20 the men were in the foothills of the Sierra Nevada Mountains near the town of Benton in Mono County, California. [14] Benton was located one hundred miles north of Keeler. [15]

The story continues with the detail provided in a letter Fred wrote on August 3 from "Camp on South Fork of Merced" to an unidentified friend in Lawrence, Kansas (altitudes are shown in brackets):

> I wrote you from Benton about two weeks ago that we were just starting to cross the Sierras to Yosemite. We are not there yet, but expect to be in two days, and as I shall be rushed for time to see the sights there, shall write you most of my letter here and finish it there. Leaving Benton on the east side of the range July 19, we spent a week reaching the summit of the range at Mammoth Pass [about 9,500 feet]. The time of actual travel was only three days, the other four were put in camping at various places. Leaving Mammoth Pass July 27, we dropped, slid and tumbled down into the valley of the San Joaquin, and ever since then have been trying to reach Yosemite. After leaving the summit of the pass there was no vestige of a trail and we have depended altogether on chart and compass but not with the most alarming success. For two days we have been hung up in a big crevice here and today found a way in which we can get out.
>
> I have seen some great sights, but it would be too big a job to write them down. I think I am competent now to compare the Rockies and the Sierras. In the matter of big cliffs and gorges it is about a stand off. In pretty, wide valleys like Estes Park, the Rockies take the bun, but when it comes to glaciers, forests of trees that are trees, and cataracts and fine river views generally, the Rockies are simply not in it at all. The grandest mountain I ever saw, besides which Long, Whitney, and Tyndall look tame, is Mt. Lyell [13,042 feet]. It takes ones

[sic] breath away to look at it. It has never been climbed and never will be, the culminating point being a spire 1,500 feet high. When it comes to describing a Sierra forest, I let out the job.

We have not reached the Sequois [sic] groves, but we rode for fifty miles at the head of the San Joaquin and Chiquito Joaquin, through a forest the average size of the trees being from four to six feet in diamater, and from eighty to 150 feet high; and in all that three days of travel I did not see one mark of an ax or a tree that had been killed by fire. But you have to see such a forest to appreciate it. [Naturalist Frank Stephens joined the Nelson party for three days on July 27 and accompanied them to the Upper San Joaquin River. Stephens took photographs of the pack train that day and additional photographs the next day. The men went over the Mammoth Pass before Stephens left the party on July 29. [16]]

The finest waterfall we have seen yet is about four miles above here where the Merced, a stream twice as large as the Grand, takes a plunge of 500 feet. Speaking of rivers reminds me that they are the most trouble we have to encounter. Of course, where there are no trails there are no bridges. The streams are large and swift with bad bottoms and we expect to drown some of the pack animals or ourselves every time we tackle one. Our mode of proceedure [sic] on reaching one of these rivulets is about as follows: Nelson and I open one of the packs and extract therefrom a demijohn containing some of the "Spirits of '76" with which we brace up our nerves, at the same time looking carefully under each others' whiskers and reminding ourselves that after all the things of this earth are but earthy. While we are thus engaged the Chinaman burns a couple of joss sticks and the Indian sneaks off behind the bushes and passes the time of day with the Great Spirit. All this done we force our horses in, draw the burros across with picket ropes, and upon reaching the other bank chant something appropriate like "The Beautiful River" or "Over There."

Ever since we have been in the mountains we have had all the venison and trout we can lie up to. The Indian killed his last deer this morning. The fish are "rainbow trout," larger and somewhat prettier than those of Estes Park.

My next will be from the Yosemite.

FRED FUNSTON.[17]

Fred's letter on August 15 to the same friend from "Yosemite" shows that he retained his capacity for awe:

I have seen it all. I can't describe it, it is beyond me. The Yosemite bridal vail [sic: veil], Nevada and Vernal falls, El Capitan, the Dome and Sentinel Rock. The Yosemite fall is in sight, half a mile away, and I can see every foot of her from where the river breaks over the cliff to where she strikes the rock 2,700 feet below. The noise of this thing is like one continued peal of thunder. It is one of those sights that makes a man want to take off his hat and not want anyone to speak to him. The prettiest fall I think is the "Nevada" where the Merced takes a plunge of 500 feet.

We entered the valley of the Mono lake trail. The descent of the trail into the valley is a marvel of engineering and cost Uncle Sam thousands of dollars. For a long distance it zigzags down an absolutely vertical rock face where it has been blasted out. At one point if one sits on his horse reaching his arm out over the edge, drop a rock it will not touch anything for one mile. The mere thought of any of the trail giving away makes a man feel religious and feel for his prayer book.

Summing it all up Yosemite is grand and terrible beyond the comprehension of one who has not seen it, for its like is not in this world. It has its draw backs. There are no fish in the Merced. The trout is a good climber but when it comes to humping himself up a cataract half a mile high he is not in it. And there are more shoddy cabins that ought to be burned and some weed patches that look bad. The woods are full of "chappies" who roam about with 32 calibered rifles hunting grizzlies a quarter of a mile from the hotel. As a simpering idiot without brains or hope of any, I hereby award the pastry to the average eastern or city tourist.

We have not had any mail since leaving Benton and will not get any for two weeks at least. Did not have our mail sent here as were not sure of getting here ourselves. My address is still Keeler. When we get down on King's river I am going to recross the Sierras alone for the mail. I am happy and enjoying myself hugely, but am dirty and ragged beyond description.

Goodbye,
FUNSTON [18]

According to Nelson, who noted that his party had gone from the head of the Merced River downriver to Yosemite Valley, "Galen Clark then superintendent of the [Yosemite] park said that this was the first record of a pack train having done this although it had often been tried before."[19] According to Billy White, this was "the first 'back door' entrance into Yosemite Valley, down the sheer side of the mountains."[20] No wonder that Nelson later described this "side Expedition" as "the most adventurous and interesting of the entire Expedition..."

In conversation during the weeks that Fred spent with Edward Nelson, Fred may have heard accounts of Nelson's experiences on behalf of the government in Alaska. Nelson, ten years older than Fred, spent several years there. He served as weather observer at St. Michaels on the Bering Sea (1877-1881) and studied zoology, ethnology, and geography and also made collections for the Smithsonian (1881-1882). In collecting specimens, he explored relatively unknown areas of western and northwestern Alaska. His explorations were not limited to Alaska since as a passenger on the U.S. Revenue cutter *Corwin* he journeyed to Siberia and other locales. His anthropological work in Alaska was significant, making a large, well-documented collection of Eskimo artifacts and learning invaluable information about Eskimo culture.

Returning to the United States, Nelson developed tuberculosis and went to Arizona for his health. There he was a rancher and county clerk in Apache County (1882-1890). He resumed his biological work when he joined the Death Valley Expedition. "Nelson has been described as a 'determined, intense worker, with great restless energy,' so completely devoted to work that neither illness nor other physical discomfort could deter him for long."[21] "[I]f there were any health setbacks for Nelson on the [Death Valley] expedition, they are not recorded in his journal or his correspondence." [22]

At Yosemite, Nelson received a wire advising that the expedition was to be disbanded, and that he and his men should proceed immediately to Lone Pine, near Owens Lake, where they would join the other explorers. Nelson's party recrossed the Sierra Nevada by way of King's River trail, and then down to Lone Pine where they arrived by about August 22.[23] There Fred had a third water experience. The camp at Lone Pine was near an irrigation ditch, and near it naturalist Frank Stephens and his wife had their tent. Mrs. Stephens had washed a number of tin pans and placed them outside to dry. Fred came walking along, and stepping into one of these pans, it slid with him into the irrigation ditch.[24]

Mrs. Stephens was not the only wife on the expedition. Not surprisingly, the now 24-year-old benedict, Frederick Coville, wanted his bride, Elizabeth, to join the expedition when it was at Lone Pine and in the Sierra Nevada Mountains. Merriam permitted this, and Vernon Bailey wrote on July 23:

> Mr. + Mrs. Coville go with me over the trail to Kern River + up that to Whitney. Palmer and Dr. Fisher go over the King River Trail farther north. 'It is going to be one of our roughest trips and a long time from mail or towns, but on the other hand one of the grandest trips to be had in all this country. We will be up among snowy peaks and thick pine forests and cold streams full of trout and game and new plants + animals.
>
> My party suits me to a dot. Dr. Fisher wants to go with me to [sic] but Palmer wont [sic] let him because he would have to go alone. I was specially anxious to get Coville. He is a great help to me + both he and Mrs. Coville are first rate company. We have two men for packers and cook, will have 9 horses and pack 4 of them. We expect to stay up in the Mts. till late in September. Will send our men down for provision as we need it and may be able to connect with mail occasionally. I can probably send out letters at intervals but do not expect to get any.

Elizabeth Coville played an interesting role on this trip:

> This has been a very quiet Sunday [August 9]. Coville is cataloguing plants, Mrs. C. has been reading to us from Longfellow + Scot [sic]. now she is reading the paper while we write. She often reads us a chapter in the Bible, and other books as we work. She never shot a gun much but the other day borrowed my gun + 4 aux. cartridges + killed 2 chipmunks + 2 birds. Yesterday she beat Coville shooting his rifle. Now she wants to kill a Bear. [25]

Fred and Coville on August 22 drove to Keeler where they packed specimens before returning to camp at Lone Pine.[26] The final leg of the expedition's journey was spent in Whitney Meadows at the base of Mt. Whitney.[27] On August 27, Coville spent the day making arrangements for breaking up the expedition, and, the next day, he, his wife, and Fred left Whitney Meadows for the town of Visalia, which they reached on September 1. In Coville's words: "We reached Visalia, where the next two days were spent disposing of the outfit; and the botanical field work of the expedition was ended."[28] The main party disbanded at Visalia on September 19.[29]

This first scientific expedition was a grand success. The scientists' collections were sent to Washington, D.C., where they were deposited in the U. S. National Museum. All total, the collections included about 1,000 reptiles and batrachians, 1,000 birds, 5,500 mammals, 4,500 insects, and, thanks to botanists Coville and Funston, 18,000 plants. Also included were a number of fishes and mollusks from the hot springs of some of the interior deserts. Additionally, there were several hundred miscellaneous specimens.[30]

Several members of the expedition, but not Fred, were memorialized by becoming eponyms for newly discovered species of snails, toads, mountain goats, frogs, lizards, and greasewood.[31] Nelson even had a previously unknown short range of mountain, near the north end of Panamint Valley, named for him.[32] Surprisingly, since he was Chinese and thus not a white man, it was Ti Sing who had the greatest honor bestowed upon him. Ti had started working as a cook in 1888 for the United States Geological Survey, a career he would follow for thirty years, and had been lent to the Death Valley Expedition, joining it with topographer Dikeman of the Geological Survey.[33] Although not a United States citizen, "he was highly regarded by the survey members ..." Eight years after the Death Valley Expedition, an employee of the U.S. Geological Survey named a 10,555-feet peak, located in Yosemite National Park, Sing Peak in Ti's honor.[34] Ti died tragically on July 19, 1918, the year after Fred's death, when a wagon in which he was riding overturned on an embankment in Bird Creek Canyon near Hollister, California.[35]

An oft-repeated tale about the expedition after it disbanded was that, of all of the expedition members, only Fred did not go insane or die. In view of the prominence of expedition members Merriam, Coville, Fisher, Nelson, Palmer, Bailey, and Dutcher, it seems extremely odd that such a story should circulate, and yet it did. As Merriam told a reporter in 1901, after Fred captured the Filipino leader Aguinaldo, "That is one of the lies which crop up annually, like the discovery of a barrel of snakes somewhere out west." Merriam, with "a smiling countenance," said that the survivors of the expedition, "although pretty badly wrecked...all appreciate these annual stories, General Funston among the rest." Merriam then identified by name various prominent members of the expedition currently living and working. "In fact, there are not any of us that have not survived."[36]

This absurd tale of Fred's sole survival and of his sanity was, surprisingly, repeated by both Charlie Scott and Billy White. They clearly should have known better, since, by contacting Merriam at his office in Washington, D. C., they could have easily learned the truth. Scott repeated the canard in 1898 and 1901 articles, except he said that "more than half were permanently disabled in body or mind...," but Fred "came out of it "sound and well..."[37] Even after Fred's death, Charlie wrote Eda Funston that Fred "alone of the entire party returned alive and without permanent disability."[38] Billy White asserted in two 1899 articles that Fred was the "only member" who was then "alive and sane."[39]

A. K. Fisher, writing many years later, provided this perspective. He stated that Edward Nelson, upon reading what White had written, "wrote a rather curt note to White stating that quite a number of that party are still alive including himself..." According to Fisher, White apologized to Nelson, and "stated that he had received the information directly from Funston."[40] If this is true, then Fred must have meant it only as a joke. Since Fred's practice was to focus attention on others rather than on himself, it makes no sense for him to single himself out for such an impressive status as the sole survivor and the sole sane person, particularly when this could so easily be proved false. In view of the harrowing experiences of not only Fred, but also of Palmer, Bailey, Dikeman, Bartlett, and the driver who went insane, I speculate that these stories became exaggerated in the retelling, and, in the end, the story of death and insanity came out totally wrong.

The best comment about this tale comes from an 1899 biographical sketch of Fred: "The privations of the six men of this expedition in Death Valley have been the theme of song and story for half a dozen years. It has been said that all save Funston are dead or in lunatic asylums; but that is a mistake. I saw most of the members a week or two ago. They are in Washington, serving the government by day and wearing spike-tailed coats by night."[41]

When the expedition was over, how did Fred feel about the experience? Unfortunately, there is no written record to tell us. He clearly benefited from the expedition's arduous challenges, including at least two perilous trips when he went for the mail at Panamint. Fred learned that he was capable of enduring and overcoming extreme physical—and mental—challenges. He had written Buck Franklin: "I have got my belly full of roughing it for a number of years to come," yet just five months later, he wrote another friend: "I am happy and enjoying myself hugely, but am dirty and ragged beyond description." What a sense of accomplishment he must have felt. That the expedition experience was positive for him is reflected by the fact that Fred, a few years before his death, told Fisher that he was strongly in favor of having a reunion of the expedition members, and that he would go anywhere in the United States to attend.[42]

What did Coville think of his assistant? A decade later, after Fred had shot to new national fame with his capture of Aguinaldo, Coville told a *Washington Post* reporter that "[t]he subsequent career of Funston was a surprise to us who knew him in the Death valley [sic] expedition, not that he was lacking in courage, for he was always willing to undertake any enterprise that gave promise of adventure, but it did not seem to us that he was built for a rough and strenuous life. He seemed never to have roughed it any, and his inexperience was often the cause of jest."[43] Reflecting a half century after the expedition, Vernon Bailey described Fred thusly: "Funston did not take scientific life very seriously, but he was full of fun and good stories, and did his work cheerfully."[44]

Fred was soon back in Kansas, presumably traveling there by train. "[M]uch to everyone's surprise" he turned up in Lawrence where he visited friends "after a long sojourn in the fatal Death Valley of California."[45] After a several days' visit, on September 14 Fred took the train home to the Funston farm.[46] *The Iola Register* briefly reported Fred's safe return "after his long wanderings."[47] But he did not stay long. By the first week of October, both he and Billy White were on the staff of *The Kansas City Journal* in Kansas City, Missouri. That Fred would return to journalism for a livelihood is not surprising; he both liked the work and was good at it. Charlie Scott complimented the two young men: White had been running the *El Dorado Republican* for two years and was an experienced journalist. Also, "his wit and logic will give an interest and value to [the *Journal*] that it has lacked for a long time." As for Fred, "Mr. Funston has had comparatively little newspaper experience. But his letters to the *REGISTER* give abundant proof that he has the faculty of seeing clearly and writing entertainingly, and we have not the least doubt that his work will win early and substantial recognition."[48]

White had been invited to join the *Journal* editorial staff by Charlie Gleed, who was involved at the time in the *Journal's* ownership and management, and who knew White from his days in Lawrence.[49] I speculate that Gleed also invited Fred to join the staff. Gleed, in his eulogy for Fred, said that he had talked with Fred after his return from the Death Valley Expedition, and had "asked him if he was ready to take a quiet newspaper job." Fred had responded, "not yet."[50] Perhaps Fred's "not yet" referred to being a journalist permanently, not just temporarily.

In his *Autobiography,* Billy White years later told of the experiences of the two young men in Kansas City. White mistakenly stated that Fred had just returned from Central America from his coffee plantation venture; in reality, this did not happen until 1895. Billy noted that he had rented a room on McGee Street, north of Twelfth Street, which had two double beds. He and Fred shared one, and the other was shared by Billy's close friend from El Dorado, Lew Schmucker, and Fred Vandergrift, a city editor for *The Kansas City Star*, who was ten years older than the others. There was a fifth man, Harve Hoover, "a railway postal clerk who was running with Schmucker." He also shared the bed with Vandergrift, but Hoover occupied only half of the bed since neither he nor Schmucker were at home on the same night. Billy recalled that he was never lonely, and with this "company of rollicking hellions" he also was not homesick or sad. After Billy finished his newspaper work for the day, he, Fred, and Schmucker "roamed the city like sheep-killing dogs." As Billy detailed it, once he was done by about 10:30 p.m., he headed to the police station where Fred was on the "dogwatch" for the newspaper. They roamed together and made friends with the people of the night—cops, dopes, and male and female toughs. By one in the morning, they walked the mile home, at times singing ribald songs. Fred liked sea songs, singing solo "Blow the Man Down." Other songs they sang together.[51] They played cards until three in the morning.[52]

The young men ate at a restaurant run by "Mother" Wosslick, "a large, well-upholstered woman, and [as] generous and hospitable as she was portly." Fred had a special recipe for bordelaise sauce which he shared with Mrs. Wosslick, who then included it in her cooking. It was Fred who introduced to his friends beefsteak and bordelaise sauce. Mrs. Wosslick also served, to the pleasure of the group, German-fried potatoes, coffee, and hot biscuits.[53]

Not surprisingly, Fred did not stay with this job long, but, even for him, it was an extremely short time. On November 1, he was once again on the payroll of the United States Department of Agriculture, this time as a special agent.[54] Later that month he was in Washington, D.C., working on the botanical collection from Death Valley.[55] Serving as special agent was certainly a logical position for him, and I speculate that it was only after he had started his work as a journalist that the Department of Agriculture offered him a position as special agent. This was also a well-paid position at $1,200 per year, a handsome sum and far more than the $12 per week he made as a reporter.[56] And, of course, there was the prospect, as a special agent, of more adventure. A better offer had come, and Fred took it.

"Going into Camp" Sierra Nevada Mountains
On left: Indian Mike (behind burro) and Edward Nelson (in front of burro)
On right: Fred Funston and Ti Sing

# Chapter Five Notes—*The Death Valley Expedition*

Epigraph: E. W. Nelson to Mrs. Frederick Funston, February 9, 1931 (Frederick Funston Papers on microfilm, hereafter FFP Micro) (Archives Division, Kansas State Historical Society).

1. For quotation: C. Hart Merriam, M.D. *Death Valley Expedition I – Journal of a trip across Southern California + Nevada including NW Arizona + SW Utah 1891*, Vol. I (March – July) (manuscript, container #4, C. Hart Merriam Papers, Manuscript Division, Library of Congress, D.C.), June 16, 1891, entry.
   For balance: Frederick V. Coville, *[Death Valley Expedition] Itinerary* (Smithsonian Institution Archives, Accession 11-253, Frederick Vernon Coville Field Books, 1890–1924, folder Death Valley Expedition, Itinerary, 1890-1891), 90.
   Periodically, the expedition shipped specimens to Washington, D.C. On one occasion, Fred sent to Francis H. Snow, his former professor who was now chancellor at the State University of Kansas, "a very rare lizard" from Death Valley ("University Items," *The Lawrence Daily Journal*, May 19, 1891).

2. U.S. Department of Agriculture, Division of Ornithology and Mammalogy, *North American Fauna No. 7. The Death Valley Expedition. A Biological Survey Of Parts Of California, Nevada, Arizona, and Utah, Part II* (Washington: Government Printing Office, 1893), 371, 376.

3. Frederick V. Coville, *[Death Valley Expedition] Itinerary*, 90.

4. U.S. Department of Agriculture, Division of Ornithology and Mammalogy, *North American Fauna No. 7. The Death Valley Expedition. A Biological Survey Of Parts Of California, Nevada, Arizona, and Utah, Part II*, 373.
   Vernon Bailey described Owens Lake: "Owens Lake is an interesting place though an abominable place in some respects. The lake water is loaded with salt + borax + soda but springs of fairly good water are common around the shore. They are all warm + have rank flavors of their own, but we dont [sic] mind such little things..."
   "There are thousands of ducks on it. Spoonbills and Gulls + Curlers + Snipe + lots of small birds around shore. They live on maggots of flies that live in the water. They are in a little brown shell in the chrysalis state; are thick all along the edge of the lake. The Indians live on the maggots too, gather them + thrash off the shells + make rice pudding of them" (Vernon Bailey to Dear Friends, December 28, 1891, Keeler, California) (Vernon Bailey Papers, Box 9, Folder 3, American History Center, University of Wyoming).

5. The source for the name "Indian Mike" is the handwritten identification on the back of a photograph of the four men with the label "Going into camp – Sierras" (T. S. Palmer photograph collection, December 1890-December 1891, The Huntington Library, San Marino, California).

6. Frederick Vernon Coville, *Botany Of The Death Valley Expedition* (U. S. Department of Agriculture, Division of Botany, Contributions From The U.S. National Herbarium, Vol. IV. Issued November 29, 1893, Washington: Government Printing Office, 1893), 273. This work contains a Catalogue of Specimens, and from that one can obtain a detailed record of where and when Fred collected specimens. In the text, I have used only Coville's brief summary of where Fred was.

7. U.S. Department of Agriculture, Division of Ornithology and Mammalogy, *North American Fauna No. 7. The Death Valley Expedition. A Biological Survey Of Parts Of California, Nevada, Arizona, and Utah, Part II*, 370.

8. Saline Valley is located northeast of Owens Lake between the Inyo Mountains

and the northern extension of the Panamint Mountains (U.S. Department of Agriculture, Division of Ornithology and Mammalogy, *North American Fauna No. 7. The Death Valley Expedition. A Biological Survey Of Parts Of California, Nevada, Arizona, and Utah, Part II*, Washington: Government Printing Office, 1893), 379.

9. F.F. [Frederick Funston], "Into The Valley Of Death," *The New York Times*, March 27, 1892.

10. "The Pacific Slope," *The San Francisco Chronicle*, July 9, 1891.

11. "The Pacific Slope," *The San Francisco Chronicle*, July 9, 1891, for Dikeman and Bartlett's experience. For Bailey's account, see Vernon Bailey, "Into Death Valley 50 Years Ago," *Westways*, December 1940. The language in brackets is from elsewhere in Bailey's article.

    Bailey had a dim opinion of Dikeman and Bartlett: "The Topographers are off towards Daggett. I dont [sic] know where + dont [sic] want to. They have been the greatest bother we have had" (Vernon Bailey to Dear Friends, June 14, 1891, Lone Pine, California) (Vernon Bailey Papers, Box 9, Folder 3, American Heritage Center, University of Wyoming).

12. "Fred Funston's Exploits," *The Kansas City Star,* February 20, 1898. The essence of this story also appeared in "Funston, Brig. Gen., U.S.V.," *The Kansas City Star,* May 7, 1899 (Frederick Funston Papers, hereafter FFP) (Archives Division, Kansas State Historical Society).

13. *The Iola Register*, July 3, 1891 (reprint from *El Dorado Republican*).

14. Frederick Vernon Coville, *Botany Of The Death Valley Expedition*, 273-274. This work contains a Catalogue of Specimens, and from that one can obtain a detailed record of where and when Fred collected specimens. In the text, I have used only Coville's brief summary of where Fred was.

15. U.S. Department of Agriculture, Division of Ornithology and Mammalogy, *North American Fauna No. 7. The Death Valley Expedition. A Biological Survey Of Parts Of California, Nevada, Arizona, and Utah, Part II*, 363.

16. Frank Stephens, handwritten log of Death Valley Expedition of 1891 (Frank Stephens Field Notes Collection, San Diego Natural History Museum Research Library, San Diego, California), July 27-29, 1891, entries.

17. Fred Funston to unidentified person, August 3, 1891. Published in *The Lawrence Daily Journal*, August 26, 1891. The newspaper did not identify the addressee of the letter.

18. Fred Funston to unidentified person, August 15, 1891. Published in *The Lawrence Daily Journal*, August 31, 1891. The newspaper did not identify the addressee of the letter.

19. E. W. Nelson to Mrs. Frederick Funston, February 9, 1931 (FFP on microfilm, hereafter FFP Micro).

20. William Allen White, "The Hero Of The Philippines," *The St. Louis Republic Magazine Section*, May 21, 1899.

21. Keir B. Sterling, Richard P. Hammond et al., ed., *Biographical Dictionary Of American And Canadian Naturalists And Environmentalists* (Westport, Connecticut: Greenwood Press, 1997), 571.

22. Matthew Laubacher, "Cultures of Collection in Late Nineteen Century American Natural History" (dissertation, Arizona State University, May 2011).

23. E. W. Nelson to Mrs. Frederick Funston, February 9, 1931 (FFP Micro). The date

of August 22 is from Frederick V. Coville, *[Death Valley Expedition] Itinerary*, 111.

24. Albert Kenrick Fisher, *Frederick Funstun* [sic] (manuscript, container #40, A. K. Fisher Papers, Manuscript Division, Library of Congress, Washington, D.C.), 6.

25. For Coville's desire to bring his wife out, see Vernon Bailey to My Dear Friends, March 20, 1891, Furnace Creek, California. Quoted paragraphs: Vernon Bailey to Dear Friends, July 23, 1891, Visalia, California, and Vernon Bailey to Dear Friends, August 9, 1891, Mineral King, California (both from Vernon Bailey Papers, Box 9, Folders 3-5, American Heritage Center, University of Wyoming).

26. Frederick V. Coville, *[Death Valley Expedition] Itinerary*, 112.

27. E. W. Nelson to Mrs. Frederick Funston, February 9, 1931 (FFP Micro).

28. Frederick V. Coville, *[Death Valley Expedition] Itinerary*, 112-113. Coville does not mention that his wife was on the expedition. Vernon Bailey noted: "I was sorry to see them go, but they were glad to get out of the woods. They are the pleasantest ones in the party" (Vernon Bailey to Dear Friends, August 30, 1891, Whitney Meadows, California) (Vernon Bailey Papers, Box 9, Folders 3-5, American Heritage Center, University of Wyoming).

    Bailey was glad to have the expedition end. He had been "camping steadily for over 14 months" since he had been on another field assignment before the Death Valley Expedition. On the night of September 19, 1891, he slept in a hotel in "the first bed up above the ground... I did not fall out of bed last night nor throw any bones on the dining room floor" (Vernon Bailey to My Dear Friends, September 20, 1891, Visalia, California) (Vernon Bailey Papers, Box 9, Folders 3-5, American Heritage Center, University of Wyoming).

29. Theodore S. Palmer, *Diary May 26, 1891 — Sept. 19, 1891* (manuscript, container #1, T. S. Palmer Papers, Manuscript Division, Library of Congress, Washington, D.C.), September 19, 1891, entry.

30. "Report of the Ornithologist and Mammalogist," *Report Of The Secretary Of Agriculture 1891*, 52 D Congress, 1st Session, House of Representatives, Ex. Doc. 1, Part 6, 267.

31. Richard E. Lingenfelter, *Death Valley & The Amargosa: A Land of Illusion* (Berkeley: University of California Press, 1986), 364.

32. E. W. Nelson to Mrs. Frederick Funston, February 9, 1931 (FFP Micro).

33. Vernon Bailey to Dear Friends, December 14, 1890, Lone Pine, California (Vernon Bailey Papers, Box 9, Folder 3, American Heritage Center, University of Wyoming).---

34. Frances P. Farquhar, *Place Names Of The High Sierra* (San Francisco: Sierra Club, 1926), 88.

35. "McAdoo's Cook Killed As Wagon Overturns," *San Francisco Chronicle*, July 21, 1918 (copy pasted on back of page 152 of C. Hart Merriam, M.D. *Death Valley Expedition I – Journal of a trip across Southern California + Nevada including NW Arizona + SW Utah 1891*, Vol. II (March – July) (manuscript, container #4, C. Hart Merriam Papers, Manuscript Division, Library of Congress, D.C.).

    For a delightful children's book about Ti Sing in 1915, see Annette Bay Pimentel, *Mountain Chef: How One Man Lost His Groceries, Changed His Plans, And Helped Cook Up the National Park Service* (Watertown, MA: Charlesbridge, 2016).

36. "Death Valley Expedition," *Marietta Daily Leader*, May 30, 1901 (reprint from *Washington Post*). In response to this question, "Did General Funston get lost and have a terrible experience in crossing the alkali desert, as widely reported?"

Merriam gave an odd answer: "I have never heard of it. He couldn't get lost. All he had to do was to keep along and pull weeds." Perhaps this dismissive attitude revealed an envy of Fred, the new national hero, on the part of Merriam, who is described by his biographer as strong willed and opinionated (Keir B. Sterling, *Last of the Naturalists: The Career of C. Hart Merriam* (New York: Arno Press, 1974), 157). Merriam did go on to provide this analysis of Fred: "But he afforded us much entertainment on the trip. He was a droll, sarcastic fellow, and his comments made us laugh."

37. Chas. F. Scott, "Remarkable Career of a Kansas Boy," *Mail and Breeze* (about March 20, 1898) (FFP). Charles F. Scott, "Frederick Funston," *The Independent*, April 11, 1901, 817.

38. Chas. F. Scott to Mrs. Frederick Funston, December 29, 1924 (FFP).

39. William Allen White, "Gen. Frederick Funston," *Harper's Weekly*, May 20, 1899. William Allen White, "The Hero Of The Philippines," *The St. Louis Republic Magazine Section*, May 21, 1899.

40. Albert Kenrick Fisher, *Frederick Funstun* [sic], 7.

41. William E. Johnson, "The Making of Brigadier Funston," *The New Voice,* May 13, 1899 (FFP).

42. Albert Kenrick Fisher, *Frederick Funstun* [sic], 7.

43. "Courage Of Funston," *The Lawrence Daily Journal*, April 23, 1901 (reprint from *Washington Post*).

44. Vernon Bailey, "Into Death Valley 50 years Ago," *Westways,* December 1940, 8.

45. "Personal Mention," *The Lawrence Daily Journal*, September 10, 1891.

46. "Personal Mention," *The Lawrence Daily Journal*, September 14, 1891.

47. "Local Matters," *The Iola Register*, September 18, 1891.

48. "Editorial Notes," *The Iola Register*, October 9, 1891.

49. William Allen White, *The Autobiography of William Allen White* (New York: The Macmillan Company, 1946), 198-199.

50. C. S. Gleed, eulogy, "Report of Select Committee," *Journal of the House*, Hall of the House of Representatives, Topeka, Kansas, February 26, 1917 (FFP).

51. William Allen White, *The Autobiography of William Allen White*, 210-211.

52. "When Funston Drew $12 Salary," *The Iola Daily Record*, January 25, 1906 (reprint from *Kansas City Journal*).

53. "Funston In K.C.," *The Kansas City Journal*, February 20, 1917 (Kansas State Historical Society, *Frederick Funston Clippings*, Vol 1). Interview of Fred L. Vandegrift, who, erroneously, stated that the group of young men, including Fred Funston, was together in the winter and spring of 1892. Fred had left in November of 1891. Vandegrift attributed Fred's departure to the call of *Cuba Libre*, which is also incorrect.

54. Jessie Dell, Commissioner, United States Civil Service Commission, to Eda B. Funston, March 19, 1931 (FFP).

55. "Country News," *The Lawrence Daily Journal*, November 24, 1891.

56. Jessie Dell, Commissioner, United States Civil Service Commission, to Eda B. Funston, March 19, 1931 (FFP). This was an appointment outside the civil service classified positions. "When Funston Drew $12 Salary," *The Iola Daily Record*, January 25, 1906 (reprint from *Kansas City Journal*).

# Part Two
**Botanist
Yakutat Bay, 1892
Alaska and the
British Northwest
Territory,
1893 – 1894**

---

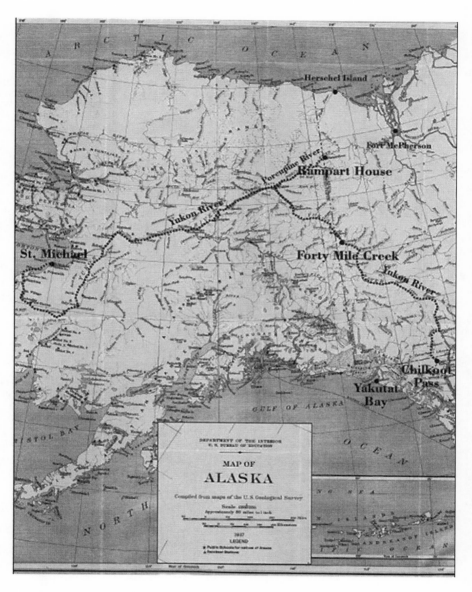

Dotted line shows Fred Funston's 1893-1894 route.

CHAPTER SIX

# "A Summer on the Alaskan Coast": Yakutat Bay, Alaska

### April 16, 1892 - October 15, 1892

**Last evening our [Carlyle] school and neighborhood had the pleasure of listening to a lecture by Mr. Fred Funston, lately returned from Alaska. To say that it was entertaining and instructive from first to last is putting it mildly.... He can give more information in an hour concerning the corns and bunions on this hind foot of our venerable Uncle Samuel than could be obtained from books in weeks or months.**

—D. M. Smith, Carlyle, November 3, 1892

Fred Funston's next adventure as a botanist occurred in a locale the antipode of Death Valley—Alaska. In a letter to a friend shortly before his departure for the far north, he described, in his usual humorous style, the object and nature of his upcoming expedition:

To make a long story short, I am on my way to Alaska. The U.S. coast survey steamer "Hassler" leaves San Francisco April 10 [1892], for the north, and the Department of Agriculture got them to agree to take me up to Yokutat [sic: Yakutat] Bay, at the foot of Mt. St. Elias, in which uninhabited wilderness of glaciers, grizzlies and mosquitos [sic], I am to do the Robinson Crusoe act until next fall, when the "Hassler" will pass by on her return south and pick me or my remains and convey me or them to the States. My work is to make a large collection of Alaskan flora, and incidentally a few animals. I shall have with me one man who is to perform the duties of *chef de cuisine, valet de chambre,* chaplain, mind reader, weather prophet, and such other things as I may give him to do when time hangs heavy on his hands. I shall have a

98

lonesome vigil up in those gloomy forests with no one to talk to but my man Friday, but there are some fine points about it, mainly that at this spot is the finest bear hunting in the world today, and one of my small ambitions has been to kill a grizzly. This place, Yokutat [sic] Bay, is right up the coast 300 miles north of Sitka, which latter place, will, I suppose, be my postoffice.[1]

On his train journey from Washington, D.C., to the West Coast, Fred stopped in Lawrence and briefly at the Funston farm and in Iola. From there he left for San Francisco on April 4. Charlie Scott noted that "[h]is appointment to the work which he goes to perform was highly complimentary as there were a great many applicants [seventy-one] and he was chosen solely on his merits, his father not knowing that the appointment was so much as talked of until after it was made."[2] *The Wichita Daily Eagle* editorialized that it "is claimed that old man Funston's boy Fred is a better man to hustle offices than his dad. The young man got himself a government job paying $125 a month without the old man's knowledge."[3] Fred was commissioned a "Special Agent of the Department of Agriculture detailed for duty to the Division of Botany thereof," with pay at the rate of $1,500 per annum, beginning April 1, 1892.[4] This was a $300 per annum increase because of his assignment to field work. *The Lawrence Daily Journal* noted that while "the work to be done will be very hard...[t]he work is not in the hands of an inexperienced hand as Mr. Funston has had two years of the hardest kind of work in the line of this expedition and has always been successful in getting what he was after."[5]

Fred had an agreement with Charlie Scott to write letters for *The Iola Register's* readers telling about his Alaskan adventure. He was slow in getting started, since it was August 20 before he wrote his first letter. This was published on September 16, and was quickly followed by two other letters published October 14 and October 28, respectively. Ironically, Fred was already back home by the time the final letter appeared in print. He also wrote letters to relatives and friends while at Yakutat Bay. After the conclusion of the expedition, Fred composed his official "Field Report," which was included as a part of a government publication by Frederick Vernon Coville, "Botany of Yakutat Bay, Alaska." Several years later, he wrote two magazine articles, both published in 1896, about his experience and about Alaska: "The Territory of Alaska. From A Commercial Standpoint" and "Along Alaska's Eastern Boundary," which covered both of his Alaskan expeditions.[6]

The story of Fred's Yakutat Bay adventures will be told primarily through his three published letters, supplemented in brackets principally by appropriate material from his other writings and other sources. Fred's first letter from Yakutat Bay on August 20 started with an apology to the *Register's* readers:

The fact that letter writing in camp is the most unsatisfactory of all occupations is the only excuse I can give for so long neglecting my promise to give the readers of the REGISTER an idea of life up here at the jumping-off place of the world.[7]

[In accordance with my commission and letter of instructions to proceed to Yakutat Bay, Alaska, and make a collection of the plants of that vicinity, I took passage from San Francisco on the Coast Survey steamer *Hassler*, having purchased a camp outfit and hired a laborer to accompany me on the trip as cook and general camp employee. The *Hassler* sailed April 16, 1892...[8]]

[The laborer, Thomas White, had been a camp hand on Professor Israel C. Russel's United States Geological Survey expedition the year before to extend surveys previously made and to ascend Mount St. Elias.[9] Also on board the *Hassler* from the U. S. Geological Survey were the McGrath and Turner parties. The McGrath party was to develop the triangulation of Yakutat Bay in connection with the work to mark the 141st meridian. The party of J. Henry Turner would perform astronomical observations at Yakutat Bay.[10]]

I shall not burden my letter with a detailed account of the long voyage...although a volume could be written on that subject alone, and shall pass by briefly our visit to Port Townsend and the pleasant stay of three days at Victoria, the pretty capital of British Columbia, a town as thoroughly English as if it were situated on the banks of the Severn instead of the coast of Vancouver's Island. From Victoria the Hassler steamed to Departure Bay, B. C., for coal and after a stay of four days entered the famous "inside passage" for Alaska.

Tourists galore and the writers of guide books have described better than I can that wonderful channel between the islands and the mainland extending from Puget Sound, Washington, to Cross Sound, Alaska, by which the largest ship ever built can steam for fifteen hundred miles on salt water and never once be in sight of the open ocean or more than two miles from land on either side. Day after day and night after night the Hassler threaded that narrow and tortuous channel, sometimes three miles and sometimes three hundred feet

wide. On either side were mountains and impenetrable forests, the former sometimes rising almost sheer for a mile from
the water's edge. The water was as smooth as glass, and for
two weeks not a cloud crossed the sky. It was like navigating
some mighty river. Time and again it seemed that it was to
end where some huge snow-covered peak blocked the way; but
when the supposed obstruction was reached it was found that
the passage made a sharp turn either to right or left, and the
little steamer kept on its way. Occasionally an Indian village
with its inevitable totem poles was passed, and the natives
gathered in groups on the beach, while their thousand or less
of dogs barked furiously at the white ship plowing through
the water. More than once deer were seen at the water's edge,
while seal were as common as coyotes in Colorado.

We anchored for several days at Port Simpson, on the extreme northern coast of British Columbia, only twenty miles
from the Alaskan line. Inside a log stockade, bastioned and
loop-holed, are the low buildings of the trading post, and
floating over them the flag of the Hudson Bay Fur Company.
Port Simpson is pretty much behind the times, and things are
done here as they were years ago, when Sir George Simpson
and Alex. McKenzie ruled the Northwest Territory with a rod
of iron. The supply ship of the Fur Company calls a few times
a year, and sometimes a sealing schooner stops for water. The
Indians, a large number of whom live in the vicinity, are allowed inside the stockade to trade, a few at a time, first carefully depositing their muzzle-loading guns and sheath knives
on the outside. This indicates a distrust of the noble red man
that pained me greatly, and shows the hard-heartedness of
this great monopoly which has in such a ruthless manner put
a stop to the great biennial looting of the trading post and
massacre of the employees which in years past has furnished
so much amusement for these simple children of the forest.[11]

[There are about a dozen white people, traders and missionaries, and more than 800 Indians. These Indians are pretty tough citizens. In front of many of their houses are carved
wooden idols, some of them thirty feet high. These are called
"totem poles." The Indians on this coast are said to be the finest wood carvers in the world.

[The Indian name of Port Simpson is Metlakatla. You
know, we have a book about the place in the library called
"The Story of Metlakatla." We have been here three days, and
put in most of our time hunting and fishing. Yesterday some

of the sailors from the Hassler in a single haul of the seine caught two tubs full of fish—salmon, mackeral, halibut, and cod.[12]]

[We can notice that we are getting pretty far north already, and at night the northern light sweeps across the sky in great waves, and the days are getting so long that we do not have much dark and then [sic: the sun] sets at nine and rises at four.[13]]

After a stay of four days at this place we resumed our voyage up the seemingly endless inside passage, the country as we went farther north becoming more mountainous, with here and there, great glaciers extending from the beach far back into the mountains. On the thirteenth day of May the Hassler, rounding the northern end of Baranoff Island, dropped anchor in the harbor of Sitka, the capital of Alaska, where she remained for several days.

Sitka, with a population of two hundred whites, mostly Russians, and some eight hundred Indians, is the center of civilization in Uncle Sam's far northern possessions. Here are the marine barracks and the gunboat Pinta, to keep the natives straight, and the big Presbyterian mission school,— in charge, of course, of a Kansas man, Mr. Alfred Docking. The Greek Church of the Russians also controls an Indian school, while the old, Russian church is one of the sights of Sitka. On a big rock near the harbor is "Baranoff Castle" the old residence of Admiral Baranoff, one of the early Russian governors. We climbed the steps and looked through the now empty rooms where years ago the frisky old Admiral and his bibulous companions used to hold high jinks through the long winter nights, and where many a luckless Thlinket caught in some petty infraction of the laws has been sentenced to death or to the knout. While we lay at Sitka the harbor was enlivened by the presence of the United States men of war "Mohican" and "Adams," on their way to Bering Sea to protect the seal rookeries from the Canadian poachers.

After a few pleasant days in Sitka we started on the last stretch of our long voyage, only to encounter a furious northeasterly gale, and be compelled to put back to Sitka for shelter or be battered to pieces. I shall not attempt a description of that storm, but merely say that the captain of the Hassler, who has been for twenty years an officer in the navy, had never seen its equal. The next start from Sitka, made two days later, was more fortunate, and everything went well. On the morning of the nineteenth of May everybody was on deck gazing at what men who have seen all that the world has to offer in the way of mountains, agree is without comparison the grandest mountain picture on the face of the earth. The day was perfectly clear, and we were running along the coast about ten miles off shore. Stretching along the coast, separated from the beach by only a narrow strip of low forest, and unobstructed by foot-hills, rose the long line of tremendous peaks that make up the so-called St. Elias Alps, among them Fairweather, Crillon, La Perouse and others more than 16,000 feet high. As far as the eye could reach, north and south, was that panorama of peaks and glaciers. The mountains were spotless white from base to summit, and the reflection of the white range in the blue water of the ocean is simply beyond description.

And along such a picture as this we steamed all of that never-to-be-forgotten day. At seven o'clock in the morning the officer on watch announced a large peak far ahead. Away in the dim distance, apparently isolated from the other mountains, was what looked like a white cone peering above the horizon. It was Mt. St. Elias *one hundred and eighty miles away*, the highest mountain on the continent north of Orizaba. The ship's course was headed straight for the peak, and at five o'clock there appeared a wide opening in the range, into which the Hassler steamed, and an hour later dropped anchor a few hundred yards off the Thlinket village in Yakutat Bay, after an eventful voyage of thirty-three days from San Francisco.

Why Dame Nature saw fit to stick away up here in this corner of the world, far beyond the route of tourist travel, with no one to gaze upon them but a few savages and an occasional explorer, the Malaspina Glacier and Mt. St. Elias, is a mystery. At the risk of overdoing the scenery business I shall attempt a brief description of these two sights. It is best, probably, to begin with a few comparisons. The great peaks of the Rockies and Sierra Nevada, having an average elevation above the sea of 14,000 feet, either rise from plateaus nearly half as high or are surrounded by foot hills and other mountains to such an extent that nearly half their height is lost. Although I have never seen the Alps, naval officers who have visited them tell me that such is the case with them as well as with the Andes. As seen from Yakutat Bay, Mt. St. Elias rises from the sea level to the tremendous height of 18,100 feet, or three and one half miles. No large peak is in the immediate vicinity, and no foot hill obstructs the view. It is a perfect mountain, rising by steep and regular ascents to a square-topped peak. Although heroic attempts to reach the summit have been made by Schwatka and Russell [sic: Russel], the mountain has never been climbed, and probably never will be. Its elevation, 18,100 feet, was definitely ascertained last year by Prof. Russell [sic], after complete and accurate observations.

People who visit the Alps and the Sierra Nevada are shown what are called "glaciers"—large patches of dirty, hard-packed snow with a ridge of stones along the edges and cracks or crevasses in the snow indicating that there is a downward motion. These glaciers are sometimes a mile or two long and several hundred yards wide and, I am told are regarded as worth a hard climb to see. We have here at Yakutat Bay what we regard as a very respectable glacier, it being the largest in the world. A few figures may give some idea of its dimensions. The frontage, from Yakutat Bay to Icy Cape is *ninety miles*, the extent from the beach to its head is from fifteen to twenty-five miles, and the thickness of the pure blue ice of which it is composed may be judged by the fact that crevasses wide enough to drop the State House at Topeka into have been sounded to a depth of *thirteen hundred* feet,—a great field of ice as large as the Second congressional district moving slowly but with irresistible force to the sea. From its surface come from time to time rumblings and boomings like distant thunder as new crevasses are formed or the old ones widened. Such is the world's greatest glacier,—the Malaspina. It was amid such sights that we were to spend the summer.

No sooner had the Hassler anchored than some thirty Indians, mostly women and children, pushed off in canoes and came on board with baskets, furs, trinkets and other native products for sale. The Thlinket village is composed of some twenty odd-looking houses in which live about two hundred people. The Alaskan builds his house on a plan peculiar to the country. Doors are dispensed with, and entrance is had through a round hole about two feet in diameter, through which the visitor wriggles himself, and as soon as he has recovered from the peculiar odor and his eyes become used to the darkness, finds squatted about on the floor about a dozen men, women and children, the men dressing skins, the women making baskets and the children wallowing in filth. In the middle of the floor a brisk fire is kept burning, the smoke escaping through a hole left in the roof for that purpose. Each house is occupied by from two to six families, who seem to get along together remarkably well.

The Thlinkets are a queer mixture,—ten parts of barbarism to one of civilization. But little attention is paid to the decencies of life. Polygamy is common, and women and children are bought and sold as are cattle in Kansas, to whomever wants to buy. By paying the price, from thirty to one hundred dollars, a man becomes the absolute owner of a woman. I saw a boy about thirteen years old sold by his father for one hundred dollars. All of this in the United States of America in this year of Grace 1892. But these people have their good points; thieving is almost unknown, and they take excellent care of the aged and infirm. In the three months that I have been among them I have yet to see the first quarrel. Three years ago the Swedish Lutherans established a mission among them, and have some thirty children in the mission school. These youngsters are taught the English language, and are compelled to keep clean and live like whites. The mission school-ma'am is a native born Kansas girl.

When dressed for some holiday occasion these Indians, especially the young men and women, are by no means bad looking. The children are healthy and fine looking, and when kept clean are remarkably pretty. The Thlinkets bear little or no resemblance to the Indians of the States; the complexion is lighter and clearer, and the features more regular and pleasing. The prominent cheek-bone is wanting, while the eyes have a decided slant. In fact a Thlinket would appear less at home at San Carlos or Pine Ridge than in Yokohama. I never saw a happier or more contented people. They have all they want to eat and wear. Salmon are so plentiful that they are killed with clubs in the streams. Yakutat Bay swarms with the hair seal, while shell fish are found by the boat load. During the summer season the woods are full of wild berries. The trader gives good prices for their furs and baskets and deals squarely with them. [The baskets, made by the Indian women, are made from the root of a tree, which is "boiled and split very fine, and are very ornamental on account of the pretty patterns woven into them. They are nearly water tight and sell from $1 to $2.50."[14]] They [the Indians] have never had any trouble with the whites and the result is that white men are liked and welcomed. This is the case more with Yakutat than with some other Thlinket villages. More than twenty years ago Sitka was the scene of a terrible battle between the Indians and a force of soldiers and sailors, and about ten years ago the man of war "Adams" bombarded and totally destroyed Killisnoo, on account of the murders of white men.[15]

[On the night following our arrival there arose a heavy southeasterly wind, accompanied by rain, which continued with great violence for five days; so that it was not until May 25 that I was able to establish my camp on shore. In order to have some place suitable for storing supplies and caring for specimens, I rented from the natives a house situated in the smaller of their two villages, on Khantaak Island: the larger village being on the mainland, distant about a mile.[16]]

In a letter to one of his old college friends dated June 8, Fred described his situation, including the status of his botanical work:

I am now well established in my first camp and shall remain here until about July, when I shall go to the upper end of the bay for the remainder of the season. Up there I shall be among the St. Elias grizzly and I am going to nip some of them. They are terrors, and the Indians are afraid to hunt them.

My present camp is near a village of Thinket [sic] Indians. They are a fine sort of people for Indians and live by hunting, sealing, and fishing.

A great sight yesterday morning was nine canoe loads of them killing seals in the bay just off my camp....

I am camped in a very pretty spot on a narrow tongue of land near the entrance to the Bay. A hundred feet from my back door are the waters of the bay, as blue and quiet as a mill pond while fifty feet from my front door the surf comes rolling in from the open ocean booming and roaring every hour out of the twenty four. For scenery in my back yard I have Mt. St. Elias and the Malaspina glacier.

The great institution up here is the long summer day. It has not been dark here for three weeks and will not be until August. At 10 p.m. the sun was a short distance below the horizon just enough to make good twilight, and is in sight again by 2 a.m. One can read ordinary print with ease at midnight.

I am doing some great work in the botanical line, and am going to surprise the people in the Department of Agriculture with my collection of posies.

I am afraid that I have made a fizzle of my Kodak work. I send you by this mail the first roll of 48 films. I do not think that more than half of them are any good. However I wish you would arrange with some photographer to develop and print all that anything can be made out of. I will pay the bill when I return or you can pay and I will refund to you. Dont [sic] let any one charge too much. Get the best rate you can. The films are 4 x 5 most of them instantaneous.

The Hassler leaves this evening for Sitka so that this letter will not be long in reaching you.[17]

Except for biweekly trips to Sitka, the crew of the *Hassler* spent the remainder of the time at Yakutat Bay sounding it and making a chart of its shores.[18] The *Hassler* provided Fred an interesting adventure in early June:

Several days ago the Hassler's steam launch having the whale boat in tow crossed to the north side of the bay and by means of the whale boat effected a landing through the surf at the place where last year the revenue cutter "Bear" lost six men by the swamping of a boat.

It was an exciting experience. The crew ran the boat in through the breakers stern first. We all had to jump at a signal from the coxwain [sic], but I got in a hurry and jumped too soon and got a hell of ducking. Capt. Harber jumped next and made it O.K. McGrath got a worse bath than I did. It was a great experience. At times the boat would be at angle of 45 degrees and slide like a duck down the big roller. One of these threw more than two barrels of water into her.

We walked along the beach at the edge of the Malaspina glacier, for half a mile and in that time saw the tracks of more than a dozen grizzlies. The tracks of one measured seven by thirteen inches. Just wait until I get over there. We reached the launch after another bout with the surf, and in three hours steaming returned to the Hassler.[19]

Fred's interest in killing a grizzly was more than for the thrill of it; he also had a monetary motivation. On July 5, he wrote to the "Supt, National Museum" in Washington, D. C., inquiring "what price the Museum will pay for good specimens suitable for mounting of the black horned white goat, [illegible] ground bear or St. Elias grizzly, white marmot, and other mammals of this region."[20] The Smithsonian Institution ("United States National Museum") responded "that it is not our practice to offer fixed sum of money for such material." Nevertheless, if Fred sent to the Smithsonian a list of what items he could furnish and what he would expect for payment, the museum would "take up matter."[21]

In a letter to his father at the end of July, Fred reported that "[e]verything is going well with me. I have had excellent health though I am living a pretty rough life and am wet to the skin nearly every day. The only means of travel in this country is by water [in a canoe] along the shores of the bay and up the rivers."[22] Fred focused on the details of canoe travel in his second letter published in *The Iola Register*:

A person who would cast his lot at Yakutat Bay, or in fact anywhere on the Alaskan coast, must of necessity become an expert in the use of the light and "nobby" spruce canoes of the country or confine his wanderings to the immediate vicinity of his own domicile. As the burro is to New Mexico and the mustang to Texas, so is the canoe to the Thlinket of Alaska. No one walks in Alaska, at least in this part of it, neither does he ride, as the horse and the mule have not yet made their advent into the tangled and gloomy forests of the far Northwest.

To me, accustomed to fine, open forests of the Rockies and the Sierra Nevada, the forests of the Alaskan coast are a revelation. The trees are not large, compared with those of the western Territories; in fact, the average size is much smaller. But it is the density of growth, the network of fallen trees in all stages of decay which cover the ground in picturesque confusion, the deep and soft spagrum [sic] or moss, and above all the dense and tangled undergrowth of black alder, "devil clubs" and wild currant bushes that makes the forests absolutely impenetrable. In some parts of the forest near Yakutat it would be a hard day's work for a man unencumbered by a load to push his way for a mile. Climbing over the slippery and moss-covered logs, and pushing his way inch by inch through thorny bushes, falling into a spagrum [sic] swamp knee deep every moment, tormented by mosquitoes and black flies, he would be likely to give up the job in disgust after half an hour's effort and never attempt it again. [One day I tried to make a short cut through the woods from a river to the beach about as far as from our house to the cross roads [a half mile] and it took me just four hours to get through.[23]]

In such a country it is no wonder that the dug-out canoe has reached a high development and that all communication is by water, either along the coast or up the numerous rivers and bays. The Yakutat canoe is acknowledged to be superior in lightness and in beauty of model to those made anywhere else on the Alaskan coast. Each canoe is made from a single piece of well seasoned white spruce. The rough work is done with an axe, and the finishing with a curiously constructed knife with curved blade. The canoes, when completed, range from ten to twenty feet in length, and from two to four feet in width. The prow is ram shaped and the sides are about an inch thick. The smaller canoes weigh not more than a hundred pounds, and can be easily dragged along the bank. There are no seats, and the occupants kneel on the bottom facing toward the prow. Light paddles above five feet long are used in place of oars. Three rapid strokes are made on each side alternately, and as the occupant faces the prow instead of the stern as in a skiff he steers the canoe easily with the paddle. [They are so light and narrow that they are very easily upset until one gets used to them but after getting used to handling them they are a great thing. At first I got upset several times but now can handle one as well as an Indian.[24] [I] even went so far as to paddle more than 200 yards standing erect.[25]]

The smaller canoes, those ten feet long, carry from one to four persons and the larger ones eight or ten. This does not include the great cedar war canoes, of which there are several in each village. The Yakutat chief has one of these forty feet long and five feet across, made from a single log. I saw this canoe at one time loaded with eighteen people, ten dogs and a large amount of camp equipage. The Thlinket does not hesitate to go far out to sea in the smallest canoes, and the Hassler passed some off Cape Manby thirty miles from land on the open ocean where the rollers were ten feet high. To one who has not seen it done it is beyond comprehension how a light canoe whose sides are only a foot above the water can ride like a duck over billows of such height.

An experience of my own will give an idea of the use to which these light canoes can be put. It became necessary in the course of my work for me to take a trip from Yakutat to Cape Manby, a distance of twenty miles, on the open ocean. I had with me my camp hand [Thomas White], a white man whose experience with canoes was about as limited as my own. The trip was made in my canoe, a craft twelve feet long, two feet wide and weighing about two hundred pounds. After waiting for several days, we made the start on a beautiful June morning, and paddling over the smooth, glassy waters of Mulgrave Bay rounded the point of Khautack [sic: Khantaak]

Island and were soon on the open Pacific ocean, where the long swell coming in made us bob up and down like a cork. The canoe would mount a big roller, and slide down into the trough of the sea as gracefully as a swan.

This was all very well as long as there was no wind, but the Alaskan weather resembles the Kansas Democracy, inasmuch as one never knows what freak to expect next. So it happened that within an hour or two after leaving camp the wind rose from the southeast, which in this country always means a gale. But we had started and were not going to return to Yakutat, to be jeered at by the officers of the Hassler, who had predicted that we would be back in an hour. It was not long before the increasing wind had kicked up an angry sea, and we had a serious job on hands [sic]. The long smooth rollers had given place to rough and boisterous waves, or "white caps," and we were tossed about in a fearful manner. Every time the canoe caught a big wave she took a lot of water over the side, and it kept me busy baling out while White paddled. An ordinary river skiff would not have lived a minute in such a sea, but the little canoe did nobly. It is true that she took in water over the side, but even a whaleboat would have done that. Often it seemed that she was going to be up-ended, but she always came down with her keel squarely underneath. Under such conditions, paddling was hard and exasperating work, and our progress in the teeth of the wind was by no means rapid.

We had been steering by Mount St. Elias, but about noon there appeared before us the low, tree-covered coast near Cape Manby, and in a few hours more we were a few hundred yards off the beach, ready for that most dangerous and trying task connected with boating on the open ocean, landing through the surf. It is a tame affair to land in a boat in the smooth waters of a harbor, but a most serious undertaking to control and steer a boat or canoe through the lines of roaring and tumbling breakers that line the coast of the open ocean. Absolute coolness and self control are more necessary than strength and skill in landing a canoe through breakers. One timid person may capsize the craft at a critical moment and drown everyone in it. It was on the identical spot where we landed that exactly one year before the revenue cutter, "Bear," lost a lieutenant and six men by the capsizing of a whale-boat in making a landing. Owing to the wind the surf was unusually high and we made preparations for an upset by removing our shoes and the greater part of our clothing. After numerous words of caution to each other not to get "rattled," we paddled into the first line of breakers and headed for the beach four hundred yards away, where the surf was booming ominously. Our great solicitude now was to keep the boat straight, that is so that the incoming rollers would strike square astern and not on the quarter, as that would throw her broadside on with the chances in favor of a capsize. We had worked her slowly and carefully and were within a hundred feet of the sandy beach, ready for the criticacal [sic] moment of going in on the last breaker, called the "curler," from the way the top curls over. I steadied the canoe as the big fellow nearly ten feet high struck us, and we slid up over it like a duck, taking on board, however, half a barrel of water. It was exciting work and hard to keep perfectly cool, and one of us— probably both—blundered and we did not get far enough in on this breaker, with the result that the next one struck us unprepared, and we got the looked for ducking. Luckily the accident happened so near the beach that the water was not more than waist deep and before the next breaker came we got out, dragging the canoe with us. We had been eight hours in going twenty-four miles—a distance which could be covered in much less time in smooth weather.

Our return two days later was made miserable by a rain storm which obscured the land so that we were compelled to steer by a pocket compass. This time we were out eleven hours.

The example given above will give a fair idea of canoeing under the most unfavorable circumstances. On the smooth glassy waters lying between Khautack [sic: Khantaak] Island and the Thlinket village it was altogether a different matter, and was a favorite exercise to take a spin of a few hours over the Auskow river to gather strawberries or to Knight Island to shoot plover.

Speaking of strawberries it may be a surprise to some people to know that away up here in the land of glaciers and icebergs, the strawberry is found in such quantities and such size and flavor as to be almost beyond belief.... The Indians nearly live on them during the season and the bears eat a great many, but with all that countless numbers rot on the vines.

There are also in the woods immense numbers of wild red raspberries called salmon berries.... In addition to the above the woods contain large numbers of huckleberries which form the leading article of food among the Indians. These various fruits with the great plenty of fish and game add not a little to the comfort of camp life in Alaska.

As would be supposed the great bug-bear here is the weather. There are some bright days and I have even seen ten consecutive days of perfectly cloudless weather at Yakutat Bay, days in which the sea was of glassy smoothness and the sky as blue as that of California.

But when the rain begins it never knows when the job is finished. At one time the water poured down in torrents and the wind blew a furious gale for eleven days and nights without cessation. During such time we remained housed up reading the magazines or entertaining our Thlinket visitors who overwhelmed us on such occasions.

A phenomenon peculiar to these northern latitudes is the long summer daylight. There was not a time from our arrival on the nineteenth of May until July 20 when one could not read ordinary print at midnight even when there was no moon.

In the interval between sunset and sunrise there was a mellow twilight in which objects at a distance were seen as plainly as at noon. On June 21 the sun was in sight for twenty-two hours and when it set at 11 p.m. sank only a few degrees below the northern horizon to appear again at 1 p.m. [sic: 1 a.m.]

Of course the corresponding season in winter is just the reverse where the sun sneaks up the fog banks in the middle of the forenoon or later and remains in sight only a few hours. So that taken as an average the Alaskan system of dividing the light and darkness is not superior to that in use in Kansas.[26]

In his July 31 letter to his "Pa," Fred told more about his life at Yakutat Bay, which included grizzly bears and the local Indians:

A week ago the Hassler steam launch took a trip to Disenchantment Bay and I went along. We steamed along the edge of a field of floating ice miles across, and were among unusual icebergs. We passed close to the foot of the Hubbard glacier, one of the largest in the world, and saw the icebergs breaking off and floating out to sea. I am going up there again in a few days and stay two weeks.

So far I have not killed a grizzly but expect to before coming home. About three weeks ago some sailors from the Hassler while out hunting met a big grizzly and fired on him. He charged them twice and they had to run, but finally killed him. The bear was struck ten times before he gave up, the ball that killed him struck him in the eye and penetrated the brain. He measured 9 ft. 4 in. long and his weight was estimated at 1800 pounds. They are dangerous brutes to handle.

So far I have got along pretty well with the Indians though they have made me some trouble but I have let them understand that I am not afraid of them. They have been having a funeral today and have been raising Cain singing, dancing and feasting. I photographed about a dozen of them this morning. The only thing that keeps them quiet is the fear of the gunboat at Sitka. It has come up here several times to cool them off in recent years. They have no government agents and live as they used to before the Russians came. There is a mission at the village where most of the children attend school. One of the missionaries, Miss Carlson is from McPherson county Kansas....

When we dont [sic] want fish, we can have clams cockles or crabs and plover. This forenoon in an hour I killed 52 plover, ten of them at one shot. So Alaska is not a bad country to live in.[27]

In the July trip on the *Hassler* to Disenchantment Bay, Fred saw enough "to be anxious for a further acquaintance and at once made preparations for a two weeks' stay." Disenchantment Bay had received its name in 1794 when it proved, upon exploration, to be only a fishhook-shaped extension of Yakutat Bay rather than the western terminus of the long-sought Northwest Passage. In his third letter to *The Iola Register,* Fred told about this further challenging adventure (without identifying it, I have divided one paragraph into two paragraphs):

A tent, a goodly store of provisions, a shot gun and two rifles, and the outfit necessary for my botanical work were loaded into two twelve-foot canoes, and a start made early on the morning of August 2. In one of the canoes was the man White, who was with me on the canoe trip to Cape Manby, while in the other, besides myself, was a mentally diluted Norwegian whose chief characteristic was a tendency to do everything at the wrong time and spend as much time as possible in doing it.

The start was made at 5 a.m. and the course lay almost

due north to the head of Yakutat Bay, a distance of twenty-five miles. The sky was perfectly clear, and a good breeze coming from the south, but not enough to make a heavy sea. Each canoe carried a light mast with a sprit-sail of forty-eight square feet of canvas. With the wind fairly behind us, it can be imagined that we did no paddling on this trip, but depended entirely on sails. Altogether, it was the most enjoyable canoe trip I have ever taken, and was not marred by a mishap of any kind. We kept up the bay about five miles off shore, and ten hours after leaving camp entered Disenchantment Bay, and three hours later landed about six miles from the entrance, directly opposite the great Dalton glacier. We had sighted a great many icebergs since noon and found Disenchantment Bay a veritable nest of them, but by hugging the shore and using our wits to good advantage avoided them and skirted along the edge of the ice field for several miles without a collision.

The place selected for a camp was at the mouth of one of the wide canons [sic] opening back into the St. Elias Alps, and as there is no surf here the landing was an exceedingly tame affair, and in an hour the tent had been pitched and a good warm supper stowed away. We were in what seemed to me the jumping-off place of the world,—away in the heart of the St. Elias Alps. Before our camp lay the blue glassy waters of the bay, seeming more like a great river than an arm of the sea. Everywhere almost straight up from the beach rose the granite mountains, steep and rugged beyond comprehension. No trees were to be seen but some stunted willows and alders grew in the sheltered canons, and on these we depended for fuel. Directly across the bay from our camp, a distance of some three miles, was the Dalton glacier, having a frontage on the water of two miles, and a few miles farther up the Hubbard glacier, with a frontage of five miles. Both these glaciers extend back into the mountains about fifteen miles,—this being only an estimate, as they have never been explored. The ice of which they are composed is about five hundred feet thick. From these glaciers come the hundreds of icebergs, large and small, that crowd Disenchantment Bay and line the western shore of Yakutat Bay as far as Cape Manby. Just beyond the Hubbard glacier is Mt. Seattle, which, like the glaciers, was named last year by Prof. Russel. This is something of a mountain in its weak way, rising to a height of nearly 16,000 feet above the waters of the bay.

A few days after our arrival I climbed a mountain about 4,000 feet high situated just back of our camp, and got a good general view of the mountain range and of Yakutat and Disenchantment Bays. From here could be seen unbroken snow fields miles across, and glaciers without number. I tried from this point to count the icebergs in sight, but it was too much like counting the stars and I gave it up after getting somewhere in the hundreds. All of this in the dog days, when people in the States were worrying themselves into premature old age trying to keep cool.

In such out of the way places as this one is generally struck with the total absence of sound and awed by the unbroken stillness that pervades the whole region. I well remember that nearly two years ago, when our little party surmounted the crest of the Panamint range and looked for the first time into the depths of Death Valley, what created the most lasting impression was not the shining white bottom a thousand feet below, nor the dim gray haze, nor the red peaks of the Funeral range, but the deathlike silence that made one almost afraid to speak. But here the case was as different as could be imagined, and avalanches in the mountains, the grinding of icebergs as they came into collision, or as a new one was formed by separating from a glacier front, the widening of crevasses, together with the everlasting screeches of gulls and other sea fowl, kept up a pandemonium of noise which for the first night of our stay made sleep impossible. Often a field of snow and ice a mile across and probably a hundred feet thick would break loose from its perch up on the mountain and come tearing down to the valley thousands of feet below, sweeping away everything in its course. If it were in a distant part of the range, thirty miles or so distant, we would hear only a series of low rumbles lasting but a few moments but if, on the other hand, it were within two or three miles, the roaring was terrific, and seemed to shake the earth, while the echoes thrown back from different parts of the range continued for several minutes after the avalanche had reached the bottom. The roar of one big slide would hardly have died away before things would break loose somewhere else; and so the show went merrily on, day and night, during our two weeks' stay.

My closest acquaintance with an avalanche was at the distance of about two miles. White and I had gone in a canoe to a rocky island in the middle of the bay to shoot ptarmigan, and were just preparing to return to camp when I chanced to look toward Mt. Seattle and saw that something was wrong. Up on a spur of the mountain which rose about 8,000 feet above the waters of the bay clouds of loose snow were being whisked about by the wind, and we could see that there was a downward movement of a large section of the snow field. The progress was at first apparently slow, but it soon gathered headway as it advanced, and then, widening like a partially opened fan, swept with terrific speed down to the bay a mile and a half in vertical height below. The path cut by the slide was about four hundred yards wide at the top, but by the time it reached the bottom had spread out to a mile. The sight, as that mass of contless [sic] thousands of tons of ice, snow and rock struck the quiet waters of the bay, beggars description. In the water where the avalanche struck were a large number of icebergs, most of them small, however, and, rather than risk suspicion of drawing the long bow, I will not say how high, in my opinion, some of these, and the surrounding water, were thrown by the force of the impact, but will leave that to be guessed. Shortly after the slide started we heard the first rumblings, but by the time it reached the bottom the roar was almost deafening. I afterward learned from the officers of the "Hassler" that it was heard distinctly on board the ship thirty-five miles distant. Of course, a tremendous agitation of the water produced a tidal wave that would have swamped any boat and would have seriously troubled a ship. Within a minute or two a wave more than ten feet high swept by the little island that we were on, followed by others gradually diminishing in size, and it was nearly an hour before we would trust ourselves in the canoe. We would have had a frolicsome time if we had been caught in a canoe when it occurred. The water was agitated nearly all night, and the ice cakes and bergs rubbing and grinding against each other rumbled and grumbled for hours. It seems that there is a screw loose somewhere when such a magnificent spectacle is witnessed by but two men and one of them,—the other fellow, not myself,—a very common and unappreciative sort of chump, when thousands of people travel around the earth to see less.

But enough of avalanches. A visit made a few days later to the Dalton glacier was full of interest. We worked our way in a canoe through several miles of floating ice to within a few hundred feet of the ice wall of the glacier front, where we lay for an hour watching pieces large and small detach themselves and float out into the water. The forming of an iceberg, while an interesting sight, is such a small affair compared with an avalanche that it seems hardly worth describing. As the pressure of the upper part of a glacier forces the lower part out into the water, the ice is undermined by the action of the waves underneath and breaks by its own weight with a crash like a field piece and, tumbling into the water, "turns turtle" two or three times and finally floats off, a full fledged berg, growing smaller and smaller every day from the action of the sun and waves, until finally it takes its last roll and dis-appears. A large iceberg breaking off creates a considerable wave, which makes fooling about in the vicinity in a small boat rather ticklish business.

We remained for two weeks in the midst of icebergs and avalanches, and enjoyed life hugely. We killed ptarmigan by the dozen. The harmless bird which bears this euphonic name is about half the size of a prairie chicken, and as a table delicacy is several points ahead of that fowl. They are found in great numbers in the low willow brush in the canons, and make first class wing shooting. We tried experiment of eating two Arctic woodchucks, animals about the size of raccoons, and found them excellent. But finally the time came to return to Yakutat, and we left Disenchantment Bay to the possession of the seals, gulls and fishhawks, launched the two canoes, got caught in a gale and knocked about Yakutat Bay all night, and finally came into our old camp tired, wet and hungry.[28]

On August 19, three days after his return to his camp, Fred wrote his mother, telling her that "[w]e had fine weather all the time and saw some of the finest scenery in the world." He also shared with her both his feelings at that time and his wardrobe needs:

I am getting mighty tired of this exploring trade, and dont [sic] think I shall ever come out on another trip though I may, as there is considerable money in it. This trip has not been so profitable to me as the Death Valley expedition, because it did not last so long, and I spent considerable money in outfitting for this trip, such as camera, shotgun and clothing.

The Hassler will leave here on her return to San Francisco about Sept 15, reaching Port Townsend Wash. about Oct 1. I shall leave the ship at Port Townsend and come home by rail, saving five days time.

I am in a rather bad fix for clothes to come home in, so I wish that you would send to me by express at Port Townsend my good suit hanging in the closet and my shirts collars and cuffs. I think that I may be mistaken and send the key to my trunk. You had better express the things in one of Pa's valises, leaving it unlocked but well strapped. If you cannot get a valise you had better make a stout package but be careful that the clothes will not get badly mashed. Two or three shirts will be enough to send.

Send it as soon as you get this and address the package Port Townsend, Washington "<u>To</u> <u>be</u> <u>held</u> <u>until</u> <u>arrival</u> <u>of</u> <u>U.S.S.</u> <u>Hassler</u>".

Write me at Port Townsend care of the Hassler whether you have sent the clothes. Any more mail sent to me here will miss me.

If any mail comes for me at home hold until I return.

I hope that attending to all these jobs will not be to [sic] much trouble for you.[29]

Fred apparently had moved into the Indian house that he rented for storage purposes, and on August 20, the day after writing his mother, he wrote to Buck Franklin: "It is raining like hell today in order to keep up the record, and all morning I have been shivering over a smoky fire, damning the climate and have just mustered up sufficient energy to schreiben a letter to my only Buck." He further noted that with the fire built in the middle of the floor of the Indian house he resided in, the smoke escaped through a hole in the roof designed for that purpose, but he lamented that "on rainy days like this a d____d sight bigger volume of rain comes through the hole than there is of smoke coming out."[30]

After describing for Buck his recent "hell of a trip" to Disenchantment Bay, Fred discussed several important subjects:

I must make the sorry confession that I have not slain a grizzly as yet. I have seen places where the ground was tracked up like a cattle corral, but they keep themselves in the impenetrable brush and it is almost impossible to hunt them without dogs. Yesterday a party of Indians came in with their grizzlies. I am going to take a hunt in a few days and believe I can have some sort of luck. Damn it! I <u>must</u> kill a bear before I leave this country.

A party of sailors from the Hassler while out hunting near Pt. Manby recenty [sic: recently] encountered a grizzly and killed him after a terrible fight. He charged them twice and was hit ten times before he gave up. His Jags measured 9 ft 4 in from tip to tip.

I have received two letters from you recently, one from

Estes Park and the other after your return to Lawrence. As to the films, when we went to change the roll we found that something was the matter with the d____d camera, and the turning business was not taking the roll off as it should so that it was not exhausted. I made a number of other exposures and about three weeks ago got the roll off and sent it to you, so you have probably received it by this time. I have no hopes of any pictures in that roll as everything went wrong with it. I fixed the "masheen" and have run off another roll, and as soon as I can rig up a dark room shall take it off and send to you. I have great hopes of them. Be sure to keep the pictures in chronological order, so that I can identify them on my return.

As the time approaches to go home I am beginning to be glad to leave this country, although my summer here has been a regular picnic....

I hear often from the estimable young woman [Maude Richards] formerly of the New England Conservatory, but now of Iola. During the coming year she is to run the music department of St. Charles College, near St. Louis.

I expect to visit the young "ooman" [sic] on my return to the States.

So E. June [Scott] thinks I am hardly up to the estimable you, in physique, does she? <u>Well</u> I'll be <u>damned</u>! What does E. J. know about my physique?

Remember me to the Sutliffe's [sic] and other friends.[31]

Immediately after getting settled at Yakutat Bay in May, Fred began collecting specimens of flora. This had continued until the time he wrote Buck. Because of the great humidity and almost daily rains, the drying papers for the specimens had to be changed two or three times each day, and often they had to be dried by hand over a fire before they could be returned to the specimen presses. During the collecting season, Fred used about ten cords of wood for these fires.

After Fred's return to his camp on August 16, the "exceptionally favorable" weather changed and "[t]he rain poured in torrents nearly every day during the latter half of August, though some collecting was done in the intervals [between the downpours]. The rainfall is said to have been heavier in the summer of 1892 than in any other since the American occupation of Alaska. From my arrival at Yakutat Bay on May 19 until my departure on September 4, a period 107 days, there were but 24 days wholly without rain."[32]

The summer had been a success for Fred. He had collected about

3,000 specimens representing 154 different species. On September 4, Fred boarded the *Hassler* for his return trip to San Francisco. Fred left ship at Port Townsend on October 3.[33] Taking the train, he arrived home on Saturday, October 15. Charlie Scott described Fred as "looking as if his long summer in Alaska has agreed with him."[34] Fred was home for the November election in which his father was re-elected to the House of Representatives. For the Science Club at the State University, he gave a lecture with fifty-four stereopticon views titled "A Summer on the Alaskan Coast." This was described as "very entertainingly given."[35] Fred left by train on November 10 for Washington, D. C., to arrange and classify the plants he had collected.[36] His $1,500 per annum salary was reduced to $1,200 per annum because of his change of assignment from the field to Washington, D.C.[37]

From his winter quarters at 213 North Capitol Street in Washington, Fred wrote three letters which have survived, all of which are significant in this story of Fred's early life, and thus are set out in full below. The first letter, dated November 27, was written to Buck Franklin:

> My dear Buck:
> I am all by my lonely tonight, and am going to put in a part of the evening talking to my ownest own. Well, Old Box of Matches, how are you anyhow. You darking old seducer, how are Gertrude, Lucinda, Effie June and other victims who have been ruined by you and then cast aside to make room for others doomed to satisfy your horrible lust, Seloh?
> Gawd, Buck, you just ought to see how I am fixed here, all by myself in a good double room, about three hundred yards north of the Capitol. I believe in being comfortable and I am going it on that score this winter, but in other directions I am hauling in my hours,—that is I am neither sporting, nor fooling with the fair ones not a little bit.
> Did you go to Lincoln [Nebraska], and if so did you see my estimable young "ooman"? [Maude Richards] What do you think of her? How does she stack up compared with Lucinda? I take the K. C. Star and see that the Doughnuts downed us at football, but that our boys braced up when it came to tackling Missouri. I have not learned the result of the Lincoln game.
> I saw a great game Thanksgiving day between Columbia Athletic Club and Georgetown College. Latter won 12-0.
> I got about 3/4 full a few nights ago, and enjoyed myself hugely but am not going to do it anymore. It don't pay.
> Well—How are the Lawrence girls? Damm [sic] it, I would

half like to live it [sic: in] Lawrence just because of the spright-
ly young dames, whom I know. By Jove, I came near getting
stuck on young Berry, the night she was at Sutliff's and sang
for us. She is a smooth little girl and not so infernally cyclonic
as her older sister.

I have just read a new book "Barbara Dering," a sequel to
"Quick or the Dead" by that suave young thing Amélie Rives
Chanler. Gawd it is an amorous story—just boiling over with
hugging and kissing bouts. I had to have a glass of ice water
within reach while I read in order to keep from going stark
mad and rushing with a frantic yell down to the Division. You
must get hold of the book and read it.

About ten days ago I wrote Kellogg to express to me my
Kodak and umbrella, but he don't seem to have done it. Wish
one of you would attend to it for me soon.

Tell Goat to write me how he made it on that election bet.
When you express those things don't forget to put on my street
number or I will never get them.

Recently I obtained several copies of the N. Y. Times of
last spring that had my Death Valley letter in it. I send you
a copy by this mail. Am going to do lots of that style of work
this winter.

Write me soon.

Lovingly

Gric [38]

Fred's reference to drinking alcohol to an excess one night, but
then concluding that "[i]t don't pay" is of particular interest in view
of his apparent collegiate drinking experiences. Whether Fred's reference to having a glass of ice water within reach to control his sexual
arousal in reading Barbara Dering's story is literally true or simply a
part of his sense of humor is impossible to determine.

The next letter Fred wrote was to his mother on December 14:

Dear Ma

I received a letter from you about two weeks ago but have
neglected answering because I am so busy. I am putting in all
my spare time now writing up my Alaska trip for the eastern
papers and it is pretty slow work.

It still looks as if I will get to go to Alaska next year for
a stay of a year and a half. I have not much fear of losing my
job with the new administration. [Democrat Grover Cleveland
had been elected President of the United States.]

I am sorry that my boxes were in such a damaged condition. I wish you would pack all of the baskets and all of the other Indian curiosities in a box and send to me by express. There are a number of people here who would like to see them and I want to give two or three of the baskets to my friends. The remainder I shall bring back with me when I come in the spring. You may leave out the sealskin cap for Edward if it fits him.

You might also put in my nightshirt which I believe was in one of the boxes. The corduroy suit, blanket, rubber blanket, rubber coat and boots you had better put away for me as I shall take them with me if I go north again next spring.

I wish you would have Pogue [his brother] nail up the box and express it to me at once.

Burt [his brother] and I were around to see Pa the other evening. He seems to be pretty well fixed.

I board at 213 North Capitol and room at 217. Hereafter you may send my mail to 217 as that will be more convenient for me.

I am taking the Register and the Kansas City Star, so that I am keeping pretty well up on Kansas news. I see that things are about as hot politically as they were at election time.

I have not been around very much since I have been here but have been to the theater twice, and last Sunday went out to the Zoo with Congressman Kribbs [1846-1938] of Pennsylvania. He and I room at the same house and have become quite chummy. He is a democrat.

I am very anxious to take that big trip to Alaska next year as it will be a great opportunity for me to save money and if I come back safe and sound from that one, think that I shall be ready to quit exploring. I dont [sic] know yet whether I shall make any Christmas presents or not this year.

Write me soon.
Your son
Fred[39]

Fred's concern about earning a living is once again apparent in the above letter when he contemplates a further expedition to Alaska as "a great opportunity...to save money." Also, he, once again, believed that he was nearing quitting exploring—but, first, just one more adventure.

The next month Fred wrote Buck a further letter dated January 29, which is, perhaps, the most revealing of all about how Fred perceived himself at age twenty-seven:

My dear Buck:

I am much obliged to you for sending the Kodak, umbrella and lantern slides.

The pictures in the Kodak were no good; the film having decomposed. It is too damned bad. I wanted the lantern slides to illustrate a talk before the Club of the Dept. of Agriculture which I have been inveigled into giving. It was to have come off last Friday night but has been postponed a week on account of the date conflicting with several other things. I have ordered a new camera, a "Premier" 5 x 7 which use [sic] cut films, or celluloid plates which are said to be a great improvement over roll films, and are of course much lighter than glass plates.

I am going to learn developing in one of the galleries here.

The prospects are quite good for my trip to the north in the spring though it cannot be considered as definitely settled for some time yet. I am more than anxious to go, and if I do, am going to bring back some photos worth seeing.

I have been having a quiet and retired life this winter, and have gazed neither upon the seductive cocktail, the elusive jackboot, nor the amorous chippy, and have trod the paths of virtue with unwavering tread.

The estimable young "ooman" [Maude Richards] at Lincoln, damn her, has shown a tendency recently to give her tootsy-wootsy the cold and clammy shake. Twas ever thus. I always was damned small potatoes with the girls. By the way, Buck, How are Gertrude, Lucinda, E. June and other victims of your capricious lust?

I would like to see some of our old Kansas girls now but the [sic] damn the girls anyhow.

What in hell is the matter with you and Kellogg that neither of you write to me this winter? Damned if it dont [sic] [illegible] me the way you two can get sometimes.

Did Kellogg ever do anything about my election bets?

Write me soon.

   Lovingly
   Gric[40]

Fred's comment about leading a quiet and retired life is particularly interesting, since he claimed not to have "gazed" upon alcohol ("the seductive cocktail"); the "elusive jackboot," perhaps referring to traveling; nor "the amorous chippy," a promiscuous woman. At the same time, he was unhappy with Maude Richards's apparent rejection of him, which reinforced his belief, and, likely, experience, that he "always was damned small potatoes with the girls." Perhaps an incredible physical and mental challenge and adventure in Alaska for a year and a half was just what Fred needed to take his mind off his lack of success with women.

Totem pole at Port Simpson, British Columbia. Photo taken by Fred Funston.

Unknown where Fred Funston took this photo.

Unknown where Fred Funston took this photo.

# Chapter Six Notes— *"A Summer on the Alaskan Coast"*

Epigraph: "Fred Funston's Lecture," *The Iola Register*, November 4, 1892. Letter to the Editor from D. M. Smith, a Carlyle resident.

1. "The Week's News," *The Iola Register*, April 1, 1892. Extract from a "private letter."

2. "The Week's News," *The Iola Register*, April 8, 1892. For the seventy-one applicants' figure, see "University News," *The Lawrence Daily Journal*, March 24, 1892. This item about Fred Funston called him "Tim Funston, an old student."

3. "Sunflower Silhouettes," *The Wichita Daily Eagle,* April 17, 1892.

4. J. M. Rusk, Secretary, United States Department of Agriculture, March 25, 1892, to Frederick Funston (Frederick Funston Papers, hereafter FFP) (Archives Division, Kansas State Historical Society). See also Jessie Dell, Commissioner, United States Civil Service Commission, to Eda B. Funston, March 19, 1931 (FFP). This was an appointment outside the civil service classified positions.

5. "Bound for Alaska," *The Lawrence Daily Journal*, March 29, 1892.

6. Frederick Funston, "Field Report," in Frederick Vernon Coville, "Botany of Yakutat Bay, Alaska," *Contributions From The U.S. National Herbarium*, Vol. III, No. 6 (Washington: Government Printing Office, 1895), 325.
   Frederick Funston, "The Territory of Alaska. From A Commercial Standpoint," *The Bond Record,* May 1896. Under the title "Alaska—The Land and the Climate," this article was one of two excerpted in *The Review of Reviews,* June 1896.
   Frederick Funston, "Along Alaska's Eastern Boundary," *Harper's Weekly*, February 1, 1896.

7. "Fred Funston Heard From," *The Iola Register*, September 16, 1892.

8. Frederick Funston, "Field Report," in Frederick Vernon Coville, "Botany of Yakutat Bay, Alaska," *Contributions From The U.S. National Herbarium*, Vol. III, No. 6 (Washington: Government Printing Office, 1895), 325.

9. Frank Oppel, *Tales of Alaska And The Yukon* (Israel C. Russel, "Mount Saint Elias Revisited") (Secaucus, New Jersey: Castle, 1986), 387.

10. "Bound for Alaska," *The Morning Call*, San Francisco, California, April 14, 1892.

11. "Fred Funston Heard From," *The Iola Register*, September 16, 1892.

12. Fred Funston to Ann E. Funston, May 9, 1892 (FFP).

13. Fred Funston to Ann E. Funston, May 9, 1892 (FFP).

14. "Fred Funston at the Science Club," *The Lawrence Daily Journal*, November 4, 1892. This article includes a summary of various points in Fred's lecture about his Alaskan experiences, and the words inserted in the text by me are largely quoted from this summary.

15. "Fred Funston Heard From," *The Iola Register*, September 16, 1892.

16. Frederick Funston, "Field Report," in Frederick Vernon Coville, "Botany of Yakutat Bay, Alaska," *Contributions From The U.S. National Herbarium*, Vol. III, No. 6 (Washington: Government Printing Office, 1895), 325.

17. Fred Funston to "Goat," June 8, 1892 (FFP).

18. "Fred Funston Heard From," *The Iola Register*, September 16, 1892.

19. Fred Funston to "Goat," June 8, 1892 (FFP).

20. Fred Funston to "Supt, National Museum," dated from Yakutat Bay, Alaska, July 5, 1892 (received July 25, 1892) (Record Unit 189, Smithsonian Institution, Assistant Secretary in charge of United States National Museum, Correspondence and Memoranda, 1860-1908, Box 42, Folder 8, correspondence concerning Frederick Funston).

21. Written instructions on how to respond to Funston's letter of July 5, 1892 (Record Unit 189, Smithsonian Institution, Assistant Secretary in charge of United States National Museum, Correspondence and Memoranda, 1860-1908, Box 42, Folder 8, correspondence concerning Frederick Funston).

22. Fred Funston to Edward H. Funston, July 31, 1892 (Frederick Funston Papers on microfilm, hereafter FFP Micro).

23. Fred Funston to Edward H. Funston, July 31, 1892 (FFP Micro).

24. Fred Funston to Edward H. Funston, July 31, 1892 (FFP Micro).

25. Fred Funston to "Goat," June 8, 1892 (FFP).

26. "Another Alaskan Letter," *The Iola Register*, October 14, 1892.

27. Fred Funston to Edward H. Funston, July 31, 1892 (FFP Micro).

28. "Our Alaskan Letter," *The Iola Register*, October 28, 1892.

29. Fred Funston to Ann E. Funston, August 19, 1890 [sic: 1892] (FFP).

30. Fred Funston to Edward C. Franklin, August 20, 1892 (FFP).

31. Fred Funston to Edward C. Franklin, August 20, 1892 (FFP).

32. Frederick Funston, "Field Report," in Frederick Vernon Coville, "Botany of Yakutat Bay, Alaska," *Contributions From The U.S. National Herbarium*, Vol. III, No. 6 (Washington: Government Printing Office, 1895), 325-328.

33. Frederick Funston, "Field Report," in Frederick Vernon Coville, "Botany of Yakutat Bay, Alaska," *Contributions From The U.S. National Herbarium*, Vol. III, No. 6 (Washington: Government Printing Office, 1895), 333.

34. "The Week's News," *The Iola Register*, October 21, 1892.

35. "Fred Funston at the Science Club," *The Lawrence Daily Journal*, November 4, 1892, and "The Week's News," *The Iola Register*, November 11, 1892.

36. "The Week's News," *The Iola Register*, November 21, 1892, and *Students Journal*, November 17, 1892.

37. Jessie Dell, Commissioner, United States Civil Service Commission, to Eda B. Funston, March 19, 1931 (FFP). This was an appointment outside the civil service classified positions.

38. Fred Funston to Edward C. Franklin, November 27, 1892 (FFP). Gric was one of Funston's college fraternity nicknames.

39. Fred Funston to Ann E. Funston, December 14, 1892 (FFP).

40. Fred Funston to Edward C. Franklin, January 29, 1893 (FFP).

CHAPTER SEVEN

# *North to Alaska and the British Northwest Territory: The Next Adventure*

### 1893 – 1894

[Y]ears before the gold rush sent men in swarms
into [Alaska and the Northwest Territory], with lurid newspaper stories of the terrible hardships endured and the dangers met in climbing the Chilkoot
Pass, hewing out boats and rafting through the
White Horse Rapids, Fred Funston made his way
over the same trail, suffered the same hardships,
encountered the same dangers and made a joke of
the whole adventure.

> —Charles F. Scott to Eda B. Funston,
> May 4, 1931.[1]

On March 9, 1893, Secretary of Agriculture Sterling J. Morton issued to Fred Funston the orders for his next assignment as a botanist
for the department.[2] A couple of weeks later, Charlie Scott told the
readers of *The Iola Register* about "Fred Funston's Great Trip," noting that Fred starts "to-day or tomorrow on the longest, lonesomest
and most dangerous [trip] he has ever yet attempted. It is to occupy
nearly two years, and involves a winter within the Arctic circle and
a long journey across an utterly unexplored country." Fred permitted
Charlie to quote directly from the Secretary's marching orders:

> After a leave of absence of seven days in Kansas, which
> is hereby granted, you will proceed to Tacoma, Washington;
> thence by steamer to Juneau, Alaska, arriving there about
> April 10. You will from that point cross the mountains by ei-
> ther the Chilcoot [sic: Chilkoot] Pass or the Taku route to the

headwaters of the Yukon river, down which you will travel to McQuestin's [sic: McQuesten's] Post. You will make this place your headquarters till about April 1, 1894, when you will proceed overland along the 141$^{st}$ meridian to Rampart House, on the Porcupine river, reaching, if possible the tundra region of northern Alaska. After remaining in this vicinity long enough to make collections of the earlier spring vegetation, you will proceed, about June 20, down the Porcupine and Yukon rivers, making collections en route and reaching St. Michaels in August. From that point you will take passage to San Francisco, there awaiting further instructions.

Although collecting botanical specimens was the principal objective of the trip, Fred was also to note, incidentally, the topography of the country, the temperature, humidity, and the physical features.[3]

These orders were based upon a six-page handwritten "Plan of proposed trip to Yukon river Alaska" prepared by Fred. He also submitted to Secretary Morton an "Estimate of expense of Yukon river trip." For the current fiscal year ending June 30, 1893, he estimated a total of $263 of expense. Included were his sleeper on the train ($20) and meals en route for seven days ($15). His camp outfit cost would be $30. Transportation cost for the steamer from Tacoma to Juneau would be $53, while transportation from Juneau to Chilkoot was estimated at $25. The cost of bearers for the portage of the Chilkoot Pass was calculated at $40. For his subsistence cost from May 1 to July 1, he estimated $60.

For the next fiscal year, which would end June 30, 1894, Fred's total estimated cost was $540, the greater portion ($360) being for twelve months subsistence.

For the final fiscal year beginning July 1, 1894, the estimated total was $90, including $40 for "Subsistence going down Yukon"; $15 for subsistence on the revenue cutter; and $35 for the "Sleeper + meals on train S.F. to Wash."[4] His monthly salary for this expedition was $185, $60 more than the Yakutat Bay expedition.[5] Hence, his annual salary was $2,220.

In selecting Fred for this mission of collecting botanical specimens, his boss, Frederick Coville, observed: "There are a whole lot of people in the United States who know more about botany than Funston does, but there is nobody who will come more nearly going where he is sent and getting what he goes after." Although Fred was offered the option of having a helper go with him, he declined, saying, "No, I don't need another man to take care of me and I don't want to take care of another man."[6]

For his trip to Alaska, Fred wore a brown corduroy suit with his self-described "fondest possession," a large Phi Delta Theta fraternity badge, pinned to the lapel of his coat; a soft-collared shirt with a Windsor tie; and a broad-brimmed felt hat.[7] After his visit in Kansas, Fred journeyed on to Tacoma, Washington, where he was the house guest of his friend, R. B. Whitaker, publisher of the *Daily Court & Commercial Index* and former Iola attorney. From there, Fred wrote on April 2 to his mother about his missing maps for the expedition:

> Dear Ma:
> I reached here three days ago and leave here tonight on the steamer for Alaska.
> Just before leaving Lawrence I found that I had lost Schwatka's report the black book with the twenty maps that I was showing to Pa the day before I started, and supposed that I had left it at home. As there was no telegraph at Carlyle, I sent a message to Charlie Scott to send a man out home to get it, and for him to mail it to me at Tacoma but up to this time I have not received it, and am afraid it will not come. Please see Charlie and if he was out any expense for livery hire in sending a man out pay him, and I will settle it along with the other things when I come back
> I think that if Charlie sent the book the reason why it did not come was because the roads have been blockaded by snow for several days, and there has been no mail from the east since I reached here.
> Your son
> Fred Funston
> P.S. I express you my valise today with my clothes in it. If it does not come in two or three weeks write to R.B. Whitaker 423 Cal. Block, Tacoma and he will look after it. Pay the express charges on the valise and charge it up to me.
>           FF
> I enclose key of valise.[8]

Charlie Scott concluded his account of Fred's upcoming "Great Trip" with this ringing endorsement and fervent prayer:

> It is a great big lonesome trip—he goes entirely alone— and a man of less experience, less endurance and less courage than Fred Funston might well shrink from undertaking it. Indeed men who have plenty of experience and nerve, who have taken part of this journey, have told Fred that $10,000 would not tempt them to go with him. And it is certainly a great distinction for a mere boy to have been chosen for so arduous

and hazardous a task. It is an expedition that will attract the attention of scientific men the world over, and if successfully accomplished it will make Fred Funston famous. And that it will be successful we do not in the least doubt. It will take a good stomach and a good heart and sound lungs, and plenty of discretion and sand and nerve and pluck, but Fred has all of these to sell. We bid him good-bye and God speed to day [sic] with every confidence that some September day in 1894 he will swing open our office door and say "Hello," as jaunty and light as if he had only been gone around the corner for an hour. It's a way he has. God go with him and bless him and keep him from all harm![9]

# Chapter Seven Notes—*North to Alaska and the NW Territory*

1. Charles F. Scott to Eda B. Funston, May 4, 1931 (Frederick Funston Papers on microfilm) (Archives Division, Kansas State Historical Society).

2. Thomas W. Crouch, *North To Alaska: Frederick Funston Above The 49th Parallel, 1892 – 1894*, 165. Copy of this manuscript with endnotes is at Allen County Historical Society Inc., Iola, Kansas. This was published, without endnotes, in 1991 in *The Iola Register*. Endnote 35 cites Secretary of Agriculture Sterling J. Morton to Frederick Funston, March 9, 1893, Washington, D. C. (Record Group 54, Bureau of Botany and Plant Industry, Division of Plant Introduction and Exploration, *Letter Press Book, March, 1893 – June, 1893, No. 9*, 5-6, 8, N.A.R.S.).

3. "Fred Funston's Great Trip," *The Iola Register*, March 24, 1893.

4. These original documents are with the original of Funston's report dated at Iola, Kansas, on May 20, 1895, which he submitted to Frederick V. Coville, botanist at the Department of Agriculture. Original at Allen County Historical Society, Inc.; copy in Frederick Funston Papers, hereafter FFP (Archives Division, Kansas State Historical Society).

5. *Letter From The Secretary of Agriculture Transmitting, In response to the resolution of the House of Representatives of January 22, 1894, a list of the special agents of the Department, together with a statement of their work and the salaries received, for the four years and six months ending December 31, 1893.* 53D Congress, 2d Session, House of Representatives, Ex. Doc. No. 243, 3. See also Jessie Dell, Commissioner, United States Civil Service Commission, to Eda B. Funston, March 18, 1931 (FFP).

6. Charles F. Scott, "Remarkable Career of a Kansas Boy," *Mail and Breeze*, about March 20, 1898 (FFP) for Coville's statement and for Fred's statement. Scott editorially quoted verbatim Fred's statement in the context of Charles Lindbergh's just accomplished transatlantic flight, Lindbergh having preferred to fly alone (*The Iola Daily Register*, May 24, 1927).

7. Ella Funston Eckdall, untitled manuscript about Funston's 1893 – 1894 expedition (Eckdall materials donated in 2003, Allen County Historical Society, Inc.). For Fred's "fondest possession," Walter B. Palmer, "General Funston's Badge," *The Scroll of Phi Delta Theta*, Volume XLI, November and December, 1916, January, March, and May, 1917, 532. Fred was quoted as follows: "When I left the University of Kansas, my fondest possession was a large Phi Delta Theta badge and it was never allowed to get out of my sight. In all my travels and experiences the badge and its associations were never forgotten. They were the greatest things in my life."

8. Fred Funston to Ann E. Funston, April 2, 1893 (Eckdall collection of letters, Allen County Historical Society, Inc.).

9. "Fred Funston's Great Trip," *The Iola Register*, March 24, 1893. The story of Fred's impending trip was told on page one in a student newspaper at the State University of Kansas under the headline "Fearless Fred." The story's introductory sentence read: "At the end of this week 'Fearless Fred' Funston will say a good bye to his friends—a good bye which may be a farewell" ("Fearless Fred," *Students Journal*, March 12, 1893).

# CHAPTER EIGHT

## *"Over The Chilkoot Pass To The Yukon"*
—By Frederick Funston

### April 3, 1893 – May 23, 1893

Fred Funston was an amateur ethnographer. Not only was he well educated through voracious reading, he also had traveled extensively in 1888 when he worked for the Santa Fe Railway as a ticket collector and journeyed as far as New Mexico and into Colorado. He possessed a curious mind and an interest in studying different peoples. According to his friend, Charlie Gleed, it was when Fred and the "hanging judge" Isaac Parker were together in 1887 in Arkansas that they discussed at great length "the relations of the United States to the Indian tribes, and to the outlaws from everywhere who took refuge in one way or another among the Indians. In this way [Fred] began the study of unusual peoples whose ways are not our ways, and whose habits and customs are incompatible with the civilization of the day" (*Trilogy*, Volume One, page 264).

Unlike many Americans who regarded the Native Americans as inferior culturally and racially, Fred frequently took a generally more balanced approach in his observations. As we have seen, in describing the Panamint Indians of Death Valley, he noted that they were "industrious and well-behaved Indians, supporting themselves by gardening, and hunting..." He was not blind to the negative effects of the United States Government upon the Native Americans: "Take it all in all, I doubt very much if there is anywhere in the United States such a well-disposed lot of Indians as this little band of Panamints, the Pueblos of New Mexico, alone, excepted. They know nothing of Government aid, missionaries, whiskey, or any of the other things which generally come from contact with the whites. If they were a band of lazy, thieving butchers like the Apaches they wouldn't have to work; this Government would feed them but as it is no Kansas farmer works harder than do these Indians, and a white man would be as safe among them as on the streets of Iola."

135

Fred also nailed the greed of many Americans and their government when he noted that the Panamints roam "at will over a country which the white man has never wanted to take from them."

Unlike his stay in Death Valley where he encountered and studied the Panamints, Fred was exposed during his more than two years in Alaska and the British Northwest Territory to many more different groups of Native Americans. As we have seen, he described the Thlinkets at Yakutat Bay as "ten parts of barbarism to one of civilization. But little attention is paid to the decencies of life. Polygamy is common, and women and children are bought and sold as are cattle in Kansas, to whomever wants to buy." Fred clearly was appalled: "All of this in the United States of America in this year of Grace 1892." Fewer than thirty years before the bloody, divisive Civil War had ended slavery in the United States at least for the Blacks, and Fred's own father had fought for nearly four years to bring about that beneficial accomplishment. At the same time that he criticized these Thlinkets, Fred pointed out their "good points": thievery was almost unknown, excellent care of the aged and infirm, and a lack of quarreling.

As will be seen in Fred's writings during the balance of his stay in Alaska and the British Northwest Territory, he expressed both compliments and criticism of various tribes. In the use of words such as "uncivilized savages" he clearly reflected the belief in the cultural superiority of the white race. When he wrote of cannibalism among some of the Indians, I am uncertain whether this was fact based or perhaps simply local lore among the white miners that cannibalism did exist among certain tribes. In his father's library, there was a book called *The Story of Metlakatla*, which gives some idea of the library's breadth and what Fred read. I have not seen a copy of this work. Two years after Fred's return home in 1894, ethnologist Dr. Franz Boas published his study of "The Indians of British Columbia" (*Journal of the American Geographical Society of New York, 1896*, Vol. 28, No. 3). Boas wrote of young men taken by the spirits who later returned home as cannibals. According to Boas, in earlier times slaves were eaten by the members of the tribe who were cannibals. Whether any of this is true, I do not know.

It is interesting to note that in the following "blended" account of Fred's "Over The Chilkoot Pass To The Yukon," nearly all of Fred's candid observations about the different tribes are contained in either his private letter to a friend or in his lengthy letters published in *The Iola Register*, not in his published article. At times, particularly in his published letters, I wonder if he is speaking in his usual tongue-in-cheek manner, including about cannibalism, expecting a smile on the face of the reader. One can imagine before his departure, Iolans and other friends kidding him about not being eaten by a cannibal. At other times, I suspect that he may have truly believed that cannibalism did exist among certain tribes.

Fred clearly admired some tribes while taking a dim view of others, which he saw as savages. He did not preach the cultural or racial superiority of the white race but his words at times reflect such an attitude. Obviously, draw your own conclusions when you have read the totality of his various writings.

* * *

"Over The Chilkoot Pass To The Yukon" was published in *Scribner's Magazine* in November 1896. It provides a graphic, but, in places, somewhat limited account of the exciting first part of the 1893-1894 Alaska and British Northwest Territory expedition. Its shortcomings likely stem from space limitations in the *Scribner's* issue. Fortunately, Fred wrote two lengthy, detailed letters in 1893 that were published that year in *The Iola Register*. The integration into the published article of excerpts from these and from another letter Fred wrote results in a richly detailed and more historically valuable account. This blended account is printed below.

In splicing this material together, I have not identified deletions and changes I have made in the published article and in the letters. Unidentified changes include adding words for ease of transition or for explanation in the text; capitalizing and de-capitalizing words; changes in punctuation and paragraphing; and corrections in spelling. Identified in brackets throughout this blended account is the material from his letters and occasional contradictions by Fred in his writings. Enjoy!

* * *

The tourists who every summer crowd the excursion steamers that sail up the long stretches of the inland passage to Alaska find their view to the north and east everywhere limited by a range of snowy peaks silhouetted like card-board against a sky as clear and blue as that of California. On the one side is a narrow strip of main-land and on the other a thousand islands, large and small, that constitute southeastern Alaska, where are the busy mining town of Juneau, and Sitka, the sleepy old capital. This is the Alaska of the tourist, famous for its great glaciers, its beautiful fiords, and its Thlinket Indians and their totem poles. But beyond the big white range is another and a totally different country, the valley of the Yukon, a great, lone land where winter reigns supreme for nine months of every year, and whose inhabitants are roving bands of fur-clad savages. Over in the British Northwest Territory, just across the coast range from Dyea

Inlet, Alaska, is a chain of lakes surrounded by snowy mountains and drained by a small stream, which, now roaring between gloomy cañon-walls and now gliding among birch-covered hills, bears away to the northwest. On either hand it receives numerous tributaries, some of them of great size, and seven hundred miles from its source leaves the British possessions and enters Alaska. After winding for 1,400 miles across this territory it pours its huge flood into Bering Sea. On the lower half of its course the river receives the waters of the Porcupine, Tanana, Koyukuk, and numerous smaller streams, until the little brook, less than ten feet wide, draining Lake Linderman, has in the 2,100 miles of its course become one of the mightiest rivers on the face of the earth—three miles from bank to bank, thirty feet deep, and with a current of five miles an hour.

[There were four of us, three miners from the States going into the interior to prospect for the yellow dust on Forty Mile Creek near McQuesten's Post.[1]] My three companions were McConnell, a grizzly old Canadian, Thompson, a miner from Idaho, and Mattern, a good-natured German, who had mined in half a dozen Western States. [I had made the acquaintance of those three men on the steamer enroute from Tacoma to Juneau, and as they seemed to be pretty decent sort of fellows, we had soon agreed to try "pot luck" as far as McQuesten's Post.[2]]

I was the only one of the party who had had any previous Alaskan experience, but all had roughed it in other countries, and we felt equal to the much-vaunted terrors of Chilkoot Pass, Miles Cañon, and the White Horse Rapids. [I, by virtue of my experience at Yakutat Bay, became a sort of Moses to the expedition, and to a large extent directed its wanderings. But I did not work on full time at the Moses business, as I had also to drag a sled and take my turn at concocting flap-jacks and other indigestible bric-a-brac.[3]] While McConnell, Thompson, and Mattern were bound for the placer gold-mining camp of Forty Mile Creek, at that time the only one on the Yukon, I had a sort of roving commission from the United States Department of Agriculture to make a botanical collection, take weather observations, and obtain any other scientific information possible, and eventually extended my journey to the Mackenzie River and the Arctic Ocean, and thence down the Yukon to its mouth, which I reached after a journey on foot and in rowboat of more than 3,500 miles.

[We reached Juneau on the morning of April 8th, and bought our outfit.[4]] Our outfit consisted of two small tents, a couple of hand-sleds, each eight feet long, with steel-shod runners; blankets, guns, ammunition that we had brought with us; a six-week's supply of flour, bacon, beans, and coffee; a whip-saw, axes, and other tools for boat-building, and my collecting material and two small cameras, the whole weighing about a thousand pounds. Our plan was to take the usual route of miners bound for the Yukon—to cross the Chilkoot Pass and descend to the frozen lakes on the other side—dragging our outfit on the hand-sleds across these lakes until we reached a point where there were trees sufficiently large to build a small boat in which to continue the journey.

[The next day we engaged a small steam tug to convey ourselves and outfit to the head of Chilkoot Inlet [Dyea Inlet in published article, apparently another name for this inlet], a hundred miles north of Juneau, the most available point on the coast from which to reach the headwaters of the Yukon. It was just daybreak on the 10th that the little tug landed us on the sandy beach at the head of the inlet, and with a parting salute from her whistle, steamed away to the southward. We watched her disappear through the fog and mist, the last we were to see of civilization for nearly two years. Surely we had done the Cortez act with a vengeance. We had burned our ships, figuratively speaking, and between us and the next habitation of civilized man lay seven hundred miles peopled only by a few half naked savages.[5]]

[About a mile back from the beach there was[6]] a small Thlinket Indian village of Dyea, whose inhabitants turn an honest penny every spring by assisting miners bound for the interior in packing their supplies to the summit of the pass. [In a short time we were waited upon by a delegation, the delegation consisting of every one that was able to walk, about a hundred of them, men, women and children, with the usual proportion of cur dogs,—three to each Indian. It was our plan to ascend the Taiya River to its source in the coast range of mountains, cross this range at Chilkoot Pass, and descend to Lake Linderman in the British Northwest Territory, and then follow the chain of frozen lakes that form the headwaters of the Yukon. The mountains that we were to cross as seen from the coast presented a cheerless prospect, looming up into the sky, white with snow from base to summit.

[Of course we knew that we would do well to get ourselves to the summit of the Pass through the deep snow without having anything to carry, and so set about engaging the Indians, who are expert packers, to bring along our stuff as far as the summit of the range, intending to drag it on our sleds from this point until we found a suitable place to build our boat. In the negotiations for packers I found that the limited knowledge of the Thlinket language that I had acquired at Yakutat last year was almost indispensable. We were anxious to start the next day, but they would not hear to it because a child had died that morning, and on the morrow the body was to be burned on a great funeral pyre, and none of them was willing to miss such a cheerful spectacle. So we idled away all of the next day, while the savages cremated the unfortunate youngster and made the woods ring far into the night with their chanting, yelling and beating of drums. It is my unbiased opinion that this is a great field for "some good earnest man" to establish a school of manners and morals, running the same as a sort of side-show to a well patronized chain-gang and whipping-post. It has been some time since I have seen a band of savages who so thoroughly need a little discipline as do these Chilkoot Thlinkets.[7] They are [a few dissolutable [sic] Indians none of whom I regretted to learn had ever attended Haskell Institute for Indians, in Lawrence, Kansas, and therefore were neither adept at baseball nor in working the Y.M.C.A. for free lunches.[8]]

[At 7 a.m. of the 12th we got started.[9]] We divided our goods into seven packs and we had engaged five men and two women to carry these loads to the summit of the pass, a distance of fifteen miles, where they were to leave us to our own devices. [Several small boys trotted along as if such little tours were an every day matter with them. The Indians carried their loads on their backs, the weight being supported by bands of deer-skin, one passing around each shoulder and one across the forehead.[10]] Several children carried on their backs light loads, consisting of food and cooking utensils for the use of the Indians, while two of the dogs also wore packs.

[My three companions dragged along the two empty sleds, while I was detailed to walk with the Indians and keep an eye on them, and carried nothing except my camera and rifle. Our route for the first five miles lay along the banks of the Taiya River [called the Dyea River in published article], a swift, turbulent stream about thirty feet wide and two feet deep, whose ice-cold waters we had to wade many times in order to avoid impassable places and thick undergrowth. As we approached the mountains small patches of snow were found here and there in the forest, and before the day was half gone we were wading in it knee deep,[11]] and from here on our progress was much impeded by it. Every two or three hundred yards the entire party stopped to rest. [When we started the sun was shining brightly and all the indications were for favorable weather, but now the sky was overcast and soon the big flakes were falling so thickly that one could hardly see a hundred yards ahead. In the evening, tired, wet, and hungry we reached the entrance to a gloomy cañon, and camped for the night.[12]] [The snow was here more than two feet deep, but we cleared off a space large enough to build a fire, and prepared our sumptuous repast of bacon, flap-jacks and coffee. We did not trouble to put up a tent, but strewing a number of spruce boughs over the snow rolled up in our blankets, not even removing our wet clothing, and slept as only worn out men can sleep,—white men, Indians, kids and dogs all in one big heap. It snowed all night, snowed as it never did and never will in Kansas, but it kept us only that much warmer.[13]]

[The next morning at the unseemly hour of five we were on our way again[14]] wading through snow from three to six feet deep to the place known as Sheep Camp, only five miles beyond. [Only one incident of note occurred during the day.[15]] [The low-browed ex-cannibal who was chief packer and seemed to have charge of the other Indians threw his load into the snow and announced that unless their pay was materially increased he and the other packers would get themselves back to the village and thus leave us in a pretty pickle. My temper had been a white heat all day long and without thinking what might be the consequences of such a move, I shoved the muzzle of a cocked Winchester into the face of the "Advisory Committee." The way the Most Serene Grand Master of the Chilkoot Salmon Taster's Association reshouldered his pack of beans and trudged along through the broad expanse of the Beautiful show that it is sometimes a good thing to have a gun in the house.[16]]

[At noon we reached the upper limit of timber, the real beginning of the Pass[17]], and only twelve miles from the coast that we had left two days before. [It was too late in the day to attempt to reach the next timber on the opposite side of the range, and so camped until the next morning. The snow was here about six feet deep on a level, but considering the circumstances we passed a fairly comfortable night.[18]] Snow had been falling and did not cease until the morning of the next day. [Just before dark there was a lull in the storm and the weather cleared up so that we got a good view of the dreaded Pass, and it was enough to make the cold chills chase one another up and down a fellow's backbone, stretching nearly a mile above us, and as steep as the roof of a house.[19]]

Roused before daybreak, we found the sky clear and the air frosty. Below us was the scattering growth of stunted spruce-trees and above the great slopes of snow and ice. Looking for a couple of miles up a large gorge flanked by precipitous snow-covered mountains, we could see at the summit, thousands of feet above, the little notch known as the Chilkoot Pass, the gate to the Yukon land. The seriousness of the work at hand was now apparent. Having had breakfast at eight o'clock, the seven Indians and ourselves began the toilsome climb upward.[20] On either hand were the huge masses of the coast range, buried in perpetual snow and ice, nobody knows how deep. The Indians, struggling under their heavy loads, stopped for breath every few moments. We four white men had the exasperating task of dragging along the two empty sleds.

As we ascended, the snow, which at lower altitudes had been soft, was found to be hard and crusted, being on the last part of the ascent more like ice than snow. At eleven o'clock we had reached the foot of the last and hardest part of the ascent. From here to the summit is only half a mile, but the angle of the slope is about forty-five degrees, and as we looked up that long trough of glistening ice and hard-crusted snow, as steep as the roof of a house, there was not one of us that did not dread the remainder of the day's work. [The Indians, in dread of avalanches, carried open knives in their hands with which to cut the lashings of their packs so that they could run in case they saw the snow above coming down on them. When I used to attend school out at Maple Grove some fifteen years ago I was considered a pretty fair sprinter, especially when I got more than I could handle in a fist fight, but this thing of outrunning avalanches was something that I never got much practice in, and to begin now was simply appalling, especially when I recall that any one of the big snow-slides that I saw in the St. Ellas range last year would make an express train ashamed of itself. But the avalanches did not come worth a cent.[21]]

As soon as the Indians ascertained that the crust of the snow was hard and unyielding they divided the packs, leaving nearly half of their loads at the foot of the ascent, intending to make a second trip for them. The two women who had accompanied us thus far now returned to Sheep Camp, and one of the men, producing a strong plaited line of rawhide, about one hundred feet long, which he had brought with him, passed it under every man's belt, lashing the nine of us together about ten feet apart. The man at the head of the line carried in his hands one of our hatchets, and as we advanced cut footholds in the ice and hard-packed snow. The slope being too steep for direct ascent, we resorted to "zigzagging"—that is, moving obliquely across the bottom of the trough for about sixty feet and then turning at right angles in the opposite direction. Our progress was painfully slow, as every step had to be cut. It was no place to indulge in conversation. There was no use in stopping, as there was no opportunity to stretch one's limbs and nothing to sit down on, so that we kept pegging away, and the hours seemed endless before we stood on the narrow crest of snow and ice that divides the valley of the Yukon from the sea. It was six and a half hours since we had left Sheep Camp and three since we had lashed ourselves together at the foot of the last ascent. On the summit all threw themselves down on the snow and remained motionless for half an hour, when the Indians started down to get the remainder of their packs that had been left at the foot of the last portion of the ascent. The trail having already been cut and not being hampered with the sleds, they were with us again in less than two hours. We had by this time taken in our surroundings. Behind us and to the right and to the left was a jumble of icy peaks, and below the zigzag trail up which we had labored so breathlessly.

But these things were now of small interest, and our gaze was fixed ahead, where, stretching away in billows of spotless white, was the valley of the great river of the north. [The view northward from the Pass would have been magnificent to anyone looking for scenery, which we were not.[22]] There was neither rock, nor tree, nor shrub, nor any living thing to break the monotony of that huge blanket of snow, the wooded shores of the lakes being concealed by a range of low hills. [The Indians, having delivered their loads were paid off and started at once on their return to the coast, first pointing out to us the direction we were to take to reach Lake Linderman. It was a comfort to see the rascals depart and to know that we were no longer dependent on their whims and caprices.[23]] The use of the two sleds that had been brought along empty was now apparent, and on to them was loaded and securely strapped down the thousand pounds of stuff that the Indians had carried to the summit. And down grade we started on the northern side of the range. For the first half mile down the glassy slope it was a wild ride. All efforts to control the sleds were fruitless, and we concluded to simplify matters by getting on board and taking "pot luck" with whatever rocks or other obstructions might be at the bottom. The route lay down the bottom of a wide gorge, so that we could not well get far out of the way. The sleds, each with two men in addition to its load of five hundred pounds, flew down grade with the speed of an express train. It was well that they were of oak and the runners shod with steel, for sometimes they would clear the snow for thirty feet at a bound. No sooner had we got started than we began to wonder how we were to stop. We found out. The sled ahead of the one I was on struck an uneven place and went over; its lashings broke, and for a few brief seconds the air was filled with rolls of blankets, sides of bacon, mining tools, and earnest, soulful profanity. Our sled coming on to a gentler slope and softer snow, was eventually stopped without disaster. In half an hour Thompson and Mattern got their sled reloaded and joined us. We were now out of the gorge and on a sort of bench or flat covered with soft snow. We got into the harness and, pushing and pulling, struggled on in the hope of reaching Lake Linderman before night.

[During the forenoon the weather had been quite favorable, but now proceeded to make another disgraceful exhibition of itself and treated us to a blizzard which lasted all afternoon and all night. The wind sweeping down from the north filled the air so full of the loose snow that we could not see fifty feet in any direction and piled up great drifts like the sand hills of the southwest. We struggled against the storm until we saw that it was hopeless to bring both sleds through, and then leaving one sled and the greater part of our stuff, loaded only our blankets and a little provisions onto the other, tried it again, all four pulling on one rope.[24] In order to mark the location of the abandoned sled a long-handled shovel was stood on end in the snow, and draped with a spare blanket.

[For a time we floundered along in this way, but made such poor progress that we saw that we would not reach timber before darkness set in. We were already numbed with cold and our clothing, which had been wet for three days, was frozen stiff. It was a plain case that if we remained out in that storm all night without a fire we would furnish a fine "lay out" for some enterprising coroner before morning, and so shouldering our blankets, which was all we could carry, and leaving the sled and provision behind, struck out down a cañon to find timber.[25]] After what seemed an endless struggle through the howling storm, [just at dark we reached a considerable grove of stunted spruce trees, about three miles from where we had abandoned the last sled, and finding a partially protected spot under the walls of the canon,[26]] and collecting some dry branches, and after many fruitless efforts, started a small fire which smoked and sputtered a great deal, but was singularly devoid of warmth. Wrapped in blankets, we huddled together all night, while the wind roared up the cañon walls and piled the snow about us. [Shortly after our arrival at this charming spot I made the joyous discovery that both my ears were frozen stiff.

[We got a little sleep during the night and awoke the next morning stiff and hungry,[27]] and weak, [for we had not eaten a mouthful[28]] of food nor water [since the previous morning.[29]] [The wind had died out and the sun was shining brightly when we started back after the abandoned sleds, the glare of the light being so strong that we wore goggles to prevent snow blindness. Going back about five miles we found, after some difficulty, the first sled abandoned yesterday.[30]] It was entirely buried, nothing but the blanket tied to the shovel being visible above the surface. The sled contained the cooking utensils and part of the provisions, and all four taking hold, dragged it slowly, a hundred yards at a time, toward our camp of the night before. It was exasperating to have with us provisions that were of no use, as it was out of the question to eat raw beans and flour. Thompson, in a frenzy of hunger, insisted on eating a raw piece of bacon, with disastrous results. Dozens of times during the afternoon we threw ourselves down on the snow from sheer exhaustion, but toward evening reached the remains of the camp at the foot of the cañon-wall. As soon as another fire could be built we melted snow for water and prepared a meal of flapjacks, bacon, and coffee, breaking a fast of thirty-seven hours, during which we had had not a wink of sleep. Without troubling to put up a tent or make any sort of camp, we drew our blankets about us and lay back in the snow for ten hours of glorious sleep. The next day [we went back to where the second sled had been left, about three miles, and brought it down with its load,[31]] a comparatively easy task, as the trail had been opened the day before.

Our worst hardships for the time being were now over. The sky was clear and the air cold enough to make exercise comfortable. [Not fifty feet from our camp a powerful spring of clear water issued from a cleft in the cañon walls, forming a stream about a foot across and several inches deep which soon disappears underneath the snow. It was the very beginning of the Yukon, one of the mightiest rivers on the face of the earth, which after a tortuous route of two thousand miles passes into Norton Sound its mighty flood, four miles from bank to bank.[32]]

Most of the sixth day from the coast was spent in recuperating our physical selves, but before evening we dragged the two sleds for a couple of miles down the ravine to Lake Linderman, the first of the chain of six lakes of the Upper Yukon. [Early the next morning we were on our way again dragging down the cañon our two heavily loaded sleds, and in less than an hour came out upon the frozen surface of Lake Linderman.[33]] Lake Linderman is six miles long and half a mile wide, and is shut in by glacier-worn granite hills. Here and there along its shores are a few small spruce and black-pine trees. All of these lakes remain frozen until early in June. [This lake, like all others on the upper Yukon, received its name from that brave but unfortunate man, the late Frederick Schwatka, who passed through this region ten years ago. When we reached it, the freshly fallen snow had nearly all been blown off from the surface of the ice, leaving only the old snow which had a heavy crust and was excellent sledding. We made good progress, and before noon had reached the end of the lake and passed down the small stream connecting it with Lake Bennett, a narrow body of water, or rather of ice, stretching to the north almost as straight as an arrow for twenty-six miles. After sledding for about five miles down this lake we camped for the night on its west shore,[34]] six miles from its head, having dragged our half-ton of stuff twelve miles. [It was now comfortably warm when the sun was shining, but water froze about an inch every night.[35]]

The following day was marked by a unique and successful experiment. A strong wind was blowing from the south, and in order to utilize it we put on to the front of each of the sleds a sort of V-shaped mast, on to which was rigged a tent-fly. [The result was that all the work we did that day was to hold back with all our strength when the wind blew too hard or when we reached a stretch of "glare ice."[36]] We went down the lake at a lively trot. It was not necessary to pull a pound. One man merely held on to the tongue of each sled to guide it and keep it from going too fast. [Much of the time we had to run to keep up.[37]] In that day we covered the remaining twenty miles of Lake Bennett and followed the bank of a short river connecting it with Lake Nares, where we went into camp. Lake Nares is the smallest of this system, being about three miles long and two miles wide. [We had covered all that remained of Lake Bennett and half of Lake Nares, twenty-one miles in all, not a bad day's work.[38]] The general surface of the country was quite broken, and to the east were lofty mountains. Wherever there was soil there were trees, mostly spruce, pine, and poplar, but the largest not more than a foot in diameter. The snow throughout this region was about three feet deep on the level. On going into camp for the night on this journey down the frozen lakes we would pull off from the ice to a grove of trees on the lake shore, and after collecting a quantity of dry wood build a fire, and then, preparing the usual rough, but appetizing, camp-meal, would lie down to sleep. The tents were not put up, and usually the only attempt at a bed was a quantity of spruce-boughs strewn on the snow. [We had only one day of the fair wind, and the next two days were spent in pulling our loads through the soft snow that covered the ice of Tagish Lake.[39]]

[For five days we dragged our heavy loads down the frozen surfaces of Lakes Linderman, Bennett, Nares and Tagish, a distance of sixty-five miles, sleeping each night in the snow without even a tent over our manly forms. This was rough, very rough...on one who only one short month before had left the luxurious ease of a Washington boarding house with its wealth of Turkish carpets, card parties, and indigestion.[40]]

[Tagish Lake is connected with Lake Marsh by a stream five miles long known as the Tagish River. Although the ice along the banks was still in place and several feet thick, it had gone out in the middle of the stream and a strong current was running. After dragging our sleds over the ice on the riverbank for about four miles we came upon a small party of miners bound for the interior who had left Juneau earlier in the spring and had stopped here to build their boats before proceeding farther down the river. Although boats built here would have to be transported over two more frozen lakes, we determined to follow the example of the others, being told that the timber here was better for that purpose than could be found elsewhere.[41]] [We went into camp a mile above Lake Marsh. The snow lay about two feet deep in the forest, but we shoveled out space sufficient for the tents, cut some spruce boughs for carpet, and were fairly well fixed. This was the first time that I had my coat or boots off since leaving the coast ten days before. I record these little incidents for the prayerful consideration of two or three good people not a thousand miles from Iola who insinuated that my trip to the Yukon was a sort of junket·or senatorial funeral. There may be oceans of fun in working in harness like a mule for fourteen hours a day and sleeping out in snow drifts at night, but my sense of humor has been so dulled that I cannot appreciate it.[42]]

On the other bank, directly opposite our camp, were the Tagish Houses. These buildings, two log structures of the Thlinket type, have no permanent occupants, but are the yearly rendezvous of bands of natives who meet on neutral ground to trade and indulge in their great annual drunk, with the accompanying feasts and dances. Here come not only the Tagish Indians, who live in the immediate vicinity, but Thlinkets from Chilkoot, Dyea, and Taku River, and Tinneh or Stick from as far away as the mouth of Pelly River. Small game was plentiful, and in an hour's walk with the gun one could always bring in a day's supply of grouse, ducks, and rabbits. The air was alive with geese and cranes on their northward migration. Near us were camped a couple of families of Tagish Indians, and a boy about ten years old spent most of his time loafing about our camp and eating such scraps of bacon and flapjacks as were thrown to him. On account of this weakness for the leavings of a rich man's table he was christened Lazarus.

We had barely settled down into this new camp before we were overtaken by a party of a dozen men bound for Forty Mile Creek, who had crossed the Chilkoot Pass three days after we did. These men went into camp near us for the purpose of building boats, and every day, from sunrise until dark, the woods rang with the sounds of whip-saws, axes, and hammers. As several of these new arrivals expected to prospect along the bars of the upper river before going to Forty Mile Creek, and Thompson wished to join them, our party was now reduced to three—McConnell, Mattern, and myself. [The tools that we had brought with us for boat-building consisted of a whip-saw, an instrument resembling a cross-cut saw except that the teeth all point in the same direction[43]] with a blade eight feet long and with a handle at either end, [an axe, hand-saw, plane, hatchet and some nails. The raw material that we had to work with consisted of a very large forest of medium sized spruce trees.[44]]

[We first constructed a "saw-pit," a heavy scaffolding about ten feet high, and then felling two good trees, cut from each a log twenty feet long, rolling these by means of skids onto the pit. Two men worked at the whipsaw, one standing on top of the pit and drawing the saw up, the other standing on the ground and pulling it down. I worked on the ground, and the other two took turns with each other working on top, each of those on top resting every half hour, they having harder work than the one on the ground.[45] The extra man busied himself planing the boards and doing odd jobs about the camp. [The whipsaw is an instrument of the devil's own invention and the five days that I stood in that pit half buried in snow and sawdust churning away until every bone ached form a separate and distinct epoch in my career.[46]] The two weeks spent in this camp were not at all unpleasant. [We rose every morning at five o'clock and began work at six, and kept it up until six in the evening[47]] with the exception of an hour at midday. [At the end of five days we had a pile of[48]] clean, straight boards [twenty feet long, ten inches wide and three-quarters of an inch thick. Now began the serious work of building a boat that could run the many rapids of the Yukon and strike a rock at full speed without splitting open. I never was much of a carpenter, my only experience in that line consisting in once having fallen off from our house with a bundle of shingles, but one of our party had served an apprenticeship at the trade, and was the only one of us who could hit a nail twice without hitting his thumb once. But we got along, and in a week more our craft was completed.[49]]

She was a flat-bottomed skiff, [twenty feet long, thirty inches deep, twenty-six inches wide at the bottom and four feet and a half at the top, and fitted with a mast and large[50]] square sail made from a tent-fly, [two pairs of oars and a steering paddle.[51]] She was very carefully put together, the seams being filled with wicking and well pitched. Although built of green lumber, this boat stood the long portage of the frozen lakes and collided with blocks of ice innumerable. [The matter of a name troubled us. We knew she must be a speedy boat and should have an appropriate name. Various things reputed to be rapid, yachts, actresses and race-horses, were discussed, but we finally agreed, and *Nancy Hanks* was penciled on her bows in honor of the famous little trotter.[52]] There was no champagne at hand so, as the boat slid over the blocks of ice on her initial plunge into the river, a pailful of Yukon water was dashed over her bow and she was christened *Nancy Hanks*.

The miners who had stopped there for the purpose of building boats completed their work at the same time, so that we left in company. Our outfit and provisions, the latter materially reduced in bulk, we stowed away in the boat, and on top were put the two sleds, that would be needed in the portages over Lakes Marsh and Labarge.

The little fleet of boats, seven in all, dropped down the Tagish River to the head of Lake Marsh, which was still frozen, and here the boats were dragged out of the water on to the ice of the lake. Two sleds were put underneath each boat, one under the bow and one under the stern, and our companions rigged large blankets as sails on to their boats in order to lighten the work of the twenty-mile portage. Then, one pulling the forward sled and one pushing behind, the six boats started out down the lake. The small sails aided very materially, there being a strong breeze astern. Before leaving camp, McConnell, who was an ingenious fellow, had rigged up a contrivance to enable us to avoid this draft-horse work, and with astounding success. This was merely a light pole, the middle of which was fastened to the bow of the boat and one end to the tongue of the forward sled, the other extending back nearly to the mast. A man standing at the bow of the boat could, by moving this pole to the left or right, control the forward sled perfectly. Two spars had been attached to the mast, one at the top and the other near the gunwale of the boat, and between them was stretched a tent-fly ten feet square. By means of a halyard the upper spar could be lowered instantly, thus shortening sail at will.

By the time that these elaborate preparations were completed the miners with their six boats had got two miles out on the ice, and now looked like a few dark spots on the white surface. Before leaving they had good-naturedly jeered at our "winged chariot," and offered, if we were not over the lake in a couple of days, to come back for us; but our time had come now. As the sail filled with the strong wind we gave the *Nancy Hanks* a shove and jumped on board. McConnell took the steering pole in the bow and away she went. The novelty of the situation made it a most exciting ride.

[The wind was so strong that we did not have to pull a pound, but started out merely walking alongside, allowing the sails to do the work. This plan did well enough for a few moments, but soon the wind increased and carried our novel craft along over the smooth ice at such a rate that we could not keep up and had to get in the boat and ride. McConnell and Mattern sat in the stern while I stood in the bow just forward of the mast and steered by means of a pole connected with the tongue of the forward sled. It was an exciting experience, and I shall never forget the sensation of flying down that long stretch of ice.[53]]

Gradually we crept up on the file of men trudging along, dragging and pushing their heavy loads, and passed them, fairly skimming over the ice. They threw their hats in the air and yelled, while a wild-eyed individual, who called himself "Missouri Bill," grasped his Winchester and proceeded to puncture the atmosphere in all directions. But even this was not glory enough. No sooner had we passed these men than we determined to make improvements. The sail was lowered and we came to a stop; the mast was taken out and lengthened six feet by lashing on to it an extra spar that we had in the boat. Across the end of this was lashed one of the boat's oars, making a spar eighteen feet above the ice. From this there was suspended a large double blanket fourteen feet long, the lower end fastened to the boat. Our speed was materially increased, at one time doubtless reaching twelve miles an hour—not half bad when one considers that the boat and its load weighed more than a ton.

The great height of the blanket sail above the surface made our novel iceboat top heavy, however, and more than once we came near going over. As we approached the northern end of the lake the ice became more uneven, with occasional drifts of hard-packed snow. Crossing several of these successfully gave us overmuch confidence and brought us to grief at last. I was steering at the time, and sighted ahead of us a drift that extended entirely across the lake. As we approached it seemed but little worse than some that we had already crossed. Mattern wanted to take in sail and examine it, but was voted down two to one, and we went at the obstruction full tilt. Just before striking I saw that the ice on the other side had a big sag, and shouted to McConnell to cut the halyards. It was too late; the sleds struck the drift and went over it beautifully, but as we went down on the other side the boat turned quartering to the wind, and over we went. [I recollect some five years ago while a ticket puncher on the Santa Fe road in the days of the train collector system, of falling off from the platform of a passenger train out on the plains of Colorado and distributing myself all over the right-of-way. The sensations in the two disasters were almost identical. Nobody was hurt, but it was a ludicrous sight to see my two companions crawling from under the sacks of flour and rolls of blankets that had fallen upon them. I struck on my hands and knees in the snow twenty feet ahead of the boat.[54]] The bolster of the forward sled and all the spars and the mast were broken, while the boat itself was badly wrenched. It required an hour to overturn the boat and reload it. We got up what nautical men would call a "jury rig," and limped over the remaining mile to the foot of the lake. It had taken three hours and forty-two minutes to run the twenty miles from the head of the lake to where we were wrecked, exclusive of the half-hour lost in putting up the additional sail. The men whom we had distanced did not overtake us, and but two of them reached the foot of the lake before dark.

Between Lake Marsh and Lake Labarge, which is the last and largest of the chain of lakes, there are fifty-five miles of river, but in this short space are the two greatest obstructions to navigation in the whole Yukon system—Miles Cañon and the White Horse Rapids. The stream was about three hundred feet wide, from two to six feet deep, and very swift. [At the time of our arrival the ice had gone out of this stream except along the banks where huge blocks were piled up, in some places to a height of ten feet, while a number of large pieces were still running in the river, adding another element of danger to navigation.[55]] These, with occasional boulders, made navigation exciting work. Spring had now so far advanced that the snow had nearly all disappeared and the weather was superb. [The *Nancy Hanks* having been fully repaired after her sleigh ride down Lake Marsh, was put into the river the morning after our arrival,[56]] and the sleds placed on board instead of underneath. [We proceeded this day very cautiously, keeping a sharp lookout down the river for rapids and ice gorges. It was exciting work, dodging rocks and cakes of ice while swept along by the current, but we had no serious mishaps and in the afternoon finding a place on the bank where the ice was not so high as usual tied up our boat and camped for the night, ate the usual bill of fare—bacon, camp bread and coffee, and stretched ourselves out on a pile of spruce boughs to sleep.[57]]

[The next morning we were on our way by daylight, looking for the entrance to the dreaded Miles cañon which we knew must be near at hand. We had gone less than a mile when we saw ahead of us a great black cliff divided by what looked like only a narrow slit through which the river rushes,[58]] and at the same time heard the roar of the river in its wild rush though the cañon. With one impulse we pulled frantically for the bank and got a line ashore and around a tree just in the nick of time. Landing, we found in camp seven men with their boats. These men had crossed the pass a week before we did and had built their boats at the foot of Lake Marsh, and were now engaged in portaging them around the cañon. This cañon was named by the late Lieutenant Frederick Schwatka in honor of General Nelson A. Miles, who had been instrumental in sending him on his trip to the Yukon in 1883. [Miles Cañon is formed by the Yukon, or, as this part of the stream is generally called, the Lewes River.[59]] The river, which has been about three hundred feet wide, suddenly contracts to about a tenth of that width, and increasing its velocity to twenty miles an hour, rushes with terrific force through a cañon with absolutely perpendicular walls a hundred feet high. The cañon is only three-quarters of a mile long, and at its lower end the river spreads out into a series of rapids, culminating three miles below in the White

Horse. [The volume of the river being enclosed in so narrow a space, the water rushes through with such velocity that it is forced up on the walls of the cañon, while down the middle is a long winrow of white "sombers" several feet high.[60]] There are two ways of passing this cañon, one by portaging over the hill on the east bank and the other by boldly running through. Some of the men whom we found encamped there were utilizing the former method. The boats were unloaded and dragged out of the water, and by means of a windlass hauled up the hill-slope a hundred feet high, and then pulled on wooden rollers for three-quarters of a mile, being finally slid down another hill to the river. The contents of the boats were carried over by the men on their backs. It is the most slavish work imaginable, and uses up the better part of four days.

[Of recent years, however, a number of men have succeeded in going through the cañon with their loaded boats. It is a most perilous, and in some respects a foolhardy undertaking, but to men already worn out by hard work it is a great temptation to avoid four or five days of pulling and hauling by taking a toboggan ride down a cataract and have it all over in two minutes. Fortunately there are no bad rocks in the channel except one near the entrance, but the great danger lies in striking the cañon walls, as the boat would be crushed like an egg shell, or in being swamped by the huge white capped waves or "sombers." The cañon's sides come down to the water as steep as a wall, so that the loss of a boat means certain death to the occupants, as it would be utterly impossible for anything to escape alive from such a torrent. A Missouri man who was with the party camped here asserted with a lurid cuss word that it would drown a catfish, and no one disputed the Missouri man's word. In the last few years several boats, three I believe, have been lost in the cañon. Others saw the men start in and heard their shrieks afterward, and the splinters of their boats were found floating in the river miles below the cañon, but not one of them was ever seen again.

[We three canvassed the situation pretty thoroughly. We watched men pulling and dragging their heavy boats up the steep hillside, sweating and swearing profusely as they toiled, and we climbed up to the top of the cañon walls and looked down on the seething torrent underneath, speculating on the chances of a boat living through it. We returned to the landing just as a big fellow, formerly a Wisconsin lumberman, announced[61]], in lurid language, [that he was going to take his boat through the cañon. All ran to the top of the cañon walls and crawled out as far as they dared to see the sight. Seated in the stern of his boat, and using an ordinary canoe paddle, he steered into the entrance of the cañon, the men on the rocks above watching in breathless silence. As soon as the boat was caught by the swift water it flew with the speed of an express train. The ex-lumberman plying his paddle vigorously to keep it on top of the windrow of white breakers and off from the cañon walls. As he passed underneath us, we waved our hats and yelled like maniacs. The boat was soon out of sight around the first bend, but in a couple of minutes we heard a rifle shot, the pre-arranged signal that he had passed the cañon in safety. This success nerved up two young fellows[62]] from Colorado, whom we had left on Lake Marsh, [who tried it with their boat. Once they missed the cañon walls barely two feet, but in a moment we heard their rifle shot and knew that they were safe. We had seen both ways of passing Miles Cañon, one taking four days and the other two minutes, and our minds were made up [63]]

We three looked at each other in an inquiring sort of way, and then without a word walked down to where the *Nancy Hanks* was moored against the bank. All took their places, kneeling and facing the bow, McConnell in the stern, Mattern amidships, and I [in the bow, all facing forward and using short canoe paddles.[64]] I must confess that I never felt sicker in my life than as we shoved away from shore and steered for the entrance. It was all over so quickly that we hardly knew how it happened. Barely missing the big rock at the mouth of the cañon, the boat started on its wild ride. [It was a great ride, the boat jumped up and down on the breakers like a bucking broncho and the black walls seemed to fairly fly past us. Just after starting we heard a lusty cheer from the cliff above, but didn't dare to look up.[65]] By frantic paddling we kept in the middle and off from the cañon walls. [We were through in less time that it takes to tell it, and landing at the foot of the cañon, fired a shot to let the others know of our success.[66]] There was not a dry spot on one of us when we got through, and the boat had taken on so much water that she nearly foundered before we could bail her out. But a great weight was off our minds, for Miles Cañon, more than all other things, is dreaded by Yukon travelers. Including those lost in 1894, an even dozen of men have had their boats swamped or crushed like eggshells against the cañon walls, and not one of them has come alive out of that wild maelstrom of water.

[For about two miles the river is a succession of rapids and whirlpools, the channel being strewn with huge boulders to strike any one of which would be pretty sure to smash a boat. For half a mile we went down through the rapids, dodging rocks and blocks of floating ice, but pretty soon it became altogether too interesting, and we tried the experiment of "lining" the boat from the shore. That is walking along the bank and letting it down ahead of us by means of a long line attached to the stern. This did well enough for a short distance, but we soon came to where such quantities of ice were piled up along the bank that walking was impossible, but here the river, although very swift was shallow enough near the banks to permit wading provided a fellow was not very particular about how high up the water struck him. So we went in and worked the boat slowly through the maze of boulders and stranded ice blocks, wading alongside and holding on the best we could. The water was generally about waist deep, though we crossed several places too deep for wading by holding onto the sides of the boat and allowing it to drift down to a shallow place where we could regain our footing. The gentle reader may form some idea of how warm the water was, or rather wasn't by the fact that we were continually shoving blocks of ice out of the way. If I ever have a visitation of inflammatory rheumatism, neuralgia, jim-jams, or in fact anything, I shall charge it up to that two hour ice water bath in Lewes River. But when we reached the last quarter of a mile of the rapids the river was too deep and too swift for even this arduous and toilsome method of navigation. Anyhow we had had enough of this joyous sport for one day and tied up for the night in order to get a good rest for the trial of the morrow. Our wet clothes were dried by standing about a big bonfire for several hours.[67]]

The head of the White Horse Rapids was next. These rapids are half a mile long, and the river has its usual width of three hundred feet except in the lower part, where the stream contracts to about thirty feet, and drops through a chute for forty yards. We looked the ground over carefully and spent all of the day after our arrival in carrying the contents of the boat through the woods, depositing them at the foot of the rapids. We determined to run the now empty boat through the rapids as far as the chute, instead of lining it. Realizing that it would be very difficult to stop where we wanted to, McConnell took his station on the bank near the head of the chute in order to take a line, which we were to throw to him as we passed. Everything worked smoothly. Mattern and I steered the boat through the rapids, and as we neared McConnell I threw a line, which he caught, and taking a hitch around the boulder, brought us to a rather sensational stop. In this ride I seated myself in the stern of the boat with the kodak and tried to make a snap shot of the rapids as we ran them, but was so excited that three of the four exposures were on the sky, the surrounding scenery, and the bottom of the boat; but of the successful one I am not a little proud.

The next day we drifted down the river twenty-five miles to the head of Lake Labarge, which was still frozen, although the ice was becoming quite soft. [Lake Labarge is the largest lake on the Lewes-Yukon system.[68]] This lake is thirty-two miles long and eight wide. Here we found in camp Mark Russell, a well-known Alaskan prospecter, and three other men, with two boats. After a delay of a day, caused by a severe storm, we began our last and longest portage, Russell and his party accompanying us. The three boats were placed on sleds, as at Lake Marsh, but no sail was raised, as there was almost a dead calm. [So we had to push and pull our load the entire length of the lake. For three days we worked like plow-horses, sleeping when night came on the ice and eating cold grub. The ice was about four feet thick and water was obtained by cutting down about three feet with an axe and then firing into this hole a shot from a heavy rifle, which would generally penetrate the remainder of the distance. It was a pretty trying time—this three day's portage of our heavy load, but we kept pegging away and on the afternoon of the 14th day of May again reached open water at the foot of the lake[69]] It was thirty-three days since we had left the coast at Dyea and we had covered but two hundred of the seven hundred miles to Forty Mile Creek. But we had left behind Chilkoot Pass, the six frozen lakes, Miles Cañon, and the White Horse; and from here to its mouth 1,900 miles, the Yukon is unobstructed save by a few unimportant rapids, and the remainder of our trip was to be a delightful excursion.

The next morning we again took our seats in the much-buffeted *Nancy*. For nine beautiful, cloudless days we drifted down the river to the northwest, rowing only enough to break the monotony of lounging about in the boat [and paying only enough attention to our craft to keep her from running ashore or striking a "sweeper" as a tree leaning over the water is called.[70]] This part of the stream from Lake Labarge to the mouth of Pelly River is often called by the miners Lewes River, although it is, as a matter of fact, a part of the Yukon. Great quantities of ice remained along the river-banks, and as the current was strong, there was sure to be an exciting time whenever we attempted to stop to go into camp. [The river through this entire region is extremely crooked and contains many islands, the current having a rate of from six to eight miles an hour.[71]] The surface of the country was rolling and hilly, backed by low mountains, and was generally wooded in the valleys, the uplands being bare. Caribou and moose were occasionally seen, but we did not succeed in killing any. [The second day after leaving Lake Labarge we passed two camps of Tagish Indians and stopped to buy some fresh meat and take a few pictures. They were a tough looking outfit, being clothed almost entirely in skins, though I regret to note that some of the rising generation seemed to have forgotten even these. These people are a pretty primitive lot, still using the bow and arrow, the latter being tipped with bone or horn. They had a number of canoes made from untanned moose skins stretched over wooden frames. Personally, they are of very slender build, and if the whole tribe had a hot bath applied by means of a fire hose at short range, they could be made quite presentable. The entire tribe of the Tagish Indians numbers less than two hundred individuals, but they are the sole occupants of a region larger than the State of Kansas. They are in every way inferior to the Tinneh Indians who live along the Yukon near Forty Mile.[72]]

We passed the mouth of the Teslin or Hotalinqua, and reached the mouth of Little Salmon River, where we found a small camp of Tinneh Indians, the first of these people we had met. They were a fine-looking lot of savages, dressed in skins and guiltless of any knowledge of English. In four days we reached the mouth of Pelly River, the site of old Fort Selkirk, burned and looted by Indians from the coast in 1850. It is a telling commentary on the intelligence of makers of maps that this obscure fur-trading post, abandoned nearly half a century ago and whose only remains are a blackened chimney, should still be marked on every map of that region. The river was now much larger, and for some distance below the mouth of the Pelly islands were numerous. [On May 21st we passed the mouth of White River coming in on the left and Stewart River on the right. White River, easily recognized by its milky flood, is a stream as large as the Missouri, whose entire basin is yet practically unknown to white men. The Yukon was now from one to two miles wide and with a terrific current.[73]] [Many villages of the Tinneh tribe of Indians were passed, and we overtook some of these people descending the river on rafts. They were very friendly and sociable and quite talkative, many of them being able to speak English. On the evening of the 22nd we passed the big Indian Village of Klon-dek, mooring close enough to the shore to exchange some chaff with the inhabitants, but declining to stop despite their urgent invitation. That evening we camped near the pile of decaying logs that was once the trading post of Ft. Reliance.[74]]

[But the 23rd was the eventful day. An amusing incident occurred just after our start that morning. We were running along pretty close to shore and sighted upon one of the river bluffs a white man, who as we afterward learned had gone up there from the post at Forty Mile to do some prospecting. When he saw us he knew at once that we were fresh arrivals from the "outside," as they call the world in general here, and rushed down to the edge of the bluff to get the latest news. "Who's President?" he shouted in a voice rich with Corkonian accent. I rose in my seat and was about to shout back to him the name of the "man of destiny," who would be Grover Cleveland, but McConnell got ahead of me and bawled out "John Payter St. John." I believe that I have never in my life heard such a volley of cuss words so artistically put together as came down off from that bluff before we got out of ear shot.[75]] [John Peter St. John, former governor of Kansas, had run for president in 1884 as a prohibitionist]. All day we were swept along between towering cliffs of red and brown rock. [We had a swift current and made fine progress this day, and at three o'clock sighted on the left bank two large log houses surrounded by a number of smaller ones, and a tall pole from which floated the British flag. It was Buxton Mission, a Church of England institution, and the Indian village. Half a mile farther down on the same side, where Forty Mile Creek joins the Yukon, was a collection of thirty or forty log cabins surrounding a big store house and another tall pole from which "old Glory" floated in the breeze. It was McQuesten's Post or Forty Mile as it is generally called, the farthest up river post of the great Alaska Commercial Company, and is situated about on the boundary line between Alaska and the British Northwest Territory. We tied up the *Nancy Hanks* to a raft and went ashore, our long journey done.[76]] We had been just forty-two days in the journey from the coast. McConnell and Mattern went prospecting for gold, and I never saw them again.

"Dyea—A Thlinkit Indian Village Where the Chilkoot route begins"

"Drawings Made From Photographs Taken by Frederick Funston" and published with his article, "Along Alaska's Eastern Boundary."

The *Nancy Hanks* with two sleds under it on one of the frozen lakes, probably Lake Marsh. Photo taken by Fred Funston.

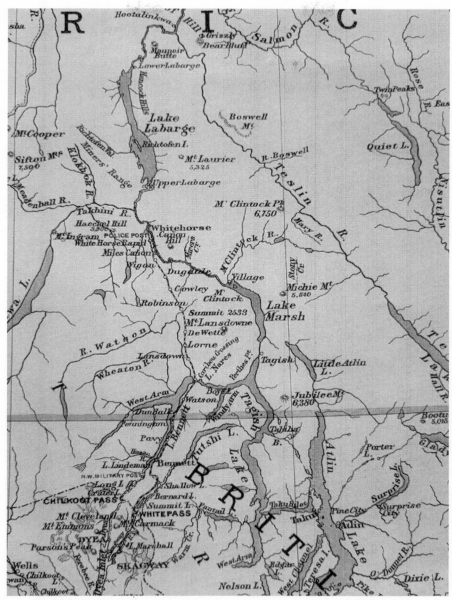

1904 map showing Dyea, Chilkoot Pass, and the chain of six frozen lakes
crossed in 1893 by Funston and his companions: Lake Linderman, Lake Bennett,
Lake Nares, Tagish Lake, Lake Marsh, and between it and Lake Labarge,
dreaded Miles Cañon and the White Horse Rapids.

DANGEROUS RAPIDS RUSHING THROUGH MILES CAÑON, NEAR CAÑON CITY, ALASKA.

Probably the miners' boats with large blankets used as sails.
Photo taken by Fred Funston.

Photo taken by Fred Funston.

Marching Up The Pass.

Passing The Miners.

Shooting White Horse Rapids.

"Drawings Made From Photographs Taken by Frederick Funston"
and published with his article,
"Over the Chiilkoot Pass to the Yukon"

# Chapter Eight Notes—*"Over The Chilkoot Pass To The Yukon"*

1-7.  "From Fred Funston," *The Iola Register*, August 25, 1893. Fred's letter dated May 28, 1893.

8.  Fred Funston to Willis Gleed, August 16, 1893 (Frederick Funston Papers on microfilm, hereafter FFP Micro) (Archives Division, Kansas State Historical Society).

9-15.  "From Fred Funston," *The Iola Register*, August 25, 1893. Fred's letter dated May 28, 1893. The chapter text based on this letter describes camping when evening came, but the published article stated instead that "at one o'clock we reached the forks of the river, seven miles from our starting point, and the Indians, throwing off their loads, said we would camp for the night. They were completely exhausted by floundering through the soft snow under their heavy packs."

16.  Fred Funston to Willis Gleed, August 16, 1893 (FFP Micro).

17-19.  "From Fred Funston," *The Iola Register*, August 25, 1893. Fred's letter dated May 28, 1893.

20.  In his May 28, 1893, letter Fred stated that at four the next morning the five Indian men left the women and children in camp and carried "half of the stuff" to the summit, where they left it and then returned for the remainder. This appears questionable in view of the details in the published account set out in this chapter. There would not have been time to go to the summit and then return by eight o'clock.

21-39.  "From Fred Funston," *The Iola Register*, August 25, 1893. Fred's letter dated May 28, 1893.

40.  Fred Funston to Willis Gleed, August 16, 1893 (FFP Micro).

41-45.  "From Fred Funston," *The Iola Register*, August 25, 1893. Fred's letter dated May 28, 1893.

46.  Fred Funston to Willis Gleed, August 16, 1893 (FFP Micro).

47-52.  "From Fred Funston," *The Iola Register*, August 25, 1893. Fred's letter dated May 28, 1893. The flat-bottomed skiff was only eighteen feet, not twenty feet (note 50) according to Fred's letter of May 30, 1894, to Charlie Scott (see Chapter Ten, second paragraph of the quoted letter) and according to the published article.

53-66.  "Fred Funston Again!," *The Iola Register*, November 10, 1893. Fred's letter dated August 3, 1893.

67.  "Fred Funston Again!," *The Iola Register*, November 10, 1893. Fred's letter dated August 3, 1893. The following sentence appears just before the beginning of the quoted language in the text: "The White Horse Rapids, beginning a few hundred yards below the foot of Miles Cañon..." This is confusing, since in Fred's published article, the beginning of the White Horse Rapids was described as three miles below the foot of Miles Cañon.

68-76.  "Fred Funston Again!," *The Iola Register*, November 10, 1893. Fred's letter dated August 3, 1893. Fred's account of the portage around the White Horse Rapids in this letter does not correspond fully with the published article, and I do not know how to reconcile the two accounts.

# CHAPTER NINE

# A Summer at McQuesten's Post (Forty Mile Creek)

## May 23, 1893 – August 25, 1893

[W]e reached the "Alaskan Commercial Company's" trading post at the mouth of Forty-Mile Creek, the lonesomest place under the stars and stripes, where the mail comes once a year, where it is daylight all summer and night all winter.

—Fred Funston, McQuesten's Post,
Yukon River, Alaska, May 28, 1893.[1]

The boundary line between Alaska and the British Northwest Territory is the 141st meridian. About eight miles east of this line the Yukon River intersects the mouth of the approximately 80-mile stream called Forty Mile Creek. Miners dug for gold in Alaska at the headwaters of this creek, while their base of operations, the village at the creek's mouth, was in the British Northwest Territory. This village, Forty Mile Creek, consisted of the miners' cabins and of the trading post of Leroy Napoleon "Jack" McQuesten; hence, the settlement was also referred to as McQuesten's Post.[2] Here Fred was to spend the summer collecting botanical specimens. He and the two miners, McConnell and Mattern, were the first to arrive that spring from the outside world, and thus "brought the year's budget of news to the three hundred white men who..." resided there. They "spent their summers in washing gold out of the gulches, and their winters in playing poker and spinning yarns."[3]

A few days after his arrival on May 23, Fred wrote his mother. Extracts from this letter are as follows. I have not indicated the places where I have omitted intervening paragraph(s):

This is not such a bad place as one might think, though I suppose it will not be so comfortable next winter. There is the trading post of the Alaska Commercial Co. in charge of Messrs. McQuesten and Mayo a church of England missionary and quite a number of Indians.

I am living in a comfortable little log cabin, where I sleep and do my work, taking my meals with the trader Jack McQuesten. McQuesten is a mighty fine fellow good company and very accommodating. He was born in Maine, but has been among the Indians of the Northwest for thirty-five years twenty years of that time on the Yukon. His wife is a Yukon Indian and they have a family of the prettiest children I ever saw.

The missionary is a queer old chap who has been in this country for thirty years.

The miners digging for gold work about eighty miles from here, so that we do not see much of them during the summer, but many of them will spend the winter near the post. They took out $100,000 last year, and it is expected that there will be a much bigger yield this year.

You can imagine how isolated this place is when I tell you that we brought in the news not only of the election but of the presidential nominations last summer.

About two weeks from now I expect to take a two weeks trip going down the Yukon a short distance in my boat to where there are some mountains, and camp, coming back whenever I feel like.

The country here is composed mostly of mountains and high hills covered with small pine and birch trees, with many wild flowers. I think I never saw prettier wild flowers than those here, the ground being covered in many places like a carpet. I send you a few that I picked.

The Yukon river at this place is about half a mile wide and very deep and swift. I don't like to fool with it very much.

The traders here have a garden of about three acres where they raise turnips, cabbage, lettuce, radishes, and early potatoes, though the potatoes are not much of a success. All that one has to do to find frozen ground is to dig down two feet even in midsummer, as the ground never thaws below that depth. As there are no horses, the garden was plowed by hitching eighteen Indians to a plow. This was one of the funniest sights I ever saw. There are many wild reindeer called caribou near here, the Indians killing them every day so that we have fresh meat constantly.

The Indians here are a very well behaved lot though once in a while some of them get drunk on a kind of liquor that they make themselves and get pretty noisy, but they are not the least bit dangerous. The other night one of them got full and began yelling in front of my cabin. The noise woke me up, and I went out and hit him a crack with an oar and he shut up in a hurry.

So far north as we are now there is no night in the summer time, it being almost as light at midnight as at noon. There will be no darkness until sometime in August. It is much more that way than where I was last year because we are farther north.

I took quite a number of photographs on my trip in here, and when the last steamer goes out this summer am going to send a number of the negatives to a photographer in Washington to be printed and have him give the pictures to Burt Mitchell to keep for me so until I return. So in this way you may see the photographs before I do.

I am feeling first rate, and never was in better health in my life.

You will hear from me again in the fall.

Your loving son

Fred Funston[4]

On July 20, Fred wrote to his mother again, and extracts follow, quoted in the fashion as before:

The steamboat has arrived on its second trip for this summer and gives me another opportunity to send out mail, probably the last for a year.

I took a trip alone into the mountains and was gone eighteen days in which time I did not see a human being. I got back safely, and expect to start out again in a few days to be gone two weeks in the same region.

Am getting along very well with my botanical collecting in spite of the fact that the weather has been unfavorable. We have had some pretty warm days twice up to 90 in the shade, but most of the time it has been rather cool with considerable rain.

This is a very interesting place to live as there are so many different tribes of Indians who come here to trade off their furs. I dont [sic] miss letters and newspapers as much I expected too [sic] though sometimes I wonder whether the cholera came and whether or not the World's Fair got started.

The latest papers brought up by the steamboat where [sic: were] those of last April and as that is about the time I left the states, there was nothing new in them for me.

Although it is now but little after the middle of summer people are getting ready for winter which begins in September. The first frost generally comes about August 15.

I am having my fur suit made—coat and hood of reindeer skin, trousers of mink skin and sealskin boots, and a big fur robe as large as a blanket to sleep in. All these things are necessary as it gets sometimes 70 degrees below zero and ordinary clothes are of no use.

I like this country immensely, and would rather live here than in Washington, that is for a year or two. I never was in better health than I am now and feel as if I could stand anything.

I have seen some big game but have not killed any yet. [At some point, Fred killed a "big lynx."[5]] I fired seven shots at a moose, an animal as large as a horse while he was swimming the river but could not hit him as nothing was above water except his head. The Indians here kill a good many moose and caribou, a kind of reindeer and that and fish is all the meat we have, but moose is as good as beef.

There are a good many Indians here but they are as harmless as children, in fact they are the best Indians I ever saw. I would as soon trust myself with them as with white men.

Here at the the [sic] post now there are almost no white people except the traders, the missionaries and myself, as all the miners are up on the head of the creek distant about eighty miles, and will not come down until the beginning of winter. These miners are pretty good sort of fellows to be with; they are very accommodating to strangers and are perfectly trustworthy.

When I go down the river next summer in a birch bark canoe I shall reach the trading post of <u>Nuklukyet</u> about halfway down the river about the time the steamboat reaches there on her way up. Here I can get my mail a month sooner than if I wait until I get to St. Michaels [near the mouth of the Yukon River]. So you may send my mail there instead of St. Michaels. Address as on card below. Send my valise with clothes as I directed before that is via San Francisco care of Alaska Commercial Co. to St. Michaels. Clothes should leave Kansas about April 15. When you send my mail I wish you would put in any papers or magazines that you think might interest me.

Charlie Scott is going to send me the Registers.[6]

Fred enjoyed an interesting diversion from plant collecting when he would drop by the blacksmith shop of John White. There, for exercise, Fred "would strike for me to steel a pick. He was a lightning striker, nearly equal to a steam trip-hammer." Fred wisely worked to keep his muscles strong, which he would need in September when he would undertake "tracking" up the Porcupine River. White later recollected the day Fred decided to boat four miles down to Coal Creek, which was located on the opposite bank of the Yukon River. "The river was up booming; so Fred got in a whirlpool at the mouth of Coal Creek and upset his boat and he swam ashore." He then walked through thick timber until he was opposite Forty Mile Creek. He was spotted and an Indian in a birch bark canoe crossed the river and brought him to Forty Mile Creek. "He was laughing and seemed to be in good humor. Well his clothes was [sic] wringing wet, but outside of that he was all right and seemed to enjoy his trip to Coal Creek." Ah, the love of adventure! Fred lost his boat in this accident.[7] Apparently this was not the *Nancy Hanks*, since he used it the balance of his Arctic expedition.

On August 16, shortly before his departure down the Yukon River, Fred wrote two letters, one to an unidentified friend in Kansas City and one to Willis Gleed, brother of his friend, Charlie Gleed. These letters provide insight into several aspects of life at Forty Mile Creek. One subject in both letters was the lack of any laws in this isolated corner of the world:

> I have enjoyed life hugely during my summer at this queer out of the way corner of the earth where the mail comes crawling in once a year. In fact I doubt if there is on the face of the earth a place inhabited by civilized men more utterly cut off from communication with the world than this arctic mining camp. It is 800 miles to the coast at Chilkoot by the way we had come into the country, and 1500 miles to the mouth of the river at St. Michaels. Once a year the steamer of the Alaska Commercial Company leaves San Francisco with goods for the traders on the Yukon, and battling her way slowly through the arctic ice pack reaches the mouth of the river and unloading her cargo hurries northward before the ice closes in again, while her cargo is brought up the Yukon by the little stern wheel steamer Arctic which makes two trips, the first bringing the mail which came up from San Francisco, and even then the latest paper is four months old. Coming as we did from Juneau via the upper Yukon we reached here

before the steamboat came from below on her first trip, and consequently brought in all the news for a year not only the elections, but the presidential nominations of 1892.

We are only a short distance from the Arctic circle, and it is considered quite the thing among the best people here to take a run and jump over the circle a few times before breakfast every morning just as a bracer. There is no law here against doing this or anything else, which is one reason why it is such a pleasant place to live. If your neighbor's dog takes a piece out of your leg you can shoot him without fear of spending the night at "headquarters" and have a chump reporter doing "dog watch" write you up in the morning paper.[8]

[If there is an officer within 700 miles of here I have not yet seen him.... If it should please any of my outcast friends up here to wipe me off the map and divide my coat of many colors among them, further than the gnawing at their hearts of sharp-toothed remorse for garnering so fair a flower, nothing would even harm them.[9]]

For his Kansas City friend, Fred described the miners:

There are not many white men here, but everyone is a fugitive from justice or domestic infelicity, and each of them claims to have come from every state in the union in the course of a winter's conversation. It is a mark of a true gentleman—just as the Kentucky man's idea of a gentleman is a man who turns his back when you drink out of his bottle—not to allude to these idiosyncrasies of nativity [,] and good breeding in the matter is not only the gateway to the best society but it is the only way to insure good health. A young man who came to Alaska some years ago and located on Yakutat Bay was so persistent in correcting conflicting statements of his elders and betters that he was killed by the Indians—they say.[10]

For *The Iola Register's* readers, Fred mentioned the "odd collection of white men who have drifted into this, the most northerly mining camp on the face of the earth." He first described the "genial, good natured prince of the upper Youkon [sic])," Jack McQuesten, who is known as the Father of the Yukon, before noting "Billy" Lloyd, whom he characterized as "a rather dissolute young Englishman who some years ago dragged a sled with the corpse of his father from Dease Lake to Calgary, more than a thousand miles through the snows of an arctic winter in order that it might find a burial place among civilized men..." The third man Fred detailed was "Bishop Bumpas, the aged missionary of the Church of England, a man who for thirty years has been pounding hymns and precepts into Indians and Esquimos and who speaks every native language from Lake Winnipeg to the Arctic ocean."[11]

Hoping to leave on the next leg of his adventure by August 25, Fred described the change in his plans to Willis:

> You may recollect that it was my original intention to winter here and go north by dog team in the early spring but I have entirely changed the plan and shall spend the winter on the headwaters of the Porcupine river, making a trip from there with dogs due north to the Arctic ocean. My plan is to leave this place about the 25th inst with a ten months supply of provisions in my boat and drift alone down to the mouth of the Porcupine river, a distance of 400 miles. Here on the site of the long abandoned trading post of Ft. Yukon is an Indian village where I shall get one or two natives to assist me in the ascent of Porcupine for two hundred miles. The Porcupine, the Yukon, and in fact all of the Alaskan rivers are so swift that no one thinks of attempting to row upstream so that the only way to ascend one of these northern rivers is by the arduous means known as "tracking" that is walking along the bank and pulling the boat with a tow line. From the experience that I have already had in the modes of navigation I find it very conductive to a ravenous appetite and a new and shocking variety of profanity. I expect the six hundred mile journey from here to Rampart House to occupy a month. Rampart House is an abandoned Hudson Bay Company's trading post situated far to the north of the Arctic circle where the Porcupine river crosses the eastern boundary of Alaska. The only white man there now is a young missionary of the Church of England, who went up about a month ago. He is a blonde with curly hair and big soulful eyes (I dont [sic] know what "soulful" eyes are but have seen the word in novels) and is what the girls in Kansas would call just the sweetest thing out. Besides the good man there are several hundred natives who are generally half starved and who include cannibalism among a number of other accomplishments and amusements.

> I half expect on my arrival to find that Bro. Totty's parishioners have made a pan roast of him, and hope to induce them to pursue a different course with me. To this end I rely somewhat on the fact that I am pretty handy with a Winchester but more on those sweet winning ways which were so popular in the salons of Lawrence and Iola as well as in the husking bees on my Deer Creek estates.[12]

In his letter to his Kansas City friend, Fred expressed similar thoughts about "tracking" with his boat: "My past experience with this sort of navigation has been such that I expect a severe strain on my physical powers and also on my limited resources for expressive, untrammeled, far-reaching profanity." The trip up the Porcupine would prove to be far more arduous than even Fred imagined. He also wrote about the planned finale of his Alaska adventure: "I shall leave Rampart House June 20, 1894, and in a small canoe I shall drift down the Yukon river to its mouth, a distance of a trifle over 1,500 miles. This trip I must take alone, with not even a native guide. It is over a country much of which is as unknown to the geographers as is Central Africa." In typical humorous fashion, Fred dealt with the possibility of his own death on the last leg of his journey:

Scattered through this country that I am to cover are innumerable tribes of uncivilized savages, who only know the government of the United States to speak to it and are not intimately acquainted with the seductive argument of a government gun boat; so should they get it in their heads to take a wing shot at me with their bows and arrows as my barque goes scooting over the rapids—why, that is my misfortune. Tell the boys at Lawrence not to drape the hall in mourning for thirty days. Rather, tell them, as Mr. Kipling says, not to

'Go down all at once. I trust
You will find excuse to "snake
Three days' casual on a bust."
Get your fun for old sake's sake.'

This country, by the way, needs a Kipling. I find my Kipling, that is packed with my dictionary and my Bible, a source of constant pleasure, accompanied sometimes by a regret that he has never turned his flash light on the natives of this far country.[13]

That Fred carried Kipling's work (*Barrack Room Ballads* and the stories of the British soldiers Mulvaney, Learoyd, and Ortheris, according to Billy White[14]) is not surprising. That his other two books were the Bible and his dictionary did surprise me. Presumably, he carried the Bible because of his religious faith, and the dictionary in order to improve his vocabulary, and, hence, the quality of his writing. Although Rudyard Kipling never went to the Arctic north, future famous author Jack London did in 1897 during the Klondike Gold Rush, and he based at least one of his published stories of the far north on Jack McQuesten.[15]

Fred concluded his two letters by conveying to both friends the size of the mighty Yukon River:

> It is almost impossible for one not acquainted with the vast extent of this northwestern country to realize the great distance and the enormous size of the rivers, as well as the total lack of means of communication. It will surprise some people who learned in the old time school geographies that the Mississippi was the largest river on the North American continent to know that it is actually puny compared with the mighty Yukon, which is next to the Amazon and the Nile the largest river in the world. The Tanana, a river of which mighty few people have ever heard is a solid mile from bank to bank twenty feet deep and with a current like a mill race. The Koyukuk another tributary of the Yukon is larger than the Ohio and the Porcupine larger than the Hudson. I venture the assertion that the Mississippi at St. Louis if turned into the Yukon below the mouth of the Koyukuk would not raise the stream six inches [and I have been up and down the Mississippi some myself[16]]. And through all this vast region comprising nearly all of Alaska and a large portion of the British Northwest Territory there is not a road or trail, other than a few dim Indian footpaths.[17]

TINNEH INDIAN WOMEN OF NORTHEASTERN ALASKA.

"Drawings Made From Photographs Taken by Frederick Funston" and published with his article, "Along Alaska's Eastern Boundary"

"Village of Forty-Mile Creek, British Northwest Territory"

"Showing Boat in which Mr. Funston made his 1600-miles Trip alone down the Porcupine and Yukon Rivers."

"Drawings Made From Photographs Taken by Frederick Funston" and published with his article, "Along Alaska's Eastern Boundary"

# Chapter Nine Notes—*A Summer at McQuesten's Post*

1. "From Fred Funston," *The Iola Register*, August 25, 1893. Fred's letter dated May 28, 1893.

2. Frederick Funston, "Along Alaska's Eastern Boundary," *Harper's Weekly*, February 1, 1896 (Frederick Funston Papers) (Archives Division, Kansas State Historical Society). Forty Mile Creek received its name because that was believed to be the distance down the Yukon River from Fort Reliance, another trading post established by McQuesten (James A. McQuiston, *Captain Jack: Father of the Yukon* (Denver: Outskirts Press, Inc., 2007), 163).

3. Frederick Funston, "Over the Chilkoot Pass To The Yukon," *Scribner's Magazine*, November 1896.

4. Fred Funston to Ann E. Funston, undated, at McQuesten's Post (probably May 28, 1893, since this is the date of his letter to *The Iola Register* which he referred to in his letter to his mother) (Frederick Funston Papers on microfilm, hereafter FFP Micro) (Archives Division, Kansas State Historical Society). An unknown hand has written on this letter "[Apr. 9. 1893]" for the date, which is impossible, since Fred stated in this letter that he had reached McQuesten's Post on May 23.

5. "Fred Funston Again!" *The Iola Register*, November 10, 1893. Extracts from Fred's letter dated August 3, 1893.

6. Fred Funston to Ann E. Funston, July 20, 1893 (FFP Micro).

7. John I. White, "Statement On Alaskan Experiences" (manuscript) (FFP Micro).

8. Fred Funston to Willis Gleed, August 16, 1893 (FFP Micro).

9. "Near The Arctic Circle," *The Kansas City Star*, November 1, 1893. Extracts from Fred's letter dated August 16, 1893, to an unidentified friend.

10. "Near The Arctic Circle," *The Kansas City Star*, November 1, 1893.

11. "Fred Funston Again!" *The Iola Register*, November 10, 1893. Extracts from Fred's letter dated August 3, 1893.

12. Fred Funston to Willis Gleed, August 16, 1893 (FFP Micro).

13. "Near The Arctic Circle," *The Kansas City Star*, November 1, 1893.

14. William Allen White, "The Hero Of The Philippines," *The St. Louis Republic Magazine Section*, May 21, 1899.

15. James A. McQuiston, *Captain Jack: Father of the Yukon* (Denver, Colorado: Outskirts Press, Inc., 2007), 231.

16. "Near The Arctic Circle," *The Kansas City Star*, November 1, 1893.

17. Fred Funston to Willis Gleed, August 16, 1893 (FFP Micro).

# Ascending the Porcupine River and Lodging at Rampart House: Fred Funston's Account

## August 25, 1893 – November 17, 1893

Fred Funston provided a detailed account of his trip down the Yukon River and then up the Porcupine River in his letter of May 30, 1894, from "Rampart House, Porcupine River, Eastern Boundary line of Alaska." Charlie Scott, the addressee, published the first part of the letter in *The Iola Register* on September 21, 1894, under the headline "Out Of The North." The balance of this very lengthy letter he published in three subsequent issues of his newspaper. The second installment, published in the October 5, 1894, issue, told, in part, about Rampart House where Fred wintered. The first installment and the first paragraph of the second installment are reprinted below, and these are supplemented by inserting in brackets material from Fred's other writings and notes made by me.

* * *

The task of crowding into one letter the experiences of a year in the Arctic region with more than 1500 miles of travel is one so manifestly impossible that I had half a mind not to attempt it but remembering my promise and fearing the wrath to come I shall do what I can in that direction.

My last letter to the REGISTER was from Forty Mile Creek on the Yukon, just before leaving that place last summer. On August 25, I loaded into an 18 foot row boat about a ton of stuff consisting of flour and other provisions and a lot of goods for barter with the natives, my botanical apparatus, rifle, shot-gun and other bric a brac, and seating myself in the stern with a steering paddle, started alone on my long journey of 500 miles to Rampart House on the Upper Porcupine river, where I was to spend the winter. The whole population of Forty Mile, traders, miners, missionaries and Indians, assembled on the river bank to see me off and showered on me advice, good wishes, blessings and misgivings in about equal proportions.

It was my plan to drift down the Yukon to the mouth of the Porcupine, about 300 miles, and then by the aid of natives, take my boat up the latter stream 200 miles by the method known as "tracking," that is, walking along the bank and towing with a long line, the current being too strong for rowing.

For six days I drifted down the big lonely river, seeing in all that time not one sign of a human being: With nothing to do but keep the boat from striking the bank, there was ample opportunity to take in the surroundings, and the ride was a most enjoyable one. The river showed off to fine advantage, being broad, deep and swift, with hills and mountains on both banks, while the weather was as perfect as if made for the occasion. At the close of each day I tied my boat to the bank, prepared a few epicurean delights, and without going to the trouble of putting up a tent, rolled down on the ground in my blankets and slept like a hired man. (A person needs lots of sleep after bartaking [sic: partaking] of my cookery.) Every night there was a heavy frost, for although only the latter part of August, the short Arctic summer was already drawing to a close. On the 31st, I reached the camp of Chief Senate's band of Indians at the head of the Yukon "flats," 220 miles below Forty Mile and 80 above the mouth of the Porcupine. Senate is or was (for we hear that he died last winter) a white haired old pirate with a visage that would give a man the ague, and made it pretty tropical for the Hudson Bay Company's traders when they first invaded his domains and established the trading post of Ft. Yukon more than 25 years ago. But the old man was shorn of his power long ago and now has turned "mug-wump" and runs down the country and talks of the good old times "befo de wah." Now when he tries to stir up his people to annihilate the two or three white men who happen to pass his camp every year, they only laugh at him and tell him to go and sleep it off. [These Alaskan Indians have a jovial, hospitable way of eating white men when their tooth gets ripe for them, so I was a little uneasy and watched the preparations for the evening meal with something more than usual interest.[1]]

From this point for more than 300 miles the Yukon is a most peculiar stream, having a width of from five to eight miles and being filled with islands, some of them hundreds of acres in extent, in fact the islands take up more space between banks than the river itself. There are also a number of sloughs or bayous branching off on either hand, so that a person not familiar with the river is apt to pass the mouth of the Porcupine unawares. This made it necessary for me to get a native at Senate's camp to accompany me as far as the river. Few of these people understand a word of English but by the vigorous use of signs I got one young fellow to agree to go with me the next day.

He had the most sorrowful countenance I have ever seen outside a cemetery and not once in the three days we were together did he crack a smile and, as all attempts to learn his name were fruitless, I christened him "Mazeppa" which he seemed to think very pretty. One can imagine how our acquaintance progressed by the fact that before the end of the first day I was calling him "Zep." Early the next morning we started out down the river, Zep caressing the oars while I steered and looked at the scenery—what there was. But my sorrows were close at hand for the dreaded fall rains had begun and lasted with slight intervals until they were stopped by the beginning of winter a month later. Within two hours we were wet to the skin and, on landing on an island, put up the tent and here on account of the storm we were compelled to remain all day and all night and were unable to build a fire or dry our clothes. Just as we stopped at this place a chum of Zep's came up in a birch bark canoe and scenting something to eat went into camp with us. He was a short heavy set fellow with a tremendous shock of hair. Zep was continually addressing remarks to this individual in a sorrowful sort of voice at all of which he laughed immoderately. By their looks and nods I could see that I was the subject of their observations, and felt decidedly creepy until I got rid of this precious pair. All three of us slept in my little 7 by 7 tent that night. The next day we made three starts when it looked as if the rain had ceased but each time it started up again and we were compelled to land and put up our tent. During all these maneuvers the young man in the birch bark canoe followed us and graced our camp with his presence especially at meal time.

The vicissitudes of the last two days with the numerous drenchings had given me a severe cold, the only one by the way that I have had on the entire trip and I lay that night in my wet blankets with a promising fever and what I fondly imagined were the preliminary symptoms of pneumonia. I knew that if I had to wrestle with that disease out here on an island in the Yukon in the midst of the fall rains, without medical attendance and no nursing but that of these two young cannibals, my chances to pull through were pretty slim. I had hoped that if I yielded up my sweet young life on this expedition it would be in some such thrilling manner as being chewed up by a grizzly or torn into small fragments by infuriated natives, but to lie out here in the brush and die of common every-day pneumonia like a person can have down in Kansas when he gets his feet wet, and have the fact get into the papers was harrowing. But the next day there was an improvement in my condition, likewise in the weather and we covered about 60 miles of the river, camping just about on the Arctic circle. The next day, Sept. 3rd, we camped at the mouth of the Porcupine river on the site of old Ft. Yukon, a long abandoned trading post, the only signs of which now are the decaying logs of the old stockade. [[I]t is only ruins now, for in a playful spell the Indians of the country rose up and had a mid-summer barbecue in which the baked meats were garnished with brass army buttons and a few shoulder straps to match.[2]] Here I was fortunate enough to find a white man, Mr. T. H. Beaumont, who had come in to trade for furs with the natives and expected to remain all winter. It had been my intention to get Indians at this place and tow my boat up the Porcupine, but Mr. Beaumont told me he was expecting soon a big five ton barge or lighter, belonging to the English mission at Rampart House, which was coming down from that place with a crew of natives for the purpose of taking up not only more supplies for the missionaries, but some trading goods he was going to trust to a young Indian in trade for furs and that there would be room for my stuff in the boat; consequently it would be better for me to leave my boat in his care and go up to Rampart House with the larger one. There was nothing to do now but settle down in camp and await the arrival of the looked-for boat. The two natives who had come down with me started on their return to Senate's camp and I spent the next eight days looking out of my tent door at the torrents of driving rain or occasional squalls of snow by which they were varied. There was nothing of interest in the vicinity, the country being as flat as a floor, a monstrous expanse of scrub spruce and birch.

On the 9th the boat arrived from Rampart House, a craft 40 feet long, 8 feet beam and 5 or 6 feet deep the entire boat being covered with a deck even with the gunwale. The boat was in charge of a very civilized young Indian who spoke good English and was withal a pretty decent fellow. He had been for several years interpreter and general handy man for Rev. C. G. Wallis, an English missionary who left this country only last summer. It was with that man Mr. Beaumont was entrusting the trading goods. The other eight Indians with him were savages, pure and simple, a wild and picturesque looking lot dressed entirely in skins of animals and guiltless of any knowledge of English or any ideas beyond eating and sleeping.

On the 11th, two days after the arrival of the Indians, we started up the Porcupine river on the two hundred mile journey to Rampart House [on what proved to be the hardest trip I ever took. The boat with its load weighed several tons...³] The Porcupine is a stream about the size of the Potomac or Hudson and has a current of six miles an hour. Of course the only method of making headway against such a current unless one is on a steam boat is by the method known as "tracking;" that is towing from the bank with a line. Fastened to the bow of the lighter was a 500 ft. line at the end of which the trackers harness themselves tandem, and pulling like plow horses, tow the boat against the powerful current, the young Indian, David, riding on the boat and steering it clear of the bank. Being a white man and a passenger I had the privilege of riding on deck, but a half day's trial of sitting there pelted by the ceaseless rains and chilled to the marrow by the north winds, was too much for me and I took a place on the tracking line and kept it the rest of the trip. Although wading nearly half the time, the hard work kept one reasonably warm, and it was infinitely better than freezing by inches on the open deck of the boat. The Porcupine is a roaring big stream nearly half a mile wide and almost without islands, the first 100 miles from its mouth being through a perfectly flat country and above this through mountains with tremendous, perpendicular bluffs, rising sheer from the water's edge for hundreds of feet. Through the flat country, our greatest trouble was caused by trees whose tops had fallen into the river, called "sweepers," and whose roots remained fast at the top of the bank, generally twenty feet above the water. Sometimes half a mile of bank had caved in, leaving a tremendous jumble of fallen trees in the water, around which it was impossible to take the boat, and it was necessary to cross the river in order to find a better bank.

These crossings were made by means of long sweep oars and were always exciting performances. So strong was the current that it was impossible to go straight across but we were always swept down stream fully half a mile, and often brought up on a gravel bar or ran into a steep bluff, or nest of sweepers and more than once it looked as if the boat and all its contents were bound for Davy Jones' locker. At these times the Indians always became greatly excited and seemed to lose their heads completely and the boat was generally allowed to take care of itself. The line also had a habit of breaking at critical moments, much to the discomfort of the one man who was on board steering. I think it is no exaggeration to say that we were wading half the time because there was no bank on which the trackers could walk, with water deep enough for the lighter near it. During all this time the rain was pouring and, in fact, everything seemed to combine to make the trip a wretchedly hard one. Under such circumstances our camps were not models of comfort, and cooking in a rain storm has some very pronounced drawbacks. [Think of wading in such water and then lying down and sleeping in clothing often stiff and frozen and always wet.[4]] But somehow we got along and, by hauling on the line ten or eleven hours a day, could make fifteen miles. In a week we were out of the flat country and in the mountains where there was no more trouble with sweepers, for the very simple reason that the river banks were of granite and so steep that no tree could grow on them. These walls of granite rise sheer from the water's edge for several hundred feet. Had they been smooth, tracking would have been practically impossible in some places, but often there were ledges or breaks where we could obtain a precarious foothold at the risk of tumbling down into the river below. That stern regard for the truth for which I am so justly celebrated, compels me to admit that in passing the worst of these places, I rode on the boat. I was brought up to believe that it was wrong, very wrong, for a man to walk on the face of a perpendicular bluff, like a fly on a pane of glass. I cannot take the time or space to describe the expedients used to get the boat around some of these cliffs that even the Indians could not scale.

On the evening of the eleventh day, we came upon the camp of about 30 Indians, the first we had seen since leaving the Yukon. They were living in hemi-spherical houses of birch bark and deer skin, about 16 feet in diameter. I took my ease in one of these primitive mansions that night with eleven Indians, men, women and children, all lying with their feet to the fire in the center, after the manner of the spokes of a wheel. Those people received us quite hospitably and set out a feed of moose meat that was not to be jeered at.

The next day was varied by an incident a little out of the usual order. About the middle of the afternoon the trackers came suddenly upon a big bear, whereat there was a great rush for the boat to get the rifles. Instead of charging the crowd as a well brought up bear would have done, he incontinently took to his heels and hid in a small clump of willows and we pelted this with stones until he ran out and was shot dead. My respect for the Alaskan grizzy was lowered several degrees by this performance. The next day a small band of caribou, as the wild reindeer of Alaska are called, was seen near the river and the Indians killed one of them. On the evening of that day, the 23rd, we reached our destination just thirteen days after leaving the Yukon. The exact distance between the Yukon and Rampart House is 213 miles, the river having been measured by Mr. J. H. Turner of the U. S. Coast Survey who spent the winter of 1889-90 at Rampart House. [Turner had been at Yakutat Bay at the same time Fred was in 1892.] We had been compelled to cross the river 111 times in that distance and being each time carried back about half a mile, had lost more than 50 miles, thus making at least, say in round numbers, 269 miles that we had towed a five ton boat against a six miles per hour current. Sometimes we were wading waist deep for hours in that icy current and for thirteen days not one of us had had on a stitch of dry clothing. It can be surmised that we were a worn out bedraggled looking crowd, when we reached our journey's end.

Rampart House, [within rifle shot of the lonely cairn of stone erected by Turner in 1890 to mark the exact point where the 141st meridian intersects the Porcupine River[5]], was for several years the most northwesterly post occupied by the Hudson Bay Company, but was abandoned in June 1893 when the trader, Mr. Firth, took charge of the post of Ft. McPherson on the McKenzie, two hundred miles to the eastward. At the same time, Rev. C. G. Wallis, a missionary of the Church of England who had been here for several years, returned home and it looked as if the Porcupine was to see the white man no more, but Mr. Benj. Totty [the curly haired blonde with the "big soulful eyes"], a young man of about 25 who had been out from England only a year, came up from Forty Mile to take Mr. Wallis' place, and reached here about six weeks before I did. So there were two of us to live out an Arctic winter among the savages with our nearest white neighbor 200 miles away, and totally cut off from communication with the outside world. The prospect was not a particularly cheering one. When the trader left here last year, he left his house, a fairly good log building, totally devoid of any unnecessary frills, however. There were several rooms, [but I have all I can do keeping myself warm in[6]] one of which I fitted up as well as possible with the means at my command the furniture consisting of a small cooking stove, two tables, a bunk and an improvised chair, [and this one [room] serves as parlor, library, bedroom, dining room and kitchen[7]], and settled down to the enjoyment of home life and domestic comforts, broken only by the trips to Fort McPherson and the Arctic ocean. The missionary's house was distant about a hundred yards and we occasionally visited each other and like a couple of house-wives exchanged receipts for such difficult feats of cooking as making tea and cooking moose steak. [Totty] [altogether does his best to give American local color to his conversation to put us on a common footing. But it is a bad job. I have thought of poker—but of course that won't do.[8]]

[Ed Funston's assessment in an 1899 interview about the Fred Funston-Benjamin Totty relationship was succinct: "'Think of Fred camping a whole winter with a preacher, and then read some of the things he says when he gets excited out in the Philippines,' and [Ed's] deep voice rang with laughter,"[9] presumably referring to Fred's love of swearing.] [Billy White was blunt: "As the winter deepened it is probable that the good brother Trotty [sic] got on Funston's nerves..."[10]]

On the day after our arrival at Rampart House winter set in with a heavy fall of snow and the river was full of ice and closed to navigation. After that the days dragged along monotonously enough. Snow fell for weeks until the whole country was literally buried in the so-called beautiful, and the plateau stretched away to the north in great rolling billows of spotless white. Day by day the sun sank lower on the southern horizon and on Nov. 16, disappeared for the last time.

I had been working myself up to a state of mild frenzy to go somewhere, no difference where, or do something, it mattered not what, to break the tiresome monotony of such an existence, and about this time an opportunity presented itself.[11] [When I heard Mr. Trotty [sic] say that he was going to send some Indians with some of the supplies he had received from Beaumont to another missionary at Fort McPherson I was glad to break away from the humdrum of the life at Rampart House, and so I went with them.[12]] For restless, adventurous Fred, his enforced stay in the isolation of Rampart House defines the phrase "cabin fever."

# Chapter Ten Notes—*Ascending the Porcupine River*

1-4.   "A Trip Up the Yukon River," *The Kansas City Star*, July 22, 1894 (Frederick Funston Papers, hereafter FFP) (Archives Division, Kansas State Historical Society). Extracts from a letter Funston wrote at Fort McPherson to an unidentified friend in November 1893.

5.   Frederick Funston, "Along Alaska's Eastern Boundary," *Harper's Weekly*, February 1, 1896 (FFP).

6-8.   "A Trip Up the Yukon River," *The Kansas City Star*, July 22, 1894 (FFP).

9.   "Fred Funston's Restless Life of Adventure," *The Chicago Sunday Tribune*, May 7, 1899 (FFP).

10.   William Allen White, "The Hero Of The Philippines," *The St. Louis Republic Magazine Section*, May 21, 1899.

11.   "Out of the North," *The Iola Register*, September 21 and October 5, 1894

12.   "A Trip Up the Yukon River," *The Kansas City Star*, July 22, 1894 (FFP).

# CHAPTER ELEVEN

# "Across the Great Divide in Midwinter"

—By Frederick Funston

## November 17, 1893 – December 8, 1893

In 1900, *Harper's Weekly* published an account written by Fred Funston about his snowshoe trip to Fort McPherson. *Harper's* identified Fred as "Brigadier General Frederick Funston," and, undoubtedly, was attempting to capitalize on the fame of the famous general. Presumably, Fred had written this article during his stay in New York City in early 1896 before his departure to fight in the Cuban revolution. My guess is that he had submitted it to *Harper's*, which purchased it but chose for now unknown reasons not to publish it. Once Fred had become famous, the magazine published it in its issue of December 22, 1900.

This article is reprinted below. On occasion, I have broken into several paragraphs one long paragraph. In brackets is information from other writings by Fred. In one place, I have deleted part of a sentence and the next sentence so that the text flows better with the inserted material. These changes are not identified.

\* \* \*

The beginning of the winter of 1893 and 1894 found me in camp with a band of the wandering Tinneh or Loucheux Indians on the site of the abandoned Hudson Bay Company trading post of Rampart House, on the Porcupine River in northeastern Alaska. I had left Dyea Inlet on the south coast five months before, and after a 1200-mile journey rid [sic] Chilkoot Pass, Forty Mile Creek, and the Porcupine River, had reached a point well inside the arctic circle, where I expected to make my headquarters during the nine-months winter. The river had begun freezing by the middle of September, and before the close of the month the scantily timbered hill-sides and the treeless plateaus that stretched back from the river-bank were buried in snow. As the season advanced, the nights grew longer and the days shorter, while the sun, sinking lower and lower on the southern horizon, disappeared for the last time in the middle of November.

Rampart House was for some years the most northwesterly fur-trading post maintained by the Hudson Bay Company, the goods for barter being brought on dog sleds from the Mackenzie River, more than 200 miles to the eastward. The furs sent out the same way were sometimes a year in reaching the Company's stores at Winnipeg, thousands of miles to the southeast. Owing to the increasing tendency of the natives to send their furs to the Yukon traders, it had been decided to abandon Rampart House, and the trader, Mr. John Firth, was transferred to Peel River post, near the Mackenzie, where I afterward met him. On abandoning the post Mr. Firth had left behind him a fairly comfortable log cabin, constructed from the small spruce trees that grow along the Porcupine River, and on my arrival I had taken possession of this house. The Porcupine River rises between the Yukon and the upper Mackenzie, and flowing first toward the north, finally bends around to the southwest, and after a circuitous course of more than 400 miles empties into the Yukon. It is somewhat larger than the Hudson, and the total area of its valley, lying partly in Alaska and partly in the British possessions, is greater than that of all the New England States combined. All of the river except its head-waters lies north of the arctic circle. The natives living in the valley of the Porcupine do not exceed five hundred, and are members of the great Tinneh race who inhabit the valleys of the Yukon and Mackenzie rivers. They were called the Loucheux by the French-Canadian explorers of the Hudson Bay Company, who were the first white men to penetrate these wilds of the far Northwest. They are well-disposed people, although savages living entirely by the chase, and are morally and mentally much superior to the plains Indians of the United States. They have no permanent villages, but are nomads, constantly roaming about like the Tartars of Asia, following the movements of the herds of barren ground caribou, whose flesh is their principal article of diet, and whose skins furnish them with clothing and material for their beehive-shaped lodges.

A member of one of the Porcupine River bands had brought up from the Yukon a considerable quantity of trading goods and established himself at Rampart House, where he remained all winter, bartering for furs with the Indians who would from time to time come in from the various hunting camps in the surrounding country. Although only a few families remained in the vicinity of Rampart House during the winter, there was scarcely a week when there were not arrivals from some of the hunting bands. These people would bring in a sled full of furs, which they would exchange for ammunition, tea, and tobacco, returning after a stay of a couple of days. This young trader had at one time been in the employ of an English missionary who had visited the country, and had also been much with Mr. Firth before the abandonment of Rampart House, and so had acquired a fair knowledge of English. He had adopted the English name David, given him by the missionary in lieu of his unpronounceable native one, and was an altogether bright and progressive young Indian. Early in November this man determined to make a trip to the Hudson Bay Company's post at Peel River, across the mountains, for the purpose of bartering some of the furs that he had acquired for goods that he had not been able to get from the Yukon traders. The distance was more than 200 miles in an almost due easterly direction, and the route for the first hundred miles lay up the Porcupine River and thence across the most northerly spur of the Rockies to the valley of the Mackenzie.

The prospect of sitting about all winter trying to keep warm, with no amusement but an occasional caribou hunt, had begun to pall on me, and I had no difficulty in making arrangements to accompany the party. There were besides David and myself three men from one of the Porcupine River bands, Chiteinda, Tabkokwat, and Kwandi, and after several false starts we finally got off on the morning of the 17th of November. There were four sleds, two laden with furs for barter, one with meat and tallow for ourselves and the dogs, and the fourth with the sleeping robes and cooking utensils.

The Esquimau sleds that I afterwards saw on the coast of the Arctic Ocean and Bering Sea were quite huge affairs, with runners, and were dragged by any number of dogs, sometimes as many as twenty. Sleds of this type are perfectly practicable along the level sea-beaches and where there is no brush, and where the snow is shallow and hard packed, but would be worse than useless in the interior, where the conditions are radically different. The Indian sled is merely a birchwood toboggan, eight feet long and twenty inches wide, and is drawn by four dogs hitched tandem. The load, usually between two and three hundred pounds, is securely lashed down in order that it may withstand the numerous upsets that frequently occur. Unless a path has already been broken by some preceding party, it is always necessary for one man to walk ahead of the leading team to make a track through the snow, as the dogs are not guided with the whip, as is done among the Esquimaux. In addition to the man walking ahead for the purpose of making a track, there is always one to look after each sled, his duties being to keep the dogs pulling steadily, untangle them when they become mixed up in their harness, and right the sled whenever it is turned over. While the Esquimau almost invariably rides on his sled, the Indian rarely does, tramping along on snow-shoes instead, the sled being utilized to carry provisions, camp outfit, and whatever goods they may be transporting.

As we fled down the bluff onto the snow-covered ice of the river in the half-twilight of a bitterly cold November morning, we were quite an imposing cavalcade, five men, four sleds, and sixteen dogs, and started at a brisk pace on our snow-shoe journey of more than four hundred miles. The sky was clear and there was scarcely a breath of wind, while the mercury was at forty degrees below zero. All of our party were clothed in the native fur costume... [I am not in the habit of disclosing the luxuries of my wardrobe through the public prints, and doubt the good taste of doing so, but it may be of interest to know how a fellow fits himself out to travel and sleep out doors in an Arctic winter, so here goes—

[Over two suits of knit underwear and a heavy flannel shirt, I wore corduroy trousers and vest, and over all this a complete suit of furs consisting of a caribou skin coat or "parkie", with hood attachment, and mink skin trousers and on my feet three pairs of woolen socks and two pairs of moose skin moccasins. My sleeping gear consisted of a robe of twenty-four lynx skins lined with a blanket.

[Of course all wore snow shoes and, as such an article is utterly unknown in Kansas, I might say that a snow shoe is a contrivance some four feet long and eight inches broad, made of rawhide woven over a wooden frame and worn on the feet to keep a person from falling into the snow up to the ears at every step.[1]] [I thought I had tried about every form of violent leg exercise from dancing the Newport to eluding the attentions of an illmannered [sic] bull-dog, but this thing of show-shoeing twenty-five miles a day was a revelation as to how terribly tired and footsore a man can get. But it is impossible to give more than the roughest outline of this trip, as it is a long story and one of terrible hardship—the worst I have ever undergone.[2]]

Kwandi took the lead, and the head team followed in his track, while each of the other four of us took charge of one of the sleds and carried a whip, which there was not much occasion to use for the first three or four days. For the first day we kept to the river-bed, and at five o'clock, which at this season in a northern latitude is long after dark, went into camp among some stunted spruce trees on the south bank. The method of establishing a nigh [sic] camp among these northern Indians is worthy of detailed description. The first thing is to unharness the dogs and turn them loose; the snow-shoes are then utilized to clear as much of the snow as possible from a space large enough to enable all five of us to lie down together, and several caribou-skins are spread on the ground. If there was a wind the sleds were arranged in order to give as much protection as possible. Any small dead spruce trees that could be found were cut down and a roaring fire built just at the foot of our impromptu bed. The big, shaggy dogs gathered about the cheerful blaze and watched the cooking operations with their appreciative eyes, occasionally varying the programme by getting into a free-for-all fight among themselves, which necessitated clubbing the more aggressive ones into submission.

Our fare was simple. On one of the sleds were about 200 pounds of dried caribou meat and several large cakes of deer tallow and ten pounds of tea. Dried meat is by no means so appetizing as the fresh article, but it would have been impossible to carry on one sled a sufficient quantity of fresh meat for our party. While we expected to kill some game *en route*, it would be rash to depend entirely on so uncertain a contingency. One whose palate has always been accustomed to the fare of civilization is apt to shudder at the thought of eating tallow, but a short period of out-door life in the arctic regions will serve to hastily bring him to his senses on that score. We had tallow as a part of every meal. It was sometimes eaten cold, but oftener melted and poured over the dried meat after the latter had been boiled. Tea is the universal beverage of the arctic traveler, if he can get it. Neither spirituous liquors, coffee, nor chocolate can in any way be compared with it as a means of keeping up the strength during the fearfully trying work of snow-shoeing day after day in arctic weather. Both white men and natives in the northern British possessions and Alaska use it in large quantities, and the former will rarely attempt a winter journey without it. It is made very strong and drunk in large quantities. At all of our camps in this journey water for boiling dry meat and making tea was obtained by melting snow in an iron kettle. Before retiring for the night the dogs were fed, an operation that required all of the party armed with clubs and whips to protect the weaker dogs from their savage fellows. At our first camp, while we were going through this exciting operation, several of the big brutes pulled one of the Indians down into the snow, and the entire pack fought all over him for a couple of minutes before he could extricate himself.

After supper we rolled up in our fur robes and lay down to sleep, I in the middle and two Indians on either side of me. It requires no little practice to enable one to arrange the robes about his face so that he can breathe with comfort and still not admit sufficient air to freeze his nose and cheeks.

We would no sooner be settled down in bed than the dogs, naturally preferring our robes to the snow, would lie down about our feet and sometimes on top of us. The only drawback to this arrangement was their mania for fighting among themselves. We would be sleeping comfortably when suddenly there would be a yelp as one dog bit another, and then half a dozen of them would fight all over our prostrate forms. This always made the Indians furious, and if the disturbance was not over in a few seconds they got up and quelled the trouble with whatever they could lay their hands on. [One night when we slept out this way it was 48 degrees below zero, and you bet if the cat didn't happen to be "in" or the clock wound up it just staid [sic] that way till morning, and if the pride of the household wanted a "grink" he stuffed snow in his face and made the best of it. Our bill of fare on the trip was dried venison, tea and tallow. People who have not eaten tallow under the shade of the Arctic circle do not know what's good. I don't blame the Indians for being cannibals; a man develops an appetite up here with the commissary store runs low which would make him look with an evil eye on his own grandfather.[3]]

In the morning we tumbled out of our robes into the stinging air, built a fire, and after a breakfast of meat, tallow, and tea, put the dogs into harness and pushed on into the darkness. Had it not been that the Indians were so thoroughly familiar with the country, it would have been impossible for us to make the journey, as two-thirds of the time that we were travelling one could not see an object as large as a man at a distance of 200 yards. Our route lay on the second day mostly on the ice of the river, though a number of short-cuts were made across bends. The country along the stream was generally flat, and covered with a jungle of stunted willow, birch, and spruce. Some distance north of the river were low mountains. Through hours that seemed endless we trudged on through the gloom, the silence broken only by the creaking of the sleds and the voices of the Indians scolding their dogs. Each day we stopped an hour at noon to prepare our mid-day meal, and one day I saw a band of seven caribou crossing the river on the ice a short distance above where we had stopped; but the Indians, with characteristic stupidity, instead of attempting to stalk them, which could have been done easily, opened fire from our position and frightened the animals, which had not yet suspected our presence. Darkness was upon us again by two o'clock and the wind had risen. I was unused to snow-shoeing, and as the Indians struck a lively gait, was soon left far behind. At nearly seven o'clock, after I had begun to wonder whether the Indians would ever stop, I heard a short distance ahead the barking of dogs and the voices of children, and found that our party had come up with a hunting band of Loucheux, and had gone into camp with them.

We left our hosts at seven o'clock the next morning and kept on our way eastward. A part of the time we were on the river-bed, and part in the great stretches of willow and scrub birch that covered the lowlands along its banks. The violent exercise of snow-shoeing twenty miles a day and sleeping in the open air had begun to tell on me badly. My muscles and joints became swollen, and I suffered at times the most excruciating pain. It was impossible to keep up with the pace set by the Indians, and I got in the habit of dropping far behind and getting into camp after the fire had been built. As long as we were in the willow brush where the snow was soft I had no difficulty in following the track of the sleds, but often for long stretches on the river or over frozen lakes the surface of the snow would be so hard crusted that the slight marks made by the sleds could not be seen in the darkness, and I often lost the track and wasted a great deal of time in groping about trying to find it again. Whenever the Indians reached the summit of a ridge or were on the surface of a lake where there was unobstructed view, one of them would occasionally stop and strike a match, which would flare up for a few seconds and serve to guide me. There were always three or four hours of twilight at mid-day, but usually a sled could not be seen more than 200 yards. We kept pushing ahead, however, and three days later reached the point at which the trail leaves the Porcupine River, and made our fifth night camp in a ravine.

The next morning the wind had died out, and at six o'clock we poked our heads from under the robes into air that stung like the cut of a whip-lash, for it was fifty degrees below zero.

All of that day for twelve long hours we pushed up hill and down hill, across frozen marshes and through miles of willow, and after a most trying day's journey of twenty-five miles, came down on the ice of a small river, a northern tributary of the Porcupine, and in an hour more were at Le Pierre House, on its north bank. Le Pierre House, like Rampart House, is an abandoned trading-post of the Hudson Bay Company. The old building once used as a trading-post was at the time of our visit occupied by a couple of families of Indians. They had a considerable quantity of caribou meat, and we determined to remain over one day to give ourselves and the dogs a much-needed rest. In six days we had covered about 125 miles—not half bad when one considers that we had to break our own track, being the first party over the trail that season. The day spent at Le Pierre House seemed to us foot-sore travellers [sic] the height of luxury.

Early on the morning of the second day after our arrival we left Le Pierre House and took a course somewhat north of east. The country was open and rolling, and there was less brush than had been encountered formerly. As soon as it became fairly light we could see ahead of us an apparently unbroken chain of not very precipitous mountains, extending from north to south. It was the northern extremity of the Rockies, within fifty miles of where they slope down to the Arctic Ocean. Although the altitude of the highest peak was not more than 4000 feet above the level of the surrounding country, the range was a most impressive one, because nowhere from base to summit was there a bit of color to break the mantle of spotless white. While we were in camp for our mid-day meal in a little hollow, I took a walk to the summit of a ridge distant about two hundred yards in order to get a better view of the range, and to my surprise saw a band of fourteen caribou, the wild reindeer of the north, scattered about on the opposite hill-side. My first impulse was to run down and tell the Indians, but upon second thought I knew that they would come tearing up the hill, followed by all the dogs, and that there would be a great deal of firing without any injury to the deer, so I walked leisurely back to camp, picked up my Winchester, and after casually remarking to David that I thought I would look about to see if there were caribou in any of the ravines, strolled off to the south to get to the leeward of the animals.

Crawling up to the summit of another ridge I again saw the herd, but by using great caution did not alarm them. The distance was about four hundred yards, and from the nature of the surface it would be impossible to approach nearer without risk of alarming the animals. The nearest deer was a big buck with tremendous antlers which was busily engaged in pawing up the snow to uncover the moss and lichens, but he was facing me and presented too small a target. Another was standing near him broadside on, but in a clump of willows, which made it a bad shot. Several were lying down, and some were distant fully five hundred yards. There was one fine-looking fellow, however, standing with his side presented and apparently lost in meditation. Of the fourteen he seemed to be the only decent target, and I set the sight at four hundred yards, rose quietly to my knee, took careful, steady aim without a rest, and fired. In the frosty air the rifle made a report like a young cannon, and the animal that I had shot at came suddenly to life and dashed off up the hill, for it was a clean miss. The bullet had whizzed uncomfortably close to the one in the willows, and he came out with a bound. The whole herd was alarmed, but the echo seemed to confuse them, and the one that had been pawing the snow wheeled about. I saw it was the last chance, took aim for a second and let drive again. He went down in his tracks, and as I stood up the remainder of the herd tore off like mad. The Indians came running up the hill, and when they saw the big buck down in the snow, all tried to embrace me at once. We cut the animal up, put a part of the meat on the sleds, gave the dogs a big feed, and moved on. That night we camped at the foot of the mountains in a little clump of willows. Except for a few willows in the ravines the country was barren and treeless.

In the morning at seven we had hitched up the dogs and reloaded the sleds, and were on our way up the ravine which the Indians said led to the pass over the range. During most of the forenoon the slope was so steep that we had to assist the dogs in dragging the sleds. Fortunately the snow on the mountain-side was quite hard packed and consequently good sledding, so that the ascent was not so serious a matter as it would otherwise have been. At high noon we were on the summit of the Great Divide which separates the valley of the Yukon from that of the Mackenzie. The view was superb and beyond description. Everywhere were mountains, all spotless white, and to the east could be seen stretching like dark bands, across the wastes of snow the timber growth that marked the courses of the Mackenzie and Peel rivers. Low down in the south were the rays of the sun, peering up from below the horizon and illuminating the sky as they do with us, an hour after sunset, and the light could be seen shining direct on the summits of some of the higher peaks. The descent led us to the bottom of a huge gorge, which was not reached until the short daylight had faded away, and we kept on for five hours more at the swinging, clumsy trot that we always affected on a down grade. Our camp for this night was a particularly cheerless one in the snow at the foot of a high cliff. The next day, in the afternoon, having kept on down the canyon to the east, we came out on the frozen surface of Peel River, here nearly half a mile wide, and crossing to the east side, kept on down the stream in a northeasterly direction for two hours, and finally saw lights in the distance and heard the barking of dogs. Half an hour later we helped the eager animals drag the sleds up the river-bank, and found ourselves in the midst of a little group of log cabins, the most northerly trading-post on the continent of North America. [And it was not a day too soon for me, as I was literally worn down to skin and bones, with every joint so stiff and sore from the unusual exercise that I could barely move without a groan. To walk 200 miles in nine days is no job to be laughed at, even if a person has a plank road with a hotel at the end of every day's journey and a beer garden every five miles, but when it comes to going up hill and down on snowshoes through the dark, sleeping out in the snow every night, and living on dry meat and tallow, and all through the cold of Arctic winter it is a pretty tough task and crowds the limit of human endurance pretty close.[4]]

This post, known throughout the Northwest as Peel River, is designated on nearly all maps by its old-time name of Fort McPherson.

It is situated on the right hand or east bank of Peel River, a short distance above its junction with the Mackenzie. The Hudson Bay Company's trader, Mr. John Firth, a fine bluff Scotchman, who in twenty years has not been south of the arctic circle, having been stationed in that time not only at his present post, but for several years each at Le Pierre House and Rampart House before those posts were abandoned. Mr. Firth, surprised and delighted to have a visitor from the outside world, took me into his house and made me his guest during our stay. [For two days I lay stretched out on a pile of caribou skins before a roaring fire, almost too tired to eat.[5]]

[The arrival of a white man across country from Alaska of course created a sensation, and the natives came from far and near to bask in my smiles and admire the frost bites on my face. As I lay there on my couch and received delegation after delegation of fur clothed savages, every one of whom insisted on shaking hands with me, I felt like some old Turkish vizier receiving homage from his subjects.

[Ft. McPherson is not a fort as the name implies but a trading post of the Hudson Bay Co., and is the most north-westerly one now occupied by them and is the only one north of the Arctic circle. The white residents are Mr. Firth, Archdeacon McDonald a Church of England man, and two Jesuit missionaries. Besides these the French traveler and hunter Count Sainville was wintering there. Very fortunately I happened to know of this latter gentleman, from having read a couple of articles of his in an English magazine describing some of his experiences in the Senegal region of Africa. Having tired of elephant and lion shooting, he has come to this country to try his luck on moose, caribou and grizzly. He is I think the finest looking man I ever saw, a magnificent blond six footer, with a military carriage, blue eyes and a tawney beard,—a queer "layout" for a Frenchman. He is a most enthusiastic sportsman and has killed big game in every quarter of the globe; he is also a very good fellow and very companionable.[6]]

The four Indians who had come with me were put up in a small house belonging to Mr. Firth, and spent the four days around the big fire, drinking tea, smoking, and exchanging gossip with the other Loucheux. The two sled-loads of furs that David had brought from Rampart House were exchanged for goods, and at six o'clock on the morning of December 1 we had the sixteen dogs again in harness, said our good-byes to Mr. Firth, cracked the whips, and started on the return to Rampart House. The moon was shining brilliantly, and the snow-covered land seemed flooded with her light. There was a sharp sting in the air, for it was forty-seven degrees below zero. All that we had to do was to follow our old trail back over hills and mountains and across lakes and rivers for more than two hundred miles. Our track had already been broken on the east-bound trip, so that better time was made. On the second night out, when we camped on the eastern slope of the divide, the mercury fell to fifty-two degrees below zero, the coldest weather encountered on the trip. At Le Pierre House we remained only one night. Two days later, as we were jogging along through the gloom, a blizzard suddenly swept down from the north, and before it was possible to unhitch the dogs or go into camp the darkness was so intense that one could not see the length of a sled. The wind had attained a hurricane velocity, and it was impossible for men or dogs to stand up against it. The air seemed full of flying snow, and above the roar of the storm were heard the shrieks of the dogs, stung into fury by the bitter cold. We simply stopped where we were, and spent all night in trying to control the maddened animals and in crouching behind the sleds to break the fury of the storm. Our faces and hands, already frost-bitten, suffered terribly; but it is useless to attempt any description of that night of horrors. After ten hours the storm ceased as suddenly as it had begun, and we hastened to the nearest clump of willows and built a fire, where we remained for a couple of hours cooking and eating.

The next day about noon I was for once walking ahead of the entire party, and came suddenly upon four Indian skin houses near the trail. It was a hunting party of Loucheux, about fifty in all. I announced my arrival by a yell, and was promptly attacked by a dozen dogs. I broke over the head of the first one a club I was carrying as a sort of staff, but they had me down in a trice, and were engaged in reducing my fur coat to ribbons when the Indians came streaming out of the houses. They knocked the dogs right and left; and a young woman, anxious to do her part, threw an iron kettle into the pack and bowled over her brother, a small boy who had valiantly taken one of the animals by his stump of a tail. I was taken into one of the houses, and as soon as it was found that I was none the worse for the scuffle there was an all-around laugh. One old dame would break out about every five minutes with a guffaw that showed her appreciation of the entertainment. In a short time my Indians came up, and we remained overnight with these people. On the night of the 8th of December we reached Rampart House, having made the return trip at an average rate of twenty-five miles a day—not bad snow-shoeing. It was twenty-two days since we had left Rampart House, and every one of the more than four hundred miles of the round trip had been tramped on snow-shoes.

[Talk of sore feet and limbs and stiff joints when every step was a torture—it nearly makes me sick to think of it. I was in a pitiful condition when we reached Rampart House—sore, stiff, worn down to skin and bone and nearly all the epidermus [sic] frosted off from my highly intellectual mug. I had...lived on food that a respectable dog would disdain. I carried my U. S. weather bureau thermometer on the trip. The maximum temperature in the twenty-two days was 31 deg. below zero. The minimum 52 deg. below. Gawd Eddie just think of your only gric sleeping out of doors when he needed but open his little eye to see the stars, with the thermometer 52 deg. below zero.[7]

* * *

In his May 30, 1894, letter to *The Iola Register*, Fred told of occurrences after the return to Rampart House. That account follows here, with material from one of Fred's later letters in brackets:

* * *

The next three months dragged by with the most tiresome monotony, broken only by a small row with the natives. Occasionally a small band of Indians would come in with their dogs and sleds and remain a day or two and depart, much to the relief of the two white men who had to put up with their insolent and everlasting begging. [Three years later he wrote: "I lay down on my bunk...and nearly cried my eyes out from sheer lonliness [sic]."[8]]

As to that rumpus with the Indians I am not particularly proud of my part in the affair, but it may be of some interest to others. The trouble was caused by a slight indiscretion on my part, that is, in giving an unusually impudent young buck a cut over the legs with a dog's whip, whereat the said Y. B. gathered together his grandfathers, uncles, aunts, cousins and other disreputable kin and announced his intention of filling me full of nice round little holes. I didn't exactly run, I withdrew like the Confederate General who "left the enemy behind by hard riding," and once within my sylvan retreat, took down my arsenal consisting of repeating rifle and double barrelled [sic] shotgun and, having barred the door, awaited developments which were not long in coming. The assembled clans gathered on the outside and procuring a stick of timber, were about to batter down the door but desisted on my positive assurance that the first gentleman who came through would be presented with about a tablespoonful of buckshot. Under such circumstances being first was rather ticklish business and the door was not broke down. The next day, everybody's temper being cooled down, the matter was arranged without shedding the blood of any of the best people.

This incident brings up the subject of the character and disposition of the Indians of Alaska. The entire valley of the Yukon and its tributaries, a region comprising the fourth part of Alaska and an immense extent of the British Northwest territory [sic], equaling the entire Mississippi valley in area, is peopled by what ethnologists, scientific men and explorers generally call the Tinneh race. These consist of a large number of separate tribes and bands, differing somewhat in language and customs, but having a sufficient degree of similarity to each other to class them as one race, or in the unique language of a Forty Mile man "the same breed of varmints." Subsisting entirely on fish and meat and clothed entirely in skins, they are of necessity hunters by occupation and lead a roving and nomadic life. Physically they are the finest savages I have ever seen, lithe and well built, almost universally healthy and strikingly good looking. In all respects, mentally, morally and physically they are superior to their near neighbors, the brutal and vicious Thlinkets on the south, and the equally degraded Eskimos on the north and west.

A year among them has satisfied me that their dangerous qualities have been greatly exaggerated. Some of them intend bad enough but as my friend Billy White would put it they "scare at the cars." After they once get it into their heads that a man is not afraid of them, they are quite a civil lot. In the matter of disposition the various tribes and bands seem to differ greatly, those at Forty Mile are as tame as cats, while the majority of those in this vicinity are well disposed though there are a few hot heads among them, like those with whom I had a rumpus.

Just at noon on January 25, while seated in the house, busy with my thoughts and a caribou stew, I was startled by a great shouting and firing of guns, accompanied by barking of dogs and a general hubbub, and rushing forth to learn the cause of the disturbance, beheld low down on the southern horizon, the smiling face of old Sol, just returning after an absence of seventy days. He looked rather sneaking and only remained in sight less than two minutes, but each day thereafter remained a little longer and rose a few degrees higher, the nights growing gradually shorter and the days longer so that before the close of March they were of equal length and by the first of May it had gone to the other extreme and was light all night.[9]

"The Indians came running up the Hill to see the big Buck."

Illustration in the published article.

Fred Funston "clothed in the native fur costume" which he had made while staying at McQuesten's Post. This photograph and those on the next two pages were taken in Kansas City, Missouri, after his return from Alaska. Likely Fred used these as illustrations in his public talks about his experiences in the frozen north.

"Over two suits of knit underwear and a heavy flannel shirt, I wore
corduroy trousers and vest, and over all this a complete suit of furs
consisting of a caribou skin coat or 'parkie,' with hood attachment,
and mink skin trousers and on my feet three pairs of woolen socks and
two pairs of moose skin moccasins. My sleeping gear consisted of a robe
of twenty-four lynx skins lined with a blanket."
Fred Funston

"Of course all wore snow shoes and, as such an article is utterly
unknown in Kansas, I might say that a snow shoe is a contrivance some
four feet long and eight inches broad, made of rawhide woven over a
wooden frame and worn on the feet to keep a person from falling
into the snow up to the ears at every step."
Fred Funston

## Chapter Eleven Notes—*"Across the Great Divide in Midwinter"*

1. "Out Of The North," *The Iola Register*, October 5, 1894. Second installment of Fred's letter of May 30, 1894. Fred's snowshoes measure four feet, one inch by 9 ¾ inches at the widest point and one inch at the narrowest. Measurements furnished by Kurtis Russell, Executive Director of Allen County Historical Society, Inc., Iola, Kansas, which owns Fred's snowshoes.

2. "Out Of The North," *The Iola Register*, October 5, 1894.

3. "A Trip Up The Yukon River," *The Kansas City Star*, July 22, 1894. Extracts from letter of Fred Funston at Ft. McPherson to an unidentified friend, November 1893 (Frederick Funston Papers, hereafter FFP) (Archives Division, Kansas State Historical Society).

4. "Out Of The North," *The Iola Register*, October 5, 1894.

5. "Out Of The North," *The Iola Register*, October 5, 1894.

6. "Out Of The North," *The Iola Register*, October 5, 1894.
   For more about a somewhat dubious character, Count de Sainville, who fathered by two different women illegitimate children while staying at Ft. McPherson, see Walter Vanast, editor, "Le Soi – Disant Comte: The Arctic Stay of Count de Sainville, A Ruined French Aristocrat Hoping To Get 'Rich' at Ft. McPherson 1889-1894" Draft 3, May 6, 2017. Available on the internet.
   From Ft. McPherson, Fred wrote his mother: "It must be a long time before this letter reaches you. There is no mail route in the country, but in a few days a train of dog sleds will start south with the year's output of furs collected at this place. So my letter will come to you through Canada, after travelling [sic] more than 2000 miles on a dog sled. It ought to reach you by May. I am in fairly good health but nothing to brag of." This letter did not reach Iola until nearly July, eight months later ("Our Arctic Explorer," *The Iola Register*, July 13, 1894. Extracts from letter of Fred Funston at Ft. McPherson to Ann E. Funston, November 23, 1893).

7. "Letter From F. Funston," *The University Courier*, September 20, 1894. This letter from Fred, whose university nickname was "Gric," was to his close friend, Edward C. Franklin. This letter was published with "expurgations."

8. Fred Funston to Charles F. Scott, May 10, 1897 (FFP). How keenly Fred must have missed Buck Franklin, V. L. Kellogg, Billy White, and Charlie Scott.

9. "Out Of The North," *The Iola Register*, October 5, 1894.

CHAPTER TWELVE

# A Snowshoe Trip to the Arctic Ocean: Fred Funston's Account

## March 10, 1894 – March 29, 1894

Fred Funston provided *The Iola Register's* readers a wonderfully detailed account of his snowshoe trip to the Arctic Ocean. This account, included in his letter of May 30, 1894, was published in the *Register* issues of October 12 and 19, 1894. It is reprinted below, and supplemental material from other writings and additional information is enclosed in brackets. On two occasions, I have broken a long paragraph into two paragraphs. These changes are not identified.

\* \* \*

[I have a great curiosity to see the Arctic ocean, and it is probable I will never have so good a chance again; and, as I didn't get to see the World's fair, I want to have something to talk about when I get home.[1]] On March 10, [1894], accompanied by one Indian and having a sled drawn by four dogs on which were carried our provisions and camp outfit, I started on what is undoubtedly one of the longest snow-shoe trips on record. Our route for the first 150 miles lay due north-west from Rampart House, over the great treeless, snow-covered plateau that stretches from the Porcupine river to the Romanzof mountains. We had brought with us on the sled dry meat for the dogs, and the same article, in addition to tallow and tea, for ourselves, sufficient to last six days, the length of time that we had expected it would take us to reach a band of Indians who, we had heard were camped in a certain locality and from whom we hoped to obtain additional supplies in order to enable us to continue our journey across the mountains. On reaching this place, we found to our dismay that the Indians had moved elsewhere and there was noting [sic] to indicate in what direction as recent snow storms and high winds had completely obliterated their trail through the snow. We were now in a pretty kettle of fish, as they say in Boston; nearly out of provisions, behind us more than a hundred miles of wintry wilderness, before us we knew not what and the thermometer 40 degrees below zero. Matters looked decidedly ugly. To take the back track and go five or six days on an empty stomach was pretty serious business when the severe cold makes such demands on one's vitality, and to push forward was only to lengthen the distance to travel in case we did finally turn back.

Our first move was to make a great circuit of about ten miles in the hope of finding signs of the trail of the missing Indians. This took all of one afternoon to no purpose, and when we bunked down to sleep that night on the leeward side of the up-turned sled our hearts were considerably heavier than our stomachs, for both ourselves and the dogs had eaten half rations. The next morning out, after a consultation we decided to push due west, the direction my Indian thought it most likely his missing brothers had taken, and then if in a days [sic] travel we found no sign of the trail, we were to kill one of the dogs for food and making a bee line for Rampart House, travel day and night until we reached it. We started without breakfast and hit a lively gait over the rolling, snow covered hills and all day my mind was tormented by visions of canine stew. The youngest and plumpest dog in that team has mighty little idea of what thin ice he skated on that day.[2]

About 1 o'clock, while we were passing through a clump of willows in a creek valley, the Indian shot a rabbit whereat we indulged in a miniature Fourth of July celebration and prepared a barbecue at once. I suppose I should blush to say it that the only part of the rabbit that got away was the hair, and the dogs didn't get anything. After that we felt more chipper and thought that in a country where there was one rabbit, there might be some of his relatives. We had seen no caribou tracks and knew there were none in this vicinity and wherever we found them, there would be Indians, for the Indians follow them in their migrations. During the afternoon we descended into the partially wooded valley of the head-waters of the Sheenjle [sic: Sheenjek], one of the northern tributaries of the Porcupine. About 5 o'clock the Indian, who was walking ahead, suddenly fired both barrels of his gun into the air and gave vent to a series of whoops that would have done credit to an Apache. He had found the long-looked-for trail. Although we now knew that we were going in the right direction, it was difficult to guess whether we would find the natives within five miles or a hundred. Following this track for a couple of hours we went into camp for the night. Just before reaching this place the Indian had shot two ptarmigan, birds about as large as a quail, and these we had for supper. The next morning we divided the last lump of tallow into several pieces about the size of a walnut and gave ourselves and the dogs one each. I will take occasion to remark right here that there is no sense in a fellow being stuck up about his grub in such a country as this. People down in Kansas who have been brought up on pumpkin pie and fried chicken, are, I know, liable to turn up their noses at a man who would make a breakfast out of a lump of deer tallow, but up here it is quite the thing and is a dish much affected by the local aristocracy.

The sled tracks through the snow which we were now following, led almost due north up the valley into the mountains, for we were now inside the Romanzof range, and on every side were hundreds of precipitous peaks and crags. That day at noon we ate the last mouthful of food on the sled, a piece of dried salmon as large as a man's hand, and to make a long story short, that night we reached the Indian camp and were most hospitably received. They were right in the midst of the caribou and had an abundance of fresh meat so that our famine was turned into feasting. In this camp were about fifty people, men, women and children, living in four houses of dressed deer skins. In shape these skin houses are round, about 16 feet in diameter, and 8 or 10 feet high in the center, and are stretched over eight poles. When the Indians wish to move camp, in order to follow the caribou, these skin houses are folded up like a tent and carried on the sleds. The cooking is done over a fire in the center, a large opening being left in the top of the tent for the escape of the smoke.

Upon my arrival I had to undergo the ordeal of shaking hands with every individual, from a decrepit octogenarian with one eye, down to the smallest babe in arms. One woman even had the monumental assurance to hold up her dirty faced young one for me to kiss, but I drew the line on that. All of the men had at some time visited the trading posts, but a number of the women and nearly all of the children had never seen a white man so that my arrival created a veritable sensation and the preparation of a feast was at once begun. From my condition I thought it would have been more appropriate to have had the feast first and the hand shaking afterwards but politeness is one of my strong points, so I said nothing.

Each family also presented me with a small present, half a dozen caribou tongues, or some other native delicacy. These presentations were always made by young comely young [sic] women, a compliment to my youth that all but moved me to tears.

At various times during the winter we had heard rumors from the Indians to the effect that a whaling fleet had gone into winter quarters somewhere on the coast of the Arctic ocean, presumably at Herschel Island, a point a hundred miles west of the mouth of the McKenzie. From Rampart House to Herschel Island can't be more than two hundred miles if one goes in a direct line about thirty degrees east of north, but I had wished to make the trip in a round-about way in order to visit these Indians, so that now, having traveled about one hundred and fifty miles in a north-westerly direction from Rampart House, Herschel Island lay about the same distance northeast of us. These Indians said that if we would wait several days until they could kill some more deer, a number of them would go with us and take several loads of fresh meat to the whaling ship to barter for cloth, tobacco and ammunition.

Although there are some disadvantages about traveling with a crowd of Indians, still I thought it better on the whole as we would go through a country with which none of us were familiar and would soon be among the Eskimo who are sometimes inclined to be a little frolicsome with their visitors. We remained with these people four days, and on two of these days I went caribou hunting with the men and distinguished myself by killing one big buck. The manner of surrounding a herd of these animals is not without interest but if I start out to tell about those caribou hunts, I can never bring this letter to a close. Anyhow a considerable number, I don't know just how many, were killed in the four days, and ten of these Indians with six sled loads of fresh meat, started off with us. We were now quite a procession, twelve men, seven sleds and twenty eight dogs. Our course lay almost due north-east across the Romanzof mountains.

On the morning of the second day we reached the summit of the divide at the headwaters of a stream that empties into the Arctic ocean [which I named Turner river[3]]. I wish that some of the people who think they have seen mountains could have been with me that morning and gazed upon the view that lay before us. On every side stretched a vast snow-covered region, limitless in extent, through which projected thousands of jagged mountain peaks. As far as the eye could reach there was a great ocean of snowy peaks, range after range, piercing the bluest of blue skies, and everything a spotless white. A more desolate or apparently lifeless land one never beheld. I was the first white man to gaze upon this scene and it is doubtful if another will, in the next hundred years, cross the Romanzof range at this place. Descending the mountains on their northern slope, we traveled rapidly down the valley of the stream I have mentioned above, crossing numerous frozen lakes. Occasionally we would see a band of caribou and get one or two of them and one day an Indian killed a mountain sheep. On the 4th day after leaving the Indian camp, we saw the first signs of Eskimos, a number of vacant snow houses that looked like overgrown bee hives, and some sled tracks.

On the evening of the next day, we came suddenly out of the mountains onto the narrow strip of low land bordering the coast of the Arctic ocean. This point, as I afterwards learned from the whalers, is almost exactly on the 141$^{st}$ meridian so that if anyone will take trouble to look on a map where the 141$^{st}$ meridian which is the eastern boundary of Alaska, strikes the Arctic ocean, he will see where we were on this day of grace March 27, 1894.

None of the Indians in my party had ever been so far away from home before and so were not sure as to the whereabouts of Herschel Island where the whalers were supposed to be, but I knew that it must be along the coast well to the eastward of us yet. So we kept on in that direction. The country bordering the beach was nearly as flat as a floor, and the snow packed very hard so that walking was a positive luxury after our weeks of floundering in the deep soft snow of the interior.

Before noon of the next day we came upon the beach of the frozen Arctic ocean. It looks as it does in pictures a great mass of icebergs jumbled together in all sorts of confusion, stretching away beyond the reach of vision. At this point were an Eskimo cache, containing a lot of sealskins, and several kyacks [sic], as their peculiar sealskin boats are called. It was evident that we must soon meet some of these people and we were in some doubt as to how they would receive us. It has not been a great many years since the Eskimos and the Indians in this region were waging a sort of guerrilla warfare caused by the former crossing the mountains into the hunting grounds of the Indians and killing caribou, occasionally stealing a child or two and doing other unneighborly acts which the Indians generally repaid by making a pan roast of every Eskimo they caught. I have in my possession a horrible looking weapon made from a large caribou antler trimmed with a piece of jagged iron, with which, several years ago, an athletic Indian battered out the thinking gear of an unfortunate Eskimo who fell into his hands.

While we were still at this place and the Indians were examining the contents of the cache, a thing which they had no business to do, we saw a dark speck coming along the beach about a mile away. In a few moments the speck grew decidedly longer, and as it drew near we saw that it was a large Eskimo sled drawn by twelve dogs. The two Eskimo in the sled were lying down and the dogs were following the old track without any driving, so that they did not see us until the dogs stopped. When the two men crawled off the sled and found themselves in the presence of eleven armed Indians, they looked about as foolish as a pair of schoolboys at their first party. But it was at once evident that neither outfit was looking for a fight and soon they were fast friends. They could not converse with the Indians except by the unsatisfactory method of signs, so that we couldn't learn how far away the ships were, but they pointed to the east. After a delay of half an hour at this place, we kept on our way following the line of drift wood along the beach and during the afternoon reached an Eskimo underground house, occupied by three men, one woman and four children.

These people were very friendly and sociable and during our entire stay the woman's face wore a smile which occupied the greater part of her countenance. This dame had herself rigged out in a costume more ludicrous than anything ever seen on the comic stage or at a masquerade. It would have made her fortune before the footlights, but I am not equal to the task of describing it. The people could give us no idea of how far away the ships were, but indicated by signs that we had better stay over night and resume our journey the next day, and this we determined to do. For several days the weather had been quite pleasant clear, calm and not more thad [sic] fifteen degrees below zero, but now there were unmistakable signs of a blizzard and as there was not room for all of us to sleep in the small underground room, the Indians rigged up a kind of wind break from their sleds, while one of the Indians and myself slept with the Eskimos. To enter this place we had to go down on our hands and knees through a hole after the manner of a prairie dog, and after groping around for a while, came into a dark room about ten feet by twelve and seven feet high. The ceiling was on a level with the snow outside and the interior was heated by a small whale-oil lamp. In this wretched hole eight Eskimos, one Indian and myself slept or tried to sleep, packed like sardines in a box. I was wedged in between a couple of those brutes so tightly I could hardly turn over. The word brute is a mild term to apply to those Herschel Island Eskimos. They apparently have no idea of decency, and seem to go out of their way to horrify people. To see those animals gorging themselves on raw frozen whale blubber was a sight that tried even the nerves of the Indians. But they seemed well disposed and tried to make us feel at home.

[ [W]hile I was out on a bleak and icy shore hunting driftwood for a fire I lost my [large Phi Delta Theta] badge. To hunt for it was out of the question as the snow was blowing and drifting, and even my tracks were being covered in a very few minutes.[4]]

Leaving this place the next morning with a terrific gale at our backs, and following the beach in an easterly direction, going all day on the trot and covering at least thirty miles, we reached Herschel Island and, rounding its southern point, saw looming up through the driving snow the masts and spars of the Arctic whaling fleet, lying fast in the ice on the east side of the island in a little cove. It was exactly twenty days since I had left Rampart House and seven since we left the Indian camp in the Romanzof mountains.

Here were the steam whaling ships "Balaeno" [sic: Balaena], "Norwhal" [sic: Narwhal], "Karleek" [sic: Karluk], "Grampus", "Jeanette", "Newport" and "Mary D. Hume", manned by three hundred white men and one hundred Eskimos. Some of the ships had been out from San Francisco three years and were going to return the coming summer; while the most recent arrivals had left there in April 1893.

[Billy White picked up the story here:

A great crowd of the men from the fleet was watching a ball game on the ice, and when Funston in his Eskimo dress spoke to a captain of one of the whalers in English there was a whaling captain who refused to believe his eyes and his ears, and Funston was obliged to show his Government commission. Then that captain took Funston to his cabin and called another captain, and they learned two-year-old news until they were glutted. Here the devil whispered something to the first captain and he whispered it to the second captain, and together they persuaded Funston to allow them to fill the flowing bowl until it ran over several consecutive times. And subsequent proceedings interested Mr. Funston no more for several hours thereafter. Whereupon the devil and the two captains went out and set about their devices. What they did and what they told made Funston's coming to that fleet a greater sensation than anything he will ever do in the Philippines. For the devil spoke these things through the mouths of the captains to men who had been away from home for three long years. England and Russia have united and declared war against the United States. New York City is captured; San Francisco is being bombarded; Russian troops are coming through Siberia to Alaska, and down through British America to Chicago; the owners of the North American whaling fleet have paid this white man $10,000 to bring this word: "Go north as soon as the ice breaks; push north; stay north, as far north as the ice will permit, for two years or until peace has been declared. Also avoid communicating with other ships."

What is the little matter of swimming a tropical torrent [in the Philippines] under fire as compared with bringing news like this, and being sound asleep and locked in a Captain's cabin when it strikes 300 homesick Yankees who want to go home and fight? Funston will never again in his life make the sensation he made in the Arctic Ocean. Nor will the devil and two captains ever have so much fun over him.[5]]

Of course, the arrival of a white man created a great stir among the whalers, and there was something of a tendency to lionize me. [If the people at Fort McPherson were surprised at my arrival you may imagine the state of mind of the whalers when I showed up. They thought it the biggest thing they had ever heard of and nearly killed me with kindness.[6]] Whalers, like miners and cow boys, are proverbially hospitable and I was handsomely treated during my four days stay. The officers were a remarkably fine lot of men, thorough gentlemen. Nearly all of them were men of considerable education, and unusually well read. Almost to a man they were from the sea-coast towns of Massachusetts and Maine. The crews were made up from nearly every seafaring nationality on the face of the earth.[7]

Funston nearing the Arctic Ocean.

# Chapter Twelve Notes—*A Snowshoe Trip to the Arctic Ocean*

1. "Near The Arctic Circle," *The Kansas City Star*, November 1, 1893. Extracts from Fred Funston's letter dated August 16, 1893, to an unidentified friend.

2. Charles Gleed, in "Romance And Reality In A Single Life. Gen. Frederick Funston," asserted that before Fred reached the Arctic Ocean, one at a time the sled dogs were slaughtered for food until only two or three dogs remained. I do not believe this to be true based on the lack of reference to it in Fred's writings. Also, Fred had only four dogs total until he joined the Indians at their camp where there was plenty of food

3. Frederick Funston's official 32-page, handwritten report dated May 20, 1895, at Iola, Kansas. Original report is at Allen County Historical Society, Inc.; copy in Frederick Funston Papers. This river was named in honor of J. H. Turner of the United States Coast and Geodetic Survey, whom Funston knew from Yakutat Bay and who in 1890 had located the 141$^{st}$ meridian where it intersects the Porcupine River near Rampart House. See also "Stories Of The Frozen Zone," *The Kansas City Star*, February 16, 1895, which described Turner "who traveled in Alaska and died in Washington a short time ago from the hardships he encountered in the frozen zone." This article reported Fred's Arctic trip lecture at the Tabernacle in Kansas City, Kansas.

4. Walter B. Palmer, "General Funston's Badge," *The Scroll of Phi Delta Theta*, Volume XLI, November and December, 1916, January, March and May, 1917, 532. There are several versions of how Fred lost his badge, but the account of Ralph W. Wilson is the most credible. It is reprinted in Palmer's story and is based on Wilson's having heard Fred tell this story at a pan-Hellenic banquet in Manila, Philippine Islands, when Wilson was a lieutenant in the United States Army. The exact day Fred lost his badge is unknown. I have inserted this story in the text at a likely point for its occurrence. Wilson also stated that "General Funston's interest and enthusiasm in fraternity matters was quite marked for a man of his age and position, and he never allowed the urgency and rush of business to blot out the memories of his college days."

    In 1899, Fred recovered his lost badge after it was found under the floor of the old ice rink in Convention Hall, Washington, D. C., when it was torn up. The badge had "Frederick Funston, Kansas Alpha" engraved on it. How this badge made it from the Arctic to Washington, D.C., is unknown.

5. William Allen White, "The Hero Of The Philippines," *The St. Louis Republic Magazine Section*, May 21, 1899. Charles Gleed, in "Romance And Reality In A Single Life. Gen. Frederick Funston," told a somewhat different story, including that it was an English whaling fleet and that Fred was sent there on behalf of the British government. Gleed also stated that Fred participated in the prank by telling details of the alleged hostilites.

    Based on his research, Thomas W. Crouch rejected the alleged British connection, and stated that Funston was correct when he described the fleet as "the Pacific Whaling Company" from San Francisco. See Thomas W. Crouch, *North to Alaska: Frederick Funston Above the 49$^{th}$ Parallel, 1892 – 1894*, endnote 94 (manuscript). Copy at Allen County Historical Society, Inc. Also, in his letter to Edward C. Franklin, Fred described the fleet as "the San Francisco Whaling fleet in winter quarters" (see next note), and Fred stated in the article reprinted in Chapter Thirteen that the seven ships were "all of San Francisco."

6. "Letter From F. Funston," *The University Courier*, September 20, 1894. This letter from Fred was to his close friend, Edward C. Franklin, and was published with "expurgations."

7. "Out Of The North," *The Iola Register*, October 12 and 19, 1894.

# CHAPTER THIRTEEN

# "Baseball Among The Arctic Whalers"

—By Frederick Funston

**March 29, 1894 – April 3, 1894**

The following account, by "Brig. Gen. Frederick Funston, U.S.V.," was published in *Harper's Round Table, 1899*, at page 434. One paragraph I have divided into two paragraphs. This change is not identified.

\* \* \*

On the 29th day of March, 1894, a party of eleven Tinneh Indians and myself, after a twenty days' snow-shoe journey across the bleak tundras and mountain ranges of northeastern Alaska, reached Herschel Island, in the Arctic Ocean, sixty miles west of the mouth of the Mackenzie River. Here, in a little cove, locked fast in the ice, were the steam-whalers *Balaena, Grampus, Mary D. Hume, Newport, Narwhal, Jeanette,* and *Karluk,* all of San Francisco. Some of these vessels had been out from their home port three years, and others only a year. The preceding October, after one of the most successful seasons in the history of arctic whaling, all had sought shelter in the only harbor afforded by this desolate coast to lie up for the winter. The ice-packs coming down from the north had frozen in all about Herschel Island, so that as far as the eye could reach was a jumble of bergs and solid floe, but behind the island where the ships lay the salt-water had frozen as level as a floor. The nine months that the whalemen were compelled to lie in idleness, while not enlivened by social gayeties, were far from monotonous. With lumber brought up from San Francisco there had been built on shore a commodious one-room house, whose most conspicuous articles of furniture were a big stove, that roared day and night, a billiard-table, and a number of benches and chairs. This was the club-room of the sixty or seventy officers of the fleet, and here they congregated to play billiards and whist, or sit about through the long arctic evenings, while the wind howled outside, smoking and spinning yarns of the many seas, or of boyhood days at New Bedford, New London, and Marthas [sic] Vineyard. There were veterans who had whaled on every ocean, and had been in nearly every port on the globe; men who recollected well the raid of the cruiser *Shenandoah,* when she burned the fleet on the coast of Siberia thirty years before, and who had been in the Point Barrow disaster, when nearly a score of ships were crushed in the ice-floe. The sailors and firemen of the fleet did not have the privileges of this house, but contented themselves with games and amusements of their own. They had an orchestra that played long and vociferously, and there was an amateur dramatic troupe that gave entertainments during the winter.

But it was on the great national game of baseball that officers and men most depended to break the tedium of their long imprisonment and furnish the necessary out-door exercise. A large number of bats and balls had been brought up from San Francisco by one of last summer's arrivals, and as soon as the ships had gone into quarters seven clubs were organized and formed into a league to play for the "Arctic Whalemen's Pennant," which was a strip of drilling nailed to a broom-handle. One nine was composed entirely of officers, another of seamen, a third of firemen, a fourth of cooks and waiters, and so on—the seven nines constituting the "Herschel Island League." A set of written rules provided that the series of games should begin after a month's practice, and continue throughout the winter, and that all must be played on schedule time, regardless of weather. Another provision was that on the diamond all ship rank was obliterated, and a sailor could "boss" even venerable Captain Murray without fear of reproof. No sooner had the harbor frozen over than the diamond was laid out and practice begun. Salt-water ice is not quite so slippery as that from freshwater, but great care had to be used by the players.

After a season of practice, during which there was much speculation as to the merits of the various nines, and no end of chaff and banter, the first game of the series was played, and in the brief twilight of an arctic December day, with the mercury thirty-eight degrees below zero, the "Roaring Gimlets" vanquished the "Pig-Stickers" by a score of 62 to 49. All winter, regardless of blizzards and of bitter cold, the games went on, three or four each week, until the schedule was exhausted, and by this time the rivalry was so intense that playing was continued, the clubs challenging each other indiscriminately. The provision in the by-laws that a club refusing to play on account of weather forfeited its position caused one game to be played at forty-seven degrees below zero, and often during blizzards the air was so full of flying snow that the outfielders could not be seen from the home-plate [the pitcher had to locate the batter by compass.[1]] Even after the sun had disappeared for the last time, and the long arctic night had begun, games were played in the few hours of twilight at mid-day, but were usually limited to four innings, as by two o'clock it would be too dark to see the ball.

All the whalemen were dressed in the Esquimau fur costume, only the face being exposed, and on their hands wore heavy fur mittens. These clumsy mittens, together with the fact that one was apt to fall on the ice unless he gave a large part of his attention to keeping his feet underneath him, made good catching practically impossible. "Muffs" were the rule, and the man who caught and held the ball received an ovation, not only from the whalers, but from the hundreds of Esquimaux who were always crowded about the rope. With the ball frozen as hard as a rock, no one was apt to repeat an experiment of catching with bare hands. One of the centre-fielders was a corpulent Orkney-Islander, whose favorite method of stopping a hot grounder was to lie down in front of it. The Esquimaux considered him the star-player of the fleet. Sliding was the only thing done to perfection, the ice offering excellent facilities for distinction in that line; and there was always a wild cheer when a runner, getting too much headway, knocked the baseman off his feet, and both came down together. The scores were ridiculously large, seldom less than fifty on a side, and sometimes twice that. On the smooth ice a good hit meant a home-run.

A most amusing feature of the games was the interest shown by the Esquimaux. With the fleet there were nearly a hundred of these people from Bering Strait and Point Barrow, and there were several villages in the vicinity of Herschel Island. These latter were Kogmulliks, the largest Esquimaux in existence, and the presence of the fleet had drawn them from all along the coast. Men, women, and children became typical baseball cranks [enthusiasts], and there was never a game without a large attendance of Esquimaux, who stood about, eyes and mouths wide open, and yelled frantically whenever there was a brilliant catch or a successful slide. At first dozens of them would break over the line and try to hold a runner until the baseman could get the ball, and it was only by vigorous cuffings that they were taught that the spectators' duties are limited to cheering and betting. They borrowed the paraphernalia and tried a few games of their own, but rarely got beyond the first inning, usually winding up in a general melée and hair-pulling. One of their umpires, who insisted on allowing a nine to bat after it had three men out in order to even up the score, was dragged off the diamond by his heels. They are naturally great gamblers, and bet among themselves on the results of the whalers' games. Many a big "Huskie" went without tobacco for a week because of misplaced confidence in his favorite nine.

A fact that impressed me very much at one of the games that I saw was that the crowd of several hundred people watching our national sport at this faraway corner of the earth, only twenty degrees from the pole, and thousands of miles from railroads or steamship lines, was more widely cosmopolitan than could have been found at any other place on the globe. From the ships were Americans, a hundred or more, men from every sea-faring nationality of Europe— Chinese, Japanese, and Malays from Tahiti and Hawaii. The colored brother, too, was there, a dozen of him, and several of the players were negroes. Esquimaux of all ages were everywhere, while the red men were represented by the eleven wiry fellows who had snowshoed with me from their home in the valley of the Yukon. One day I noticed that in a little group of eleven sitting on an overturned sled watching a game, there were representatives of all the five great divisions of the human race.

There are no men on earth who are more hospitable and more thoroughly good-fellows than these whalers of the Arctic Ocean, and it was hard to leave them; but we finally got away, and started on the long tramp over the snowy wastes toward the Yukon. Just before we left a notice was posted in the club-house which, with many "whereases," "aforesaids," and other legal formula, recited that the "Auroras" thought they knew something about ball, and hereby challenged the "Herschels" to meet them on the diamond within three days.

**Chapter Thirteen Note—"*Baseball Among The Arctic Whalers*"**

1.   "Letter From F. Funston," *The University Courier*, September 20, 1894. This letter from Fred was to his close friend, Edward C. Franklin, and was published with "expurgations."

HARPER'S ROUND TABLE

THE WHALERS PLAYING BASEBALL ON THE ICE
Drawing made from photograph taken by General Funston at Herschel Island.

HE BET ON THE WRONG NINE
From a photograph by General Frederick Funston.

# CHAPTER FOURTEEN

# *The Return Trip and Rampart House Again: Fred Funston's Account*

### April 3, 1894 – June 18, 1894

Our story continues with the concluding four paragraphs of Fred's letter of May 30, written at Rampart House, which had been serialized in *The Iola Register*, the last installment appearing in the October 19 issue.

* * *

After a pleasant visit of four days, I started on the return to Rampart House. In a week we reached the Indian camp, and after a rest of one day started for Rampart House and reached it in seven days more, after an absence of thirty nine days, and just fifteen from leaving the ships. The round trip was something more than six hundred miles and every rod of it was traveled on snow shoes. Although longer by two hundred miles, it could not be compared in hardship to the Ft. McPherson trip, as it was made at a time of year when there was plenty of daylight. Although we had some cold weather, the thermometer at one time reading 42 below zero, it was as a rule much warmer than that, averaging probably 20 below.

After my return to Rampart House, on April 17, nothing of particular interest occurred. The weather grew gradually warmer and on May 6 the mercury crossed the zero line for the last time. On the 9th was the last snow storm and a week later it began thawing slowly. The ice has just broken up in the river, and the long nine-months Arctic winter has reached its end. While on the subject of the weather, I might say that the lowest temperature recorded by the thermometer during the winter was 62 degrees below zero, —this by a very fine and

216

accurate U.S. Weather Bureau instrument. Rev. Totty had an ordinary scrub thermometer which I think he must have won in a raffle, that reached at the same time 73 below zero.

Mr. Totty is just preparing to start for the Yukon in his boat with a crew of natives to meet the yearly steam boat and get his supplies and will take this letter with him so that it will make connection with the steamboat for St. Michaels and thence go to San Francisco direct, without any delay.

As to my future movements, I leave here June 20, with either a boat or a raft, I don't know which yet, and drift down the Porcupine to its junction with the Yukon, two hundred miles and shall get the boat which I left there last September and in it drift down the Yukon to its mouth 1000 miles farther, and then with the aid of one or two Eskimos, run up the coast to St. Michaels about 70 miles and taking passage on the revenue cutter, "Bear", returning from her yearly cruise, shall reach home in October. When I reach St. Michaels I shall have traveled something more than 3500 miles since leaving the coast at Chilkoot Inlet north of Juneau in April 1893, and every rod on foot or in a row boat. Of course I take the most pride in those two snow shoe trips, aggregating 1000 miles or more. A thousand miles is a pretty tiresome distance even if one rides in a Pullman car, but allow me to say that when he measures it out step by step on snow-shoes through the pitiless cold of an Arctic winter, living on dry meat and tallow and bunking down in the snow every night, it is a long, long way. But I am bragging in public, which I have been told is not the thing to do. [1]

\* \* \*

Not only did Fred write his lengthy May 30 letter to *The Iola Register*, he also wrote two other letters that day, one to each of his parents. Each letter provides unique information about Fred's situation. They are reprinted here:

Dear Mother

On my visit to the trading post of Ft. McPherson last November I wrote you a letter which I suppose you have received before this time. [2]

I have taken some long trips during the winter and have had some pretty rough times but I shall not attempt to go over them all in a letter. I have written my experiences at length for the Register as I thought that would save me writing a number of long letters. I think it was the best place to do that as I can kill a good many birds with one stone. Of course I would have to write to some of my friends and it is terribly tiresome to write a lot of long letters containing about the same stuff.

The main news that I have to communicate is that I am alive and well, extremely so. I have not heard a word of news since I left home nearly a year and half ago, but hope that all of the folks are in the same condition, but I cannot help feeling somewhat uneasy, having been gone such a long time and hearing nothing.

By the time I reach St. Michaels I shall have traveled more than 3500 miles since leaving the coast at Chilkoot Inlet in April '93, and shall have seen more of Alaska than any man, white man or Indian, who ever lived.

During the winter I have traveled on snow shoes more than 1000 miles and have slept out of doors in the snow with the thermometer 52 degrees below zero, so you can imagine that it has been a pretty hard life. But for the particulars of my trips you had better read my Register letter.

I leave here about June 20 for St. Michaels a distance of 1300 miles and shall make the trip alone in a row boat, but there is no particular danger about it. About July 10, I shall get my mail at Nuklukyet and shall reach St. Michaels late in August, and if I connect with the revenue cutter shall be home in October. If the revenue cutter does not call at St. Michaels, I shall be in a pretty fix and will have to remain there all winter, but that is not very likely. I shall write Pa how to find out what has become of me if I am not home by November.

My plan is to spend a short leave at home, then go to Washington, remaining only long enough to make out my report and finish the business connected with my trip, and resign my job and start out with a sort of illustrated lecture on my trip and make some money out of this business. I can make more that way in a month than out of my present salary in a year. But I dont [sic] care to have anything said about this.

Now, I am going to speak about a matter which I am afraid will not please you overmuch. When I was at Forty Mile last summer the Alaska Commercial Company's agent, Mr. L. N. McQuesten who has been on the Yukon for twenty years, and whose wife is an Indian woman, asked me if I would take his little girl Mary, about eleven or twelve years old out with me, and have her live in our family for a couple of years and go to school or if you or Pa are not willing I can try to find a home for her somewhere else.

She will be worth more than it costs to keep her by the help she will be about the house. She has lived ever since she was five years old with the English missionaries and is a remarkably well behaved and nice looking little girl and speaks English well. She is but very little darker than full blooded white children. The little girls at the mission school are well trained in house work so that she will be very handy about the house.

Mr. McQuesten wants to send her away from here in order that she may be brought up among white people and all of her playmates at Forty Mile are Indians. His plan is to send her to San Francisco this summer on the Commercial Co.'s steamer and have her remain there until I come down on the revenue cutter when I will bring her east.

It was last August that he spoke to me about this so of course he may have changed his mind in the meantime. When I reach San Francisco, I shall telegraph you, and if the little girl is with me shall say so.

If you cant [sic] keep her maybe Pogue [his brother] would like to take her into his family. I believe he is a married man now.

I shall see Mr. McQuesten when I go down the river, returning from his yearly trip to St. Michael's.

I pulled a few gray hairs out of my beard the other day, and I am not yet 29.

Give my love to all the folks and excuse such a short letter.

Your loving son

Fred Funston[3]

Mary McQuesten (1884-1916) did not go to Allen County with Fred. Instead, in 1897 her father moved his entire family to a mansion in Berkeley, California.[4]

To his father, Fred gave instructions on how to locate him if he was not home by November. He also disclosed detail about the current state of his health:

Dear Pa

The departure of the missionary for the Yukon on his boat with a crew of natives gives me the opportunity of sending out some mail. I shall not attempt anything in the way of a long letter to you. I thought the best way to give the folks at home and my friends both at Iola and Carlyle a good account of my experiences was to write them up in full for the Register, and thus get a big lot of work off my hands in one long letter. I had to make a long report to the Dept, and that with the Register letter has made me terribly tired of writing almost the same stuff over twice.

As you will see by my Register letter, I have extended my trip far beyond my instructions and by the time I reach St. Michaels next fall shall have traveled 3500 miles since leaving the coast at Chilkoot Inlet in April '93. This is just one thousand miles more than the trip as originally planned. This will please the folks at Washington very much as they gave me authority in my letter of instructions to extend my trip if I saw fit, but they did not expect me to do it, as they thought they had already cut out a pretty big job for me. The 1000 miles of snow shoeing and the camping out with the thermometer from 20 to 52 degrees below zero, and living on dry meat and tallow banged me up pretty badly, but I'll be allright [sic] when I get at some civilized grub and in a decent country again.

I had a pretty serious row with the Indians last winter, and came very near shooting into a crowd of them who were going to knock in the door of my house because I had given a buck a crack with a dog whip.

I left my small boat down at the Yukon 200 miles below here last Sept. and so now have no boat to go down the Porcupine in and the missionary is going too early for me, and I am not sure yet how I shall descend this river. There is an old boat here that used to belong to the Hudson Bay Company, but it is too large and very rotten and leaks like a sieve, and I dont [sic] exactly like to trust myself in it on such a dangerous river as this, but the only other way to go down is on a raft of logs. Whether I go on this boat or on a raft, I shall take a couple of natives with me. After I reach the Yukon I shall be allright [sic] as I can then get the boat which I left there last fall and keep on down the river alone to St. Michaels 1100 miles farther.

The Dept. was to make arrangements with the Treasury Dept. to have the revenue cutter call at St. Michaels for me when returning from her annual cruise to the Arctic ocean, and I am to meet her there about Sept 1. It is barely possible that there will be some hitch about this arrangement or that I shall not reach St. Michaels in time to meet the cutter, and in that case will get left up there. In case I reach St. Michaels and find that the revenue cutter has already gone I shall wait until everything is frozen up and then get an Eskimo to go with me and strike out in a southeasterly direction and come out on the southern coast of Alaska and get home in April or May 1895.

In case I should not turn up next fall you need not be particularly scared but if you do not hear from me by Nov. 15, you had better communicate with the Supt. of the Revenue Marine, Treasury Dept, and learn at what date the cutter called at St. Michaels, if she called at all, and whether she heard anything about me. But the chances are that I shall make connection allright [sic], and if I do you can look for me home in October, or at least hear from me.

There is no particular danger about the trip down the Yukon, but the seventy miles on the open sea that I have [to] cross after leaving the mouth of the river in order to reach St. Michaels is a little bit ticklish when one has to do it in an ordinary river skiff. But when I reach the mouth of the Yukon, I shall get one or two Eskmos to [go] up to St. Michaels with me, and shall not attempt it unless the weather is favorable.

The natives in the lower Yukon have a rather bad reputation but I dont [sic] anticipate any trouble with them.

If the photographs that I have been taking are a success so that I can make good steiopticon [sic] views with them I am going to resign my job and start out with an illustrated lecture, and make a pile of money out of this thing. My trip is without doubt the longest on record made by a white man alone in the Artic[sic] regions, and if properly advertised will be a big thing. Frederick Schwatka, whose trip on the Yukon was childs [sic] play compared with mine, cleared $25,000 lecturing in two years; and he did not have any photographs to illustrate his talk with.

I would be a rank fool to let go by such an opportunity to make money but I dont [sic] want the folks in the Dept. of Agriculture to get an inkling of my intentions. I shall have plenty of money saved up by the time I get home to cover all the preliminary expense without going in debt.

I have not heard a word of news from home or the outside world since I left home in March '93 but of course hope that all the folks are alive and well. I have not heard of course the result of your contest with Col. Moore [Ed's re-election in 1892 to Congress had been challenged by his Democratic opponent].

I shall get my mail at Nuklukyet, a trading post and Indian village on the Yukon about July 10 as I sent word to St. Michaels to have it brought up there on the steamboat.

We had it dark up here all of the time in the middle of the winter and for 70 days did not see the sun, but in the summer time it is light all night. I am writing this letter at 1 a.m. and the sun is shining.

As I do not know whether Congress will be in session when this reaches home I send to Carlyle and if you are in Washington the folks can forward it to you.

Your son [no signature][5]

Fred had the solitude of his stay at Rampart House to contemplate his life and its direction. He concluded that botanizing for the government was no longer attractive to him, particularly when he had the opportunity, based on his most recent Alaskan experiences, to make a substantial amount of money by lecturing. As he had written his father, "I would be a rank fool to let go by such an opportunity to make money..."

At the same time, Fred was desirous that his employer, the Department of Agriculture, not learn of his plans. He obviously was a valuable employee, having well fulfilled his boss Frederick Coville's observation that "there is nobody who will come more nearly going where he is sent and getting what he goes after." It would be better for Fred that the Department not know of his plan to resign until he could announce it after his return home, minimizing Coville's opportunity to attempt to dissuade him from resigning.

Front of business card which belonged to Fred Funston. The North American Transportation & Trading Co. was formed in 1892 and the following year established its first trading post at Fort Cudahy.

Reverse of business card which belonged to Fred Funston.

## Chapter Fourteen Notes—*A Snowshoe Trip to the Arctic Ocean*

1. "Out Of The North," *The Iola Register*, October 19, 1894.

2. Fred Funston's letter to his mother was dated November 23, 1893, at Ft. McPherson, and survives in the form of extensive extracts published in *The Iola Register*, July 13, 1894. His mother had shared extracts from his letter with Charlie Scott, who headlined his story, "Our Arctic Explorer." Fred started his letter, as published, "I think you will be surprised to have a letter from me in this corner of the world..."

3. Fred Funston to Ann E. Funston, May 30, 1894 (Frederick Funston Papers, hereafter FFP) (Archives Division, Kansas State Historical Society).

4. James A. McQuiston, *Captain Jack: Father of the Yukon* (Denver, Colorado: Outskirts Press, Inc., 2007), 74. Biography of Leroy Napoleon "Jack" McQuesten (1836-1909).

5. Fred Funston to Edward H. Funston, May 30, 1894 (FFP).

CHAPTER FIFTEEN

# Homeward Bound: Descending the Porcupine and Yukon Rivers

## June 18, 1894 – October 20, 1894

Fred Funston...in the University was known as "Timmie." His two years' trip alone to Alaska gained for him the title of "Fearless Fred"...
— *The Lawrence Daily Journal,* January 10, 1895.[1]

It is a great achievement and one that required not only prudence and sagacity and intelligence of a high order, but no end of physical endurance and courage and "sand."
—Charles F. Scott, October 16, 1894.[2]

One of the most remarkable features about this journey is the absence of fuss and feathers with which it was planned and carried out. There was no clanging of symbals [sic] and beating of drums, and no lurid interviews to give it a tinge of the melodrama, but the fact remains that this journey of nearly 4,000 miles through the desolute wastes of Alaska, is an accomplishment beside which every other attempt at Alaskan exploration is mere child's play.
—*The Washington Post* [3]

After Fred's return to Rampart House from the Arctic Ocean, the weather rapidly grew warmer, and on May 15 the snow began melting, and was gone by June 5.[4] By May 27, the ice in the Porcupine River was breaking up, and by June 2 the river was clear. The return of the sun, which was now above the horizon nearly all of the time, caused rapid vegetation growth. By mid-June the sun was visible at midnight.

These improved conditions allowed Fred to resume plant collecting on June 6. He also began implementing the details for his departure down the Porcupine River. When the trader from the Hudson Bay Company had abandoned Rampart House, he left behind an old boat, the one Fred had described in his letter to his father as "too large and very rotten and leaks like a sieve, and I dont [sic] exactly like to trust myself in it on such a dangerous river as this... " [5] With an Indian's help, Fred patched this up, and stored on board "all of my camp and collecting outfits and personal effects... " On June 18, Fred left Rampart House in this boat "homeward bound." He and the Indian who accompanied him took turns steering and sleeping in the bottom of the boat. No rowing was necessary because of the very strong current, and the two men stopped only to cook meals.

On June 21, at 3 a.m., after three nights and two days of drifting, the men reached the junction of the Porcupine and Yukon Rivers. It had been nine months and ten days since Fred had left the *Nancy Hanks* in the care of the fur trader, T. H. Beaumont. Both were still there, and the boat was in good shape. Fred camped there for a couple of weeks, collecting plants as best he could despite almost incessant rain and swarms of mosquitoes.

Fred made preparations to descend alone the Yukon River to its mouth, a distance of more than a thousand miles. He wisely left in Beaumont's care the collections that he had made and everything else that he would absolutely not need on the last leg of his journey. Beaumont was instructed to turn these items over to the captain of the Alaska Commercial Company's steamer *Arctic,* when it next came up the Yukon, which would transport them to the trading post at St. Michaels.

On July 3, Fred loaded his small boat with "my collecting outfit, tent, camp utensils, photographic apparatus, guns ect [sic], and entirely alone started out drifting down the river, camping on shore at night and collecting any plants that I had not collected heretofore, as well as duplicating some that I had already." For the first six days, he was in the "Yukon Flats," where the river was very wide with numerous channels and the river banks were low and flat, though mountains were visible in the distance.

At 10:30 p.m. on July 8, he left the "flats" and was again in the mountains. The balance of the trip "the river is enclosed in one channel and generally has high banks." Fred's journey was "greatly bothered by high winds and rain storms... " but, at 9 p.m. on July 12, he passed the mouth of the Tanana River, the largest southern tributary of the Yukon River. He had seen few natives so far, but now a short distance from the river mouth was a large, temporary, Indian fishing camp of more than 150 people.

The next night, at 11 p.m. on July 13, Fred stopped at the trading post and Indian village of Nuklukyet and went into camp pending the arrival of the steamer *Arctic*. While waiting, he collected plant specimens to the extent that the weather and mosquitoes would permit. The *Arctic* arrived on the night of July 20 from St. Michaels and Fred received his mail, "the first word that I had heard from civilization for sixteen months."

After an additional two days in camp, he resumed his descent of the Yukon. "High winds blew up the river almost constantly and greatly delayed my progress." He passed a number of Indian fishing camps which generally contained no more than a half-dozen families. On July 27, Fred passed the mouth of the Koyuluk River, "the greatest tributary of the Yukon." On July 28, he reached the village of Nulat where he found a Jesuit priest, Rev. Father Judge, and a number of Indians. After staying there for three days, he resumed drifting down the river, passing along the way several Indian villages and a Holy Cross Mission maintained by the Jesuits. "As I descended the river the increasing poverty and squalor of the natives was very noticable [sic] and there was little resemblance between these people who rarely have anything but fish to eat and who are so scantily clothed, and the well clad meat eating Indians of Forty mile [sic] Creek." According to Charlie Gleed, Fred "was often shot at by the straggling tribes along the banks, but his rifle, opposed to the arrows of the natives, was effective in keeping assaulting parties at a safe distance."[6] As he drifted down the Yukon, Fred at times talked to himself out of "a half-mad fear that he might lose the use of his vocal organs."[7]

Although Fred's incredible 3,500-mile solo expedition was nearing its end, there was always the opportunity for disaster as long as he was on the river. In mid-August, his luck ran out:

> On August 17 while near the village of Andrieffski just above the beginning of the delta [of the Yukon River], a high wind arose, and I attempted to land on an island to remain until it subsided. As I approached the land one of rowlocks of the boat flew out of the socket, and before it could be replaced the boat was swept by the strong current into the tops of a number of cottonwood trees that had been thrown into the river by the caving in of the bank. The boat was turned over instantly, and into the Yukon went my tent blankets, rifle, shotgun, camera, cooking utensils, collecting outfit, all of the collections made since leaving the mouth of the Porcupine river, and every pound of my provisions. I saved myself

by clinging to the trees, and held onto the boats [sic] line, and eventually dragged it above the obstruction and after five hours of hard work got it turned over and bailed out with my hat.

The only thing saved was a box wedged tightly under the seat which contained one of my cameras, note books and weather instruments.

The oars were fastened to the boat so that they could not fall out, and after it was righted I rowed over to the right hand bank and about three miles below where the accident occurred found more natives with whom I remained over night, and who gave me more dried fish. The next day about thirty miles farther down the river I fell in with Father Robart a French Jesuit priest who gave me some more provisions and a blanket.

Although his luck had run out as far as saving most of his possessions, Fred had escaped uninjured, and his charmed life continued for nearly another twenty-three years.

Four days later, Fred "reached the Eskimo village of Coatlik at the mouth of the Yukon on the shores of Bering sea, having traveled something more than 3500 miles since leaving the coast at Taiya River seventeen months before." As a child more than fifty years ago, I marveled at what Fred had accomplished—and endured—on his odyssey, and I marvel even more today at this extraordinary physical and mental feat.

Two days later, Fred boarded the steamer *Arctic*, when it came down the river from Forty Mile Creek. The *Arctic* took him the seventy miles to the Alaska Commercial Company's trading post at St. Michael where he remained until September 13. From there, the United States revenue cutter *Bear* took him to Unalaska, where he transferred to the revenue cutter *Corwin*. After experiencing heavy gales off of the California coast during which the ship's starboard davits were carried away and two of its boats were smashed,[8] the *Corwin* reached San Francisco on October 15. Likely, Fred telegraphed the news of his safe return to Iola, probably to Charlie Scott, who would have relayed this welcome news to Fred's family on the farm.

Traveling by train, Fred reached home on Saturday, October 20, after an absence of nineteen months. The joy and happiness at the Funston farm likely was deeply moving. "Fearless Fred" had done the impossible alone and returned safely. This joyous reunion was undoubtedly tempered by sadness. Grandma Mitchell was not there to welcome her grandson, having died three months before.[9] Ed Funston was now an ex-congressman, having been unseated nine days after Grandma Mitchell's death by the Democratic-controlled House of Representatives, the result of the contest over his 1892 re-election.[10] Positive change on a large scale, however, had occurred on Christmas Day the prior year when a gas well drilled in Iola opened up the Iola gas field and led to the fabulous "gas boom" years of dramatic population growth and prosperity for Allen County. Iola's 1,500 population would reach 14,000 by 1907 before the gas boom faded. In its wake, it left a town and county very different—and better—than that of Fred's childhood.

Despite "rain and pitchy darkness," nearly thirty of Fred's Iola friends drove to the Funston farm in the evening to welcome home the erstwhile explorer, and to "make manifest their joy at his safe return." Charlie Scott noted: "It is a great achievement and one that required not only prudence and sagacity and intelligence of a high order, but no end of physical endurance and courage and 'sand.'" He closed his *Register* account of Fred's return with these words: "The main fact now, and the one which brings the greatest joy to the hearts of all who know him, is that the boy is home again, safe and sound, and that he accomplished all, and more than all, that he was sent to do."[11]

A week after Fred's safe return, a public reception was held at the Grand Army of the Republic Hall.[12] The venue was packed (*The Kansas City Star* reported that 700 attended[13]), and included in the crowd were Billy White and his wife.[14] Charlie Scott captured the mood: "It was a spontaneous expression of interest and pride that was deeply gratifying to the young explorer, who spoke feelingly of his appreciation and gratitude." With "a pleasant talk of half an hour," Fred exhibited to the large audience his collection of curiosities and mementoes from his trip.[15]

Three days later, Fred was again in the public eye, this time at the Richards's mansion where he was an usher in the wedding of Maude Richards and the Reverend Leslie Fenton Potter. [16] Yes, the same Maude Richards who was for a time Fred's "ooman" and about whom he had written Buck Franklin in the winter of 1892-1893 before leaving for his second Alaska expedition. One wonders if the inevitable attention focused on the now-famous Fred Funston rivaled that paid to the bride.

On November 6, Fred left for Washington, D. C., to report to his superiors about his trip.[17] On October 31 his employment as a special agent with the Department of Agriculture had ceased, Fred apparently having already submitted his resignation prior to leaving for Washington.[18] He was back home by Christmas, and was visited by

his good friend, Buck Franklin.[19] Fred ended a momentous year in
the comfort of home, family, and friends—a far cry from his Christmas the prior year in the isolation, darkness, and bitter cold of the
Arctic winter.

# Chapter Fifteen Notes—*Homeward Bound*

1. *The Lawrewnce Daily* Journal, January 10, 1895.

2. "The Week's News," *The Iola Register,* October 26, 1894.

3. Reprinted in "Personal Mention," *The Humboldt Union,* January 19, 1895.

4. Except as otherwise noted in these notes, this chapter is based on Frederick Funston's official 32-page, handwritten report dated May 20, 1895, at Iola Kansas. Original report at Allen County Historical Society, Inc.; copy in Frederick Funston Papers, hereafter FFP (Archives Division, Kansas State Historical Society). His camera was a large box one, 14.25" long, 9" high, and 7.5" wide. Measurements furnished by Kurtis Russell, Executive Director of Allen County Historical Society, Inc., which owns the camera.

5. Fred Funston to Edward H. Funston, May 30, 1894 (FFP).

6. Charles S. Gleed, "Romance And Reality In A Single Life. Gen. Frederick Funston," *The Cosmopolitan Illustrated Monthly Magazine,* July 1899.

7. William Allen White, "Frederick Funston's Alaskan Trip," *Harper's Weekly,* May 25, 1895 (FFP).

8. "From The Bering Sea," *The Salt Lake Herald*, October 9, 1894 (story is datelined San Francisco, October 8).

9. "Obituary," *The Iola Register*, July 27, 1894. Elizabeth Mitchell died on July 23, 1894; "her age [nearly 84] had left her very weary."

10. "Funston Ousted At Last," *The Iola Register*, August 3, 1894; "The Disfranchisement Of Allen County," *The Iola Register*, August 10, 1894; and "E. H. Funston, Private," *The Iola Register*, August 17, 1894, editorial in which Charlie Scott noted that in Ed's twenty-five years of public service "not even a suspicion of corruption has been whispered against him..." When Charlie Scott jokingly asked Ed how it felt to be just Ed Funston, 57-year-old Ed responded, "Fine! I never was happier in my life. Come out and see me pitch hay!"
    Ed lived another seventeen years, farming and speaking at various public events. He created national news in July 1905 when Iolan Charley Melvin dynamited three illegal saloons in Iola. Sixty-eight-year-old Ed condemned publicly the Iola police for not enforcing the Kansas prohibition law and thus causing the dynamiting. The upshot was a physical altercation with an Iola policeman and Ed's arrest. He was fined $5 for carrying a concealed weapon and $5 for disturbing the peace by using loud and boisterous language and for making insulting remarks in reference to the citizens of Iola; i.e. the Iola policeman. Before rendering his decision on the two charges, the judge acknowledged the correctness of Ed's belief in the enforcement of the prohibition law. This Funston incident was such a cause célèbre that it was the subject of an article in the nationally distributed New York magazine, *Leslie's Weekly*, August 24, 1905. The article began: "That Frederick Funston, now a brigadier general in the regular army, who achieved distinction in the Philippines, came honestly by his fighting proclivities was evidenced by a recent incident in Iola, Kan."
    For more information about the exciting story of the dynamiting and subsequent events, see "The Night of July 9-10," which I researched and wrote in my capacity as Executive Director of the Allen County Historical Society, Inc., and which was published in the Society's quarterly publication *Gaslight* in 2009.
    David Haward Bain in *Sitting in Darkness: Americans in the Philippines* (Boston: Houghton Mifflin Company, 1984), 18, stated: "Edward Funston was something of a temperance fanatic, known in his later years to berate strangers and neighbors angrily on Iola streets for ignoring the county [sic: state] prohibition

laws, and doing so with sufficient zeal that he was arrested once for creating a disturbance and charged with resisting arrest." From Bain's multiple notes for pages "18-21," I cannot determine the source for the allegation that Ed Funston "in his later years" berated "strangers and neighbors angrily." I have found no evidence of that but am always willing to learn if someone has evidence to that effect.

11. "The Week's News," *The Iola Register*, October 26, 1894.

12. "Reception To Fred Funston," *The Iola Register*, October 26, 1894

13. "Fred Funston Greeted," *The Kansas City Star*, October 28, 1894.

14. "The Week's News," *The Iola Register*, November 2, 1894

15. "The Week's News," *The Iola Register*, November 2, 1894.

16. "Potter-Richards," *The Iola Register*, November 2, 1894. Fred gave his first after-dinner speech prior to the wedding. As he recalled some years later in another after-dinner speech, "it was upon the celebration of the occasion of the approaching marriage of a girl at whose shrine I worshipped and whom I had intended to marry, but who was to wed a bald-headed minister" ("The Merchants Of Leavenworth Feted Funston," *The Leavenworth Weekly Times*, December 3, 1908).

17. "The Week's News," *The Iola Register*, November 9, 1894.

18. Jessie Dell, Commissioner, United States Civil Service Commission, to Eda B. Funston, March 18, 1931 (FFP).

19. "The Week's News," *The Iola Register*, December 28, 1894.

# AFTERWORD

In fiction, a popular theme is the future young hero or heroine who has to undergo a continuing challenge. He hates the task at first but then comes to love the work and, in the process, becomes a new man. Such was the case with Fred Funston. After only two months of struggle on the arduous Death Valley Expedition, he was ready to quit. "I have got my belly full of roughing it for a number of years to come." Yet, after five more months, he knew that this was the right job for him. "I am happy and enjoying myself hugely, but am dirty and ragged beyond description."

The expedition was also a financial success for him since there were few places where he could spend his wages and thus was able to save for future needs. He was doing a calling he liked that, at the same time, provided financial independence.

That Fred went to Yakutat Bay the next year for a different but similar experience is not surprising. It provided a good income and at the same time appealed to his restless, adventurous spirit, which liked tackling unknown and unexpected trials. Near the end, however, he was tiring of the experience. "I am getting mighty tired of this exploring trade, and dont [sic] think I shall ever come out on another trip though I may, as there is considerable money in it." "As the time approaches to go home I am beginning to be glad to leave this country, although my summer here has been a regular picnic." He realized that field botanist was a job that he was good at and which appealed immensely to him for both monetary and personal reasons.

The most demanding adventure followed with his year and a half in Alaska and the British Northwest Territory. By the end of that experience, he knew that he had definitely had enough of this kind of roughing it and could make a substantial income from his experiences by "a sort of illustrated lecture on my trip and make some money out of this business. I can make more that way in a month than out of my present salary in a year." Independent and practical-minded Fred would be able to retain his financial independence after he left government employment. Whether he would enjoy a speaking tour was a question yet to be answered.

After nearly three years of experiences in Death Valley, Alaska, and the British Northwest Territory, Fred was more rugged physically and mentally. Perhaps the clumsiness of his early years had gone away. He also was clearly resourceful in making, and surviving, these travels. Each venue of botanical operations was different, and

Fred had to determine, usually on his own, the necessary steps to successfully meet each challenge. There were no guidebooks to consult. On his own, he successfully overcame extraordinary obstacles. His self-reliance is much to be admired.

Contemporaries described Fred as "fearless," a trait he showed during those nearly three years. The sobriquet of "Fearless Fred" is frequently associated with Fred in his capacity as a United States Army officer. Yet, it was used earlier to describe him in college, Death Valley, Alaska, and the British Northwest Territory. Being "Fearless Fred" was a part of his image to others, and perhaps of his self-image. It was well earned. Why he was lacking in fear, I do not know. Perhaps it was simply part of his innate personality. Perhaps it was the consequence of a supreme and justified self-confidence in his own abilities.

Fearlessness, however, does not necessarily mean the absence of nervousness. As Fred articulated it as a soldier, "I always had the nervous jim-jams before I went into a fight [during battle], and I always had nervous prostration after it was over." During the battle, however, he was apparently without fear, perhaps because he was totally focused on the actual fighting, allowing no opportunity to feel fear.

Fred had strengthened himself both physically and mentally through successfully overcoming the dangerous obstacles of the arid and arctic climates. Restless, adventurous, fearless, independent, self-reliant, joking, self-deprecating, witty, resourceful, pragmatic, kind, Fred Funston was now ready for the ultimate experience—the crucible of fighting in the revolutionary forces for *Cuba Libre*, which completed the creation of the man he was to be.

---

# UPDATED ACKNOWLEDGMENTS
## for *Becoming Frederick Funston Trilogy*

**My great thanks to the following:**

Members of the Funston family: first and foremost, for their invaluable assistance and friendship, the late Frank Funston Eckdall and his daughter, Deborah (Eckdall) Helmken. Also, Martine Funston, Ellen (Lees) Stolte, the late Don Funston, Dale Funston, and the late Greta Funston. Each of these assisted me in one or more essential ways. Although she died long before I started work on this trilogy in 1995, I am grateful to Fred Funston's sister, Ella (Funston) Eckdall, whose writings and scrapbooks on her brother's life provided much important material and, at times, information that otherwise would have been lost forever.

Mitchell family: Burt Bowlus, grandnephew of Lida (Mitchell) Funston, mother of Fred Funston.

Brenda Cash, Resource Sharing Head, Southeast Kansas Library System, performed great work obtaining through interlibrary loan numerous essential materials. Also, Roger Carswell, then Director of Iola Public Library, for an essential item that he obtained.

In 2010, a "fluke" stroke left me with only one functioning hand and mobility challenges. My longtime friend, Bill Crowe, made innumerable trips to the Kansas State Historical Society, Topeka, Kansas, to review various collections and to obtain copies of needed materials for this trilogy.

Rick Danley worked for me part-time from 2016-2019. He helped me organize and use my ever-growing collection of materials; checked microfilm at the Iola Public Library; and read and helpfully critiqued the entire trilogy manuscript after its completion.

John E. Miller, historian, professor, and author, who died unexpectedly in 2020, my friend since graduate school days in history at the University of Wisconsin-Madison. John read several years ago the manuscript as completed to that date and validated the worthwhileness of this work.

Jarrett Robinson, my comrade in arms for more than twenty-five years in our belief in the importance of preserving and publicizing the details of the life of a worthy man, Fred Funston. Among other help, Jarrett shared with me helpful "finds" on the early years of Funston's life. Jarrett also was a great sounding board on certain chapters of volume three.

Members of my family helped in various ways: Nancy, my wife, in multiple ways, including the title of Volume Two, *Heat and Ice*; David Toland, our son, and his wife, Beth Toland; Elizabeth (Toland) Smith, our daughter, and her husband, Bart Smith; and our grandchildren, Caroline Toland and William Toland.

Bob Hawk prepared the excellent map showing Fred Funston's route through Alaska and British Northwest Territory and the map of Cuba and assisted with the technical aspects of numerous photographs. Bob, long an admirer of Fred Funston, played an essential role in the creation of the Funston Home Museum and the Funston Museum and Visitors' Center.

*American Hero, Kansas Heritage* was made possible in part by the Center for Kansas Studies, Washburn University, Topeka, Kansas, which funded formatting and design costs. Carol Yoho used her valuable computer and design skills on this book. And special thanks to Thomas Fox Averill, noted Kansas author and emeritus professor of English at Washburn University, whose belief in this book made its publication a reality and who provided great editorial assistance.

As to *Heat and Ice*, Washburn University Center for Kansas Studies continued its financial support; Tom Averill contributed again his support and editorial role; and Carol Yoho once again did the formatting.

Amy Albright, professional graphics designer, was responsible for the cover for Volume Two.

Thea Rademacher, owner of Flint Hills Publishing, Topeka, Kansas, enthusiastically published volumes one and two and promises to keep that enthusiasm going for volume three.

Andres Rabinovich translated Prats-Lerma's crucial account about Funston's Cuban military experiences.

Barbara Diehl faithfully typed nearly all of my manuscript from my handwritten draft, and made changes and corrections in the typed draft, and Terri Jackman faithfully typed the balance and made needed changes and corrections throughout the typed draft.

For their help: Sally Huskey, Richard Zahn, Ed Fitzpatrick, Margaret Robb, the late Dorothy (Carnine) Scott, the late Emerson and Mickey Lynn, the late Winifred Bicknell, Scott Jordan, the late Ed Kelly, William Berry, Donna and the late Ray Houser, Katherine Crowe, Curator of Special Collections & Archives at University of Denver Libraries, Gary LaValley, Archivist for the United States Naval Academy, Kurtis Russell, Executive Director of Allen County Historical Society, Inc., and Allen County Register of Deeds Jacque Webb and her successor, Cara Barkdoll.

The excellent staff at Kenneth Spencer Research Library, including Becky Schulte, Sherry Williams, the late Mary Hawkins, and Kathy Lafferty; Barry Bunch of University Archives; Kevin L. Smith, Director of Libraries; Brian D. Moss, Head Reference Librarian, all at the University of Kansas.

The excellent staffs at Manuscript Division, Library of Congress; Kansas State Historical Society; Special Collections and Archives, Emporia State University; Lyon County History Center & Historical Society; Elwyn B. Robinson Department of Special Collections, Chester Fritz Library, University of North Dakota; Government Documents, North Dakota State University; Department of Rare Books and Special Collections, Princeton University Library; The Rutherford B. Hayes Presidential Library and Museum; American History Center, University of Wyoming; Smithsonian Institution Archives; University Archives of University of Pennsylvania; U. S. Army Heritage & Education Center, Carlisle, Pennsylvania; Special Collection, Sheridan Libraries, Johns Hopkins University; and the Kansas Supreme Court Law Library.

My parents, the late June and Stanley Toland, encouraged and supported my interest in history starting in my childhood. I am definitely a product of that influence, and I shall always be grateful to them.

---

# BIBLIOGRAPHY

## Collections

Allen County Historical Society, Inc., Iola, Kansas
    Eckdall collection of letters

American Heritage Center, University of Wyoming, Laramie, Wyoming
    Frederick V. Coville Collection
    Vernon Bailey Papers

Kansas State Historical Society, Topeka, Kansas
    Frederick Funston Papers (Manuscript Collection 33, and Microfilm: MS75 – MS77)

Library of Congress, Manuscript Division, Washington, D. C.
    A. K. Fisher Papers
    C. Hart Merriam Papers
    T. S. Palmer Papers

Smithsonian Institution Archives, Washington, D.C.
    Edward William Nelson and Edward Alphonso Goldman Collection

The Huntington Library, San Marino California
    Papers of Theodore Sherman Palmer

## Dissertation

Laubacher, Matthew, "Cultures of Collection in Late Nineteenth Century American Natural History" (Arizona State University, May 2011).

## Manuscripts

Coville, Frederick V., *Botanizing In Death Valley in 1891 And Forty Years Afterward* (American Heritage Center, University of Wyoming).

Coville, Frederick V., *[Death Valley Expedition] Itinerary* (Smithsonian Institution Archives).

Crouch, Thomas W., *North to Alaska: Frederick Funston Above the 49th Parallel, 1892 – 1894* (Allen County Historical Society, Inc.).

Fisher, Albert Kenrick, *C.H. Merriam a narrative of Death Valley Exp* (container #40, A. K. Fisher Papers, Manuscript Division, Library of Congress, Washington, D.C.).

Fisher, Albert Kenrick, *Frederick Funstun* [sic] (container #40, A. K. Fisher Papers, Manuscript Division, Library of Congress, Washington, D.C.).

Funston, Frederick, *Itinerary of Frederick Funston 1891* (Smithsonian Institution Archives, Washington, D.C.).

Funston, Frederick, untitled, handwritten 32-page report dated May 20, 1895, at Iola, Kansas (original at Allen County Historical Society, Inc.; copy in Frederick Funston Papers at Kansas State Historical Society).

Merriam, C. Hart, M.D., *Death Valley Expedition I – Journal of a trip across Southern California + Nevada including NW Arizona + SW Utah 1891*, Vol. I (March – July) (container #4, C. Hart Merriam Papers, Manuscript Division, Library of Congress, Washington, D.C.).

Nelson, Edward W., *Death Valley Journal*, December 11, 1890 – August 24, 1891 (Smithsonian Institution Archives, Washington, D.C.).

Palmer, Theodore S., *Diary May 26, 1891 – Sept. 19, 1891* (container #1, T. S. Palmer Papers, Manuscript Division, Library of Congress, Washington, D.C.).

Palmer, Theodore Sherman, *Diary, Death Valley expedition 1891, Dec. 11, 1890 – May 25, 1891* (Call No. HM50827, The Huntington Library, San Marino, California).

Stephens, Frank, *Frank Stephens Field Notes, 1891*, February 3, 1891 – September 21, 1891 (San Diego Natural History Museum, San Diego, California).

White, John I., "Statement On Alaskan Experiences" (Frederick Funston Papers on microfilm) (Archives Division, Kansas State Historical Society).

## Select Books and Articles, including Newspaper Articles

"A Trip Up The Yukon River," *The Kansas City Star*, July 22, 1894.

Bailey, Vernon, "Into Death Valley 50 years Ago," *Westways,* December 1940.

Brown, F. C. and Arthur W. Palmer, "Frederick Vernon Coville (1867-1937)," *Cosmos Club Bulletin*, Vol. 20, No. 1 (January 1967).

Coville, Frederick Vernon, "A Winter Storm in Death Valley," *The Youth's Companion,* July 8, 1897.

Coville, Frederick Vernon, "Botany Of The Death Valley Expedition" (U.S. Department of Agriculture, Division of Botany, *Contributions From The U.S. National Herbarium*, Vol. IV. Issued November 29, 1893, Washington: Government Printing Office, 1893).

Dix, R S., "Death Valley," *Chautauqua* (August 1891).

Farquhar, Frances P., *Place Names Of The High Sierra* (San Francisco: Sierra Club, 1926).

F. F. [Funston, Frederick], "Into The Valley Of Death," *The New York Times*, March 27, 1892.

"Fred Funston's Restless Life of Adventure," *The Chicago Sunday Tribune*, May 7, 1899.

"Funston, Brig. Gen., U.S.V.," *The Kansas City Star*, May 7, 1899.

[Funston, Fred,] "Another Alaskan Letter," *The Iola Register*, October 14 and 28, 1892. Funston's second 1892 trip letter (date not shown) to the *Register*.

Funston, Fred, "A Wedding In The Mohave Desert," *University Review*, Vol. 13, no. 3, November 1891.

Funston, Fred, "Death Valley," *The Iola Register*, July 17, 1891.

Funston, Fred, "Death Valley," *The Iola Register*, September 11, 1891.

[Funston, Fred,] "Fred Funston Again!," *The Iola Register*, November 10, 1893. Funston's second 1893-1894 trip letter dated August 3, 1893, to the *Register*.

[Funston, Fred,] "Fred Funston Heard From," *The Iola Register*, September 16, 1892. Funston's first 1892 trip letter dated August 20 to the *Register*.

[Funston, Fred,] "From Fred Funston," *The Iola Register*, August 25, 1893. Funston's first 1893-1894 trip letter dated May 28, 1893, to the *Register*.

[Funston, Fred,] "Our Arctic Explorer," *The Iola Register*, July 13, 1894. Funston's letter dated November 23, 1893, to Ann E. Funston.

[Funston, Fred,] "Out Of The North," *The Iola Register*, September 21, 1894. Funston's third 1893-1894 trip letter dated May 30, 1894, to the *Register*; published in four installments in the weekly issues of September 21, October 5, 12, and 19, 1894.

Funston, Frederick, "Across the Great Divide in Midwinter," *Harper's Weekly,* December 22, 1900.

Funston, Frederick, "Along Alaska's Eastern Boundary," *Harper's*

*Weekly*, February 1, 1896.

Funston, Frederick, "Baseball Among the Arctic Whalers," *Harper's Round Table, 1899.*

Funston, Frederick, "Field Report," in Frederick Vernon Coville, "Botany of Yakutat Bay, Alaska," *Contributions From The U.S. National Herbarium*, Vol. III, No. 6 (Washington: Government Printing Office, 1895).

Funston, Frederick, "Over The Chilkoot Pass To The Yukon," *Scribner's Magazine*, November 1896.

Funston, Frederick, "The Territory Of Alaska. From A Commercial Standpoint," *The Bond Record,* May 1896.

Gleed, C. S., eulogy, "Report of Select Committee," *Journal of the House*, Hall of the House of Representatives, Topeka, Kansas, February 26, 1917.

Gleed, Charles S., "Romance And Reality In A Single Life. Gen. Frederick Funston," *The Cosmopolitan Illustrated Monthly Magazine*, July 1899.

Johnson, William E., "The Making of Brigadier Funston," *The New Voice*, May 13, 1899.

Kansas Historical Society, Kansapedia (www.kshs.org).

*Letter From The Secretary of Agriculture Transmitting, In response to the resolution of the House of Representatives of January 22, 1894, a list of the special agents of the Department, together with a statement of their work and the salaries received, for the four years and six months ending December 31, 1893*. 53D Congress, 2d Session, House of Representatives, Ex. Doc. No. 243, 3.

Lingenfelter, Richard E., *Death Valley & The Amargosa: A Land of Illusion* (Berkeley: University of California Press, 1986).

"McAdoo's Cook Killed As Wagon Overturns," *San Francisco Chronicle*, July 21, 1918.

McQuiston, James A., *Captain Jack: Father of the Yukon* (Denver: Outskirts Press, Inc., 2007).

"Near The Arctic Circle," *The Kansas City Star*, November 1, 1893.

Oppel, Frank, *Tales of Alaska And The Yukon* (Secaucus, New Jersey: Castle, 1986).

Palmer, Walter B., "General Funston's Badge," *The Scroll of Phi Delta Theta*, Volume XLI, November and December, 1916, January, March and May, 1917.

"Report of the Ornithologist and Mammalogist," *Report Of The Secretary Of Agriculture 1891*, 52 D Congress, 1ˢᵗ Session, House of Representatives, Ex. Doc. 1, Part 6.

Schmidly, David J., *Vernon Bailey: Writings of a Field Naturalist on the Frontier* (College Station: Texas A&M University Press, 2018).

Scott, Charles F., "Frederick Funston," *The Independent*, April 11, 1901.

Scott, Chas. F., "Remarkable Career of a Kansas Boy," *Mail and Breeze* (about March 20, 1898).

Spears, John R., "Trees of the American Desert," *Harper's Weekly*, July 9, 1892.

Sterling, Keir B., *Last of the Naturalists: The Career of C. Hart Merriam* (New York: Arno Press, 1974).

U.S. Department of Agriculture, Division of Ornithology and Mammalogy, *North American Fauna No. 7. The Death Valley Expedition. A Biological Survey Of Parts Of California, Nevada, Arizona, and Utah, Part II* (Washington: Government Printing Office, 1893).

White, William Allen, "Frederick Funston's Alaskan Trip," *Harper's Weekly*, May 25, 1895.

White, William Allen, "Gen. Frederick Funston," *Harper's Weekly*, May 20, 1899.

White, William Allen, *The Autobiography of William Allen White* (New York: The Macmillan Company, 1946).

White, William Allen, "The Hero Of The Philippines," *The St. Louis Republic Magazine Section*, May 21, 1899.

Young, Louis Stanley, and Henry Davenport Northrop, *Life and Heroic Deeds of Admiral Dewey* (Philadelphia: Globe Publishing Co., 1899).